GEOLOGY
OF THE
LAKE SUPERIOR
REGION

D1564722

GEOLOGY
OF THE
LAKE SUPERIOR
REGION

Gene L. LaBerge

PENOKEAN PRESS

Copyright © 1994 by Gene L. LaBerge
Library of Congress Catalog Number 93-080796
ISBN 097240880-0

No part of this book may be reproduced by any mechanical, photographic, or electronic process, or in the form of a phonographic recording, nor may it be stored in a retrieval system, transmitted, or otherwise copied for public or private use, without written permission from the publisher

First published by Geoscience Press in 1994.

Publisher's Cataloging in Publication
(Prepared by Quality Books Inc.)

LaBerge, Gene L.
  Geology of the Lake Superior region / Gene L. LaBerge.
  p. cm.
  Includes bibliographical references and index.
  ISBN 097240880-0

  1. Geology—Superior, Lake, Region—Guidebooks.
QE78.L33 1994   551'.09774'9
                                                  QBI93-22279

Published by:
Penokean Press
P.O. Box 1432
Oshkosh, Wisconsin 54901-1432

Manufactured in the United States of America
Cover design by Paulette Livers Lambert, Boulder, Colorado
Typography by Shadow Canyon Graphics, Evergreen, Colorado

8 7 6 5 4

CONTENTS

PREFACE

In this book I have attempted to describe in chronological order the major events in the geological history of the Lake Superior region. It is one of the most thoroughly studied areas of Precambrian rocks in the world, and contains a number of "classical" rock sequences and mineral deposits. I have used a regional approach to the history because all of the events are not recorded in any given state. For example, the discussion of Archean rocks centers on northern Minnesota, whereas events in the Proterozoic history are better exemplified by the rocks in Wisconsin and Michigan.

I have presented explanations for the geological events in terms of the principles of plate tectonics. Therefore, whenever possible, I have shown analogies to present day geological features and processes that illustrate events in the geologic past. I have tried to integrate a discussion of the processes (basic physical geology) into the historical perspective in which the events occurred. Although I have written the book using as little technical jargon as possible, a knowledge of basic geologic terms and processes is necessary to understand and appreciate the story being told. For this purpose a glossary of some of the more important terms is included.

During some thirty summers of field work in the Lake Superior region I have had the pleasure of talking with hundreds of people about the geology in one area or another. I have found that most people have an interest in, and curiosity about the geological events that have produced the rocks and landforms in their area. I have tried to answer their questions orally; sometimes successfully, sometimes not. It became apparent to me that while there are vast libraries of geologic information written for professional geologists (and intelligible to few others), there is virtually nothing written for the interested layperson or nonprofessional student of geology. It is for these people that I have written this book. Although geological events are long and complex I hope the readers will make the attempt to understand the history, for it gives us a much better appreciation of the area in which we live. I am also sure they will find it as exciting and awe-inspiring as I have.

I have tried to write this book using the same philosophy with which I teach; namely, that it is open at the top. To this end I have included technical data and concepts that will tax the comprehension of some readers. It is intended to make them aware of how complex the earth really is and how geologists attempt to deal with these complex problems. Hopefully readers will be stimulated to think more about these complexities and to learn more about them.

ACKNOWLEDGMENTS

Many people have contributed to this book, some directly, and others by providing invaluable background and discussions. I wish to acknowledge with appreciation the discussions with the late Carl E. Dutton (U.S. Geological Survey), Cedric I. Iverson (U.S. Steel Corporation), Paul E. Myers (University of Wisconsin–Eau Claire), the late Ralph W. Marsden (University of Minnesota–Duluth), the late Stanley A. Tyler (University of Wisconsin–Madison), Klaus J. Schulz (U.S. Geological Survey), John S. Klasner (Western Illinois University), David M. Michelson (University of Wisconsin–Madison), Paul K. Sims (U.S. Geological Survey), Meredith E. Ostrom (Wisconsin Geological Survey), Norris W. Jones (University of Wisconsin–Oshkosh), plus numerous colleagues in the mining industry and in various geology departments in the Lake Superior region. Thanks also to the numerous students from Oshkosh who have joined me on field trips, some in unbelievably bad weather, to various parts of the Lake Superior region. Their questions about the relationship of rocks from one area to another were a great incentive to try to find answers to these "simple" questions. Students in my Geology of Wisconsin course at Oshkosh also contributed many meaningful questions and discussions, and provided a "sounding board" for most of the ideas presented here.

Marcile Simm, Betty Rasmussen, and the late Katherine G. Nelson provided valuable reviews of the manuscript. The several versions of the manuscript were typed by Pamela Spaulding, Sarah Margis, Becky Steinberg, and Mary Fahley. James LaBre provided invaluable assistance with the photographic efforts of the author during the project. The assistance of all of these people is gratefully acknowledged.

Finally, my wife, Sally, has provided unfailing assistance and moral support throughout the project.

DEDICATION

To my family, my wife Sally, my children Michelle, René, and Laura,
all of whom have done so much with me,
and who have made it all worthwhile.

1

INTRODUCTION

Photograph of the surface of the Moon, a scene probably like that of the early surface of the Earth. (Apollo 8 photograph from NASA.)

The Lake Superior region is that portion of central North America that surrounds Lake Superior. It includes portions of Ontario and the states of Minnesota, Wisconsin, and Michigan. This region contains a broad spectrum of geological features that were formed by a wide variety of geologic processes. Some features originated as volcanic islands in an ancient sea; some were the result of major compressive forces that produced large folds and faults in the rocks; still other features were layers of sedimentary rocks produced when warm, tropical seas covered this part of North America; and finally the area was covered by thousands of feet of glacial ice that scoured the landscape and left distinctive deposits over most of the region. In addition, the Lake Superior region is the site of the largest iron ore deposit and one of the largest copper deposits in the United States. These deposits have played a major role in the settlement and economic development of the area.

These and other geologic phenomena were formed by events that occurred over an immense span of geologic time. Some events occurred more than 3 billion years ago, others occurred as recently as ten thousand years ago. Yet each event has left an indelible imprint on the rocks or landforms in the Lake Superior region.

The purpose of this book is to describe and discuss the various geological events that have occurred in the region. Each event is discussed in its place in the general time sequence. The geological processes that produced the various events are also discussed. It is hoped that this approach will provide the reader with an historical sequence of the many diverse events that have affected the region. This approach is somewhat different from describing the geological features in a number of different geographic areas within the region. To begin the story we need to go back in history to a time when the earth was much younger than it is today and work our way toward the present.

▲ THE BEGINNING ▲

Picture, if you will, the earth's surface, as it existed millions of years ago, pockmarked like that of the moon from countless thousands of impacts by large and small meteorites. (See figure at beginning of the chapter.) No atmosphere or oceans were present. The earth consisted of a random mixture of meteorites accumulated when it formed some

4,600 million years ago. Then, as the earth gradually heated inside from the decay of radioactive elements, the interior reached the melting temperature of the rocks. This ushered in the most spectacular display of volcanic activity in earth's history. The interior of the earth gradually melted, and the iron and nickel from many of the meteorites sank to the center of the earth, forming its core. The lighter weight materials rose to the surface, erupting as an almost endless string of volcanoes. Thus a basaltic crust was formed on the earth, separated from the core by a partially molten mantle of somewhat heavier magnesium-rich peridotite.

Vast quantities of gas and steam were brought to the surface by the volcanic activity and gradually accumulated to form the primordial atmosphere. Most of the water vapor condensed and fell back to earth and began eroding some of the volcanic ash, filling in the depressions, and spreading out in an ever-deepening layer of water. These waters formed the first oceans on earth and, along with the volcanic activity, filled in the earlier impact craters, modifying forever the surface of the earth (Figure 1–1). Occurring about 4,000 million years ago, this major

Figure 1-1: Photograph of the Earth from the Moon, showing the atmosphere and hydrosphere that has so completely changed the surface of the Earth during the course. (Apollo 8 photograph from NASA.)

event—the melting of the interior of the earth–brought about the differentiation into a core, mantle, and crust, at the same time forming the atmosphere and the first oceans. Thus the major features of the earth formed early in its history, and in a sense, set the stage for all the later events.

At somewhere around 4,000 million years ago we can picture the part of North America destined to become the Lake Superior region as a vast expanse of lifeless ocean with chains of volcanic islands similar to the present-day Aleutian Islands. These islands had been built up gradually by countless thousands of volcanic eruptions, first flowing out onto the sea floor, then adding successive layers one on top of the other until the pile of lava flows finally reached the surface. The molten basaltic rocks probably originated in the earth some 30 to 50 miles below the floor of the ocean. Several millions of years elapsed between the onset of volcanic activity and the emergence of the volcanic islands. Once the volcanic piles extended above the surface of the primordial ocean, waves began to beat against the rocks. Rains, falling on the naked volcanic ash and lava flows, began eroding the islands and carrying the debris back into the oceans. Since erosion was rapid and the ocean bottom dropped off rather steeply around the islands, sediments had little chance to undergo chemical weathering or sorting. Thus began the record of the first sedimentary rocks.

The sediments were carried into the deep oceanic basins surrounding the volcanic island by the following series of events. The sediments probably accumulated near the mouths of rivers that flowed down valleys cut into the volcanic islands. However, frequent earthquakes associated with the recurrent volcanic activity would shake the sediments loose and cause massive submarine landslides that carried the sediments out into the deeper parts of the oceanic basins. There the sediments would settle; coarsest (heaviest) particles first and finest mud last (perhaps weeks later).

This picture was repeated over and over again. The result was the formation of thick sequences of monotonously uniform sediments called *graywackes* (from their typical gray color) whose chemical composition was much like that of the volcanic rocks from which they were derived. Finally, great batches of granitic magma melted and accumulated in the upper parts of the mantle. The lower density of these magmas (compared with the surrounding and overlying basalts) caused them to rise upward toward the surface, intruding the overlying volcanic and sedimentary rocks. The intrusions caused much deformation and metamorphism of the intruded rocks, forming schists and gneisses. Blocks of the overlying rocks broke loose in the process and sank into the rising magma. These granitic intrusions formed some of the first large batholiths and some of the first continental crust, for we observe that continents are made up mainly of granitic rocks. From this violent and precarious beginning, the rocks that have recorded the geological events occurring in the Lake Superior region were formed.

In this book I present the sequences of events during the nearly 4,000 million years of geologic history. Where possible I discuss the events in the order in which they occurred, but in certain cases events are presented out of chronological order.

The Precambrian geology of the Lake Superior region, like that of many other places, is considered by some to be "the crystalline basement" or the "basement complex" that is too old and too complex to understand. While the rocks are indeed old and complex, they can be understood if one is willing to make the effort. Within the past twenty years significant advances have been made toward unraveling the long and complex history of the geology of the Lake Superior region. Crucial information has also been provided by a wide variety of studies. These include regional and detailed geologic mapping of exposed rocks along with chemical studies of rock suites to understand how they originated. Other studies involved isotopic age dating of rocks to determine when they formed, as well as regional gravity and aeromagnetic surveys. It is the interpretation of data provided by <u>all</u> of these techniques however, that has made possible the following understanding of the sequence of events that has formed the Precambrian rocks underlying all of the region and that are exposed extensively in the northern half of the area. Although these data, collected by many geoscientists, are still sketchy, they suggest an interesting sequence of volcanic activity, sedimentary basin formation, and mountain-building deformations. These developments appear to be associated with the intrusion of huge granitic batholiths and long intervals of erosion.

Geological events and the rocks produced by them have not been the same throughout geologic time. While most physical processes have remained the same (for example, water has always run downhill), there have been significant chemical changes in the earth with time that reflect a general chemical evolution of the earth. Thus, while studying present-day processes helps us interpret events of the past, we cannot make a rigid comparison of present processes with those that occurred 2,000 million years ago. As a consequence of the general evolution of the earth, certain rock types have formed during a particular interval of time, and due to fundamental changes in the chemistry of the earth, did not form during subsequent times.

▲ GEOLOGIC TIME ▲

The immensity of geologic time is perhaps the most difficult aspect of geology for nongeologists to comprehend. Most people tend to think in terms of a human lifetime of something less than one hundred years. In the time frame of a human life most features of the earth appear to be unchanging. Events that occurred 500 to 1,000 years ago are considered to be extremely ancient. Yet in the context of earth history they are so recent that they would hardly represent a single tick of a clock.

It is important to remember that the earth is constantly changing. The changes are so slow and gradual, however, that hundreds, or thousands of centuries are necessary to produce noticeable changes. In the context of earth history, even a thousand centuries is a very short time. The result is that changes and processes that proceed so slowly that we can scarcely detect them produce profound effects over the seemingly endless span of geologic time.

A consequence of these endless, gradual changes is that a wide variety of geological processes occur in the same area over a long span of geologic time. As we will see, the Lake Superior region was covered repeatedly by vast expanses of glacial ice quite recently in its history. Before that it was a land area with a warm climate and the home of a wide variety of dinosaurs. Still earlier in its history the Great Lakes area was covered by warm tropical seas in which corals lived in abundance, and long sandy beaches bordered the oceans. And still farther back in history a lofty mountain range extended across the region with many active volcanoes. And the history goes back even beyond this.

This brief list illustrates some of the very diverse geological events that have occurred in the same area. Each event is recorded in the rocks that were produced by geological processes that operated during that particular interval of time. In addition to *rock-forming* events, the geological record is also punctuated by several long periods of erosion. Erosion removed huge volumes of rock that gradually disintegrated at the earth's surface. In effect, since the erosion removed the geological record of rock-forming events, the record left is one of erosion.

In summary, the rock types, the distribution of rock units, landforms, rivers, lakes, mineral deposits, and so forth, are our heritage from the various geological events that have occurred throughout geologic time. Let us now examine what we mean by geologic time.

Geologic time is subdivided into a number of major units or eras based largely on the fossil record of life on earth. Figure 1—2 can be used as a general reference for the subdivisions used in this book. The major dividing

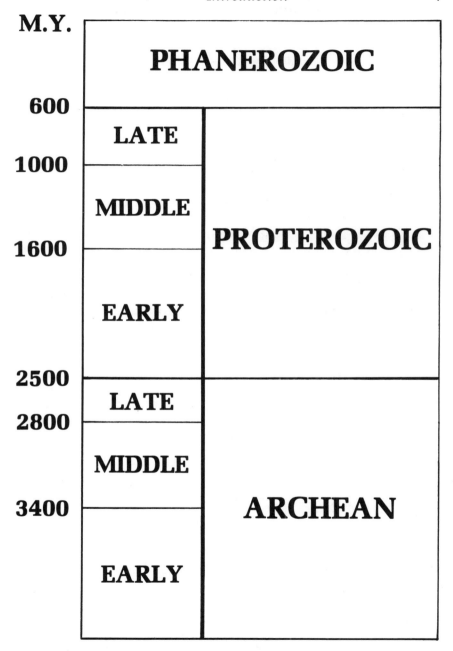

Figure 1-2: Representation of the major divisions of geologic time that will be used in this book.

point in geologic time occurred approximately 600 million years ago, when animal fossils made their first appearance. This event ushered in the Cambrian period of the Paleozoic era, the beginning of the Phanerozoic eon. All time before this is referred to as the Precambrian, which constitutes some 4,000 million (4 billion) years. The Precambrian has been divided into two major blocks of time (eons), the Archean and Proterozoic. The Archean has been further divided into Early, Middle and Late Archean. Similarly, the Proterozoic has been divided into Early, Middle, and Late Proterozoic. The Archean lasted about 2,000 million (2 billion) years, from the origin of the earth some 4,600 million years ago to 2,500 million years ago. The Proterozoic also lasted about 2,000 million years, beginning about 2,500 million years ago and ending with the beginning of Cambrian time about 570 million years ago.

The last 570 million years includes three eras, the Paleozoic era, from 570 million to 225 million years ago, the Mesozoic era, from 225 million to 65 million years ago, and the Cenozoic era, from 65 million years ago to the present. The development of abundant animal life at the beginning of Cambrian time has enabled much more detailed subdivision of geologic time into shorter intervals called *periods*. Rocks formed in a particular period can generally be recognized on the basis of fossils contained in them (if they are sediments) or by radioactive age dating, which can establish the age of igneous rocks.

▲ THE ROCK CYCLE ▲

Earth processes are very large-scale, are diverse, and result in profound changes in rocks. We must remember, however, that these earth processes neither create nor destroy the materials that make up the earth. Rather they change the materials (rocks) from one form to another. The various processes that change the rocks, and the rocks produced by these processes, are called the *rock cycle* (see Figure 1–3).

Rocks are stable in the environment in which they form. When subjected to conditions that are markedly different from those at which they formed, rocks are usually unstable and break down. Typically, rocks are altered to new minerals that are stable under the new set of conditions.

For example, *igneous rocks* are formed by the cooling of molten materials that were produced deep within the earth. The minerals that crystallize from these molten materials (called *magmas*) are stable at temperatures ranging from about 600°C to 1,100°C, the observed temperature range of

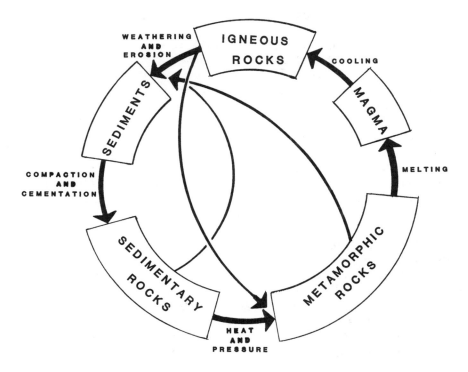

Figure 1-3: The Rock Cycle.
The diagram illustrates the changes that take place when rocks are subjected to
conditions that are different from those under which they formed.

molten rocks. Where the molten rock escapes to the earth's surface, it cools rapidly and forms a wide variety of *volcanic rocks.* Much of the molten material, however, cools and crystallizes before it reaches the surface. This magma cools much more slowly, which allows for larger crystals to form. These coarser-grained igneous rocks are called *intrusive rocks.*

When igneous rocks are exposed at the earth's surface the minerals in them are exposed to conditions very different from those at which they formed. Temperatures are much lower, may fluctuate daily or by seasons, much water is available, often as an acidic solution, and oxygen from the air is available to attack certain elements (such as iron). The heating and cooling, wetting and drying, additions of oxygen and water, cause the rocks to break down ("weather") into smaller particles. Water (from rain) soaking through the fragments removes some ingredients in solution. The smaller size of particles allows surface waters to carry materials away in streams.

The materials transported by streams are eventually deposited to form a variety of "new" rocks called <u>sedimentary rocks</u>. Sedimentary rocks are quite different from igneous rocks in appearance and chemical composition. Original ingredients in the igneous rocks respond differently to the transport in water. Quartz is quite insoluble, is hard, and tends to travel in grains of sand. Most other minerals are chemically altered and take on a new form. The common feldspar minerals are converted to clay minerals that are exceedingly fine-grained. Clay minerals are a major component of soils, and they are transported by streams and deposited in the oceans.

Because clay particles are much smaller than sand, they are carried farther offshore before they are deposited. The clay (mud) is eventually converted to a rock called shale. Because clay minerals are very abundant, shale is a common sedimentary rock.

The chemical ingredients that were dissolved out of the igneous rocks during weathering travel even farther before they are deposited. The surface environment thus results in a *reorganization* and *sorting* of the ingredients in the igneous rocks. While "new" rocks are formed in the surface environments, all of the original ingredients must eventually be accounted for. For example, calcium, perhaps the most notable compound carried in solution, although certainly not the only one, is precipitated out of solution from sea water mainly by biological processes. Various marine organisms remove calcium carbonate to make their skeletons. These deposits are converted to rocks called limestone.

Weathering and deposition are continuous processes, however, and, with time, the sedimentary rocks are buried under an ever thickening series of layers. The sequence of sedimentary rocks may reach thicknesses of tens of thousands of feet. When this occurs, the deeper layers are subjected to conditions that are different from those under which they formed. The earth becomes hotter at increasingly deeper levels from the surface, and the weight of overlying rocks adds much pressure to the rocks. The increased temperature and pressure causes the rocks (and the minerals within them) to adjust to these new conditions. The result is a <u>change</u> in the minerals to form "new" rocks called *metamorphic rocks*. Under relatively low temperature conditions the original rocks are not changed much. As temperatures and pressures increase, however, the rocks change more and more from their original nature. Water is driven out of hydrous clay minerals as the temperature increases, and new metamorphic minerals form with little or no water in their structure.

Initially the sedimentary shales are converted to *slate* with little change in overall composition. As temperatures increase the minerals become coarser and individual mica flakes become visible. The rocks are then called *schists*, and contain distinctive metamorphic minerals, such as garnet, staurolite, kyanite, and sillimanite. At still higher temperatures (perhaps 600° - 700°C) the original shale is converted to a *gneiss* that has a mineral content similar to granite. At these temperatures the rocks may begin to melt, to produce magma that forms igneous rocks, thus beginning the cycle over again.

▲ THE THEORY OF ▲
PLATE TECTONICS

The geologic history of the Lake Superior region (like that in all areas) is recorded mainly in *rock-forming* processes or events. These processes include igneous activity (both volcanic and intrusive), sedimentary processes, metamorphism, and the various settings in which rocks can be uplifted, depressed into the earth, or deformed. Many of the rocks formed during the Precambrian, particularly during Archean time, have been difficult to explain by older geological theories. Although the rocks on continents have been studied for well over one hundred years, until recently no clear unifying principle has been proposed to explain their origin, their distribution, and the structures within them.

Recently a new geological concept has been proposed that seems to bring together in a logical manner the many different aspects of geology. The theory is called *plate tectonics*. It incorporates two fundamental factors relating to the earth: that the earth's surface is composed of a number of discrete, large "blocks" or "plates", and the recognition that these plates are <u>moving</u> with respect to one another. Most rock-forming events are related to the plates, especially to processes occurring along the boundaries of the plates. Let us look briefly at the nature of the plates and the geological process associated with them to provide a background for interpreting and explaining the geologic history of the Lake Superior region.

THE PLATES

Our present understanding of the nature of the plates has come from a variety of totally independent geological studies. We have known for years that earthquakes occur in well-defined zones in the oceans and on the continents. Furthermore, most volcanic activity on earth is closely related to these earthquake zones. We now believe that the earthquake zones mark the edges of the plates, and that the earthquakes are produced by movement of the different plates on opposite sides of the boundary. Thus, in simple terms, the boundaries of the plates are outlined on the earth's surface by earthquakes and/or volcanic activity. At the present time some plates are thousands of miles across while others are much smaller, as shown in Figure 1–4. But how thick are the plates, and what are they composed of?

Various geologic studies, including studies of the way earthquake waves travel through the earth, indicate that the plates consist of a relatively rigid layer of the earth about 100 kilometers (60 miles) thick. This rigid layer is called the *lithosphere* and is underlain by a rather soft, plastic layer about 200 kilometers (122.48 miles) thick called the *asthenosphere*. The asthenosphere is the plastic layer on which the plates move about on the earth's surface at a rate of one to several centimeters per year. Beneath the asthenosphere the earth again behaves in a rigid manner.

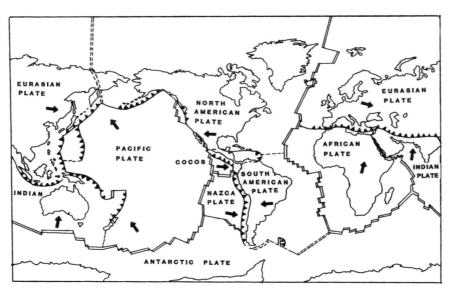

Figure 1-4: Major plates of the world.
The types of plate boundaries are: A. Midoceanic ridges at which the plates move apart are represented by double lines. B. Transform fault boundaries are shown by single lines. C. Trenches and subduction zones are marked by lines with teeth on one side. The teeth point down the descending slab. Dashed lines are used where the exact location or nature of the boundary is uncertain.

The lithosphere consists of *crust* and the upper part of the *mantle*. Two fundamentally different types of crust form the upper part of the lithosphere. Basaltic (or oceanic) crust that averages about 10 kilometers (6 miles) thick underlies the ocean basins. Granitic (or continental) crust up to 40 kilometers (25 miles) thick underlies the continents. Underlying the crust is the upper mantle, believed to be composed of peridotite, which is much denser than either the basaltic or granitic crust. Thus the lithospheric plates consist mainly of peridotite overlain by granitic or basaltic crust (Figure 1–5).

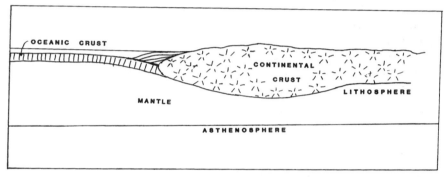

Figure 1-5: The relationship of the asthenosphere, lithosphere, and crust. Above the soft asthenosphere is the lithosphere, which includes both the rigid upper mantle and crust. Two types of crust are recognized: a thin dense oceanic crust and a thicker light continental crust. The base of the crust is called the Moho Discontinuity.

Much of the data supporting the concept of plate tectonics has come from studies of the sea floor since the mid-1960s. Dating of rocks and sediments obtained by drilling into the ocean floor has shown that the rocks on the ocean floor are relatively young; the oldest rocks yet found are only about 200 million years old. Furthermore, the rocks on the ocean floor become progressively younger toward the "mid-ocean ridges," a chain of submarine volcanic mountains that extends through all oceans. Rocks along the crest of these oceanic ridges are still forming today, as evidenced by volcanic activity at many places along the chain. Thus, new basaltic crust is continually forming at the oceanic ridges and moving away. These data have led to the concept of *sea-floor spreading,* which proposes that the lithospheric plates are moving about on the surface of the earth.

PLATE MOTIONS

If, as the data indicate, the plates are moving, then there are three possible motions occurring along their boundaries. The plates may be spreading (moving apart), converging (moving toward one another), or they may be sliding past one another, as illustrated in Figure 1–6. The geological processes along the different types of plate boundaries are very different and each produces distinctive rock types.

At spreading boundaries, the crust moves apart and *new crust* forms when basaltic magma, formed in the partially molten asthenosphere, rises to the surface and fills the ever-widening "crack" between the plates. Since most spreading plate boundaries are ocean basins, the basalt is extruded onto the ocean floor and pillow lavas result. The hot basalt reacts with the seawater, altering the basalts somewhat. On the other hand, where spreading occurs on a continent, the granitic crust is split apart and long, fault-bounded valleys are formed with associated volcanic activity. An outstanding modern-day example of this is in eastern Africa, where a long series of lakes occupies the depression caused by spreading plates. Further north the Red Sea was formed by spreading plates and the oozing of basaltic rocks onto the sea floor. A similar spreading plate boundary that occurred in the Lake Superior area approximately a billion years ago is discussed later.

Plates that are sliding past one another produce large-scale fault zones along which numerous earthquakes occur. Because of the large amount of grinding that occurs along the sliding plate boundaries, huge volumes of rock are pulverized along the fault zones. When the crushed materials are cemented together to form rocks they are called *mylonites* (from the Greek word for "milled"). Probably the best known boundary where two plates are sliding past one another today is the San Andreas Fault zone in western California. The western side of the fault is moving north at a rate of some two inches per year. Therefore, the western side of the fault has moved northward nearly 400 miles in the last 50 million years. This type of plate motion produces distinctive types of rocks that can be recognized even in the ancient terranes of the Precambrian shields.

Since the surface area of the earth is essentially constant, it is obvious that if new crust is being formed along spreading plate boundaries, older crust must be "consumed" elsewhere. Thus, along boundaries where plates are converging, crustal materials are destroyed. In most instances where plates converge, one of the plates buckles down and "descends" back into the deeper levels of the earth. These areas are referred to as *subduction zones* and are the site of numerous earthquakes, and much igneous activity as material melted from the descending

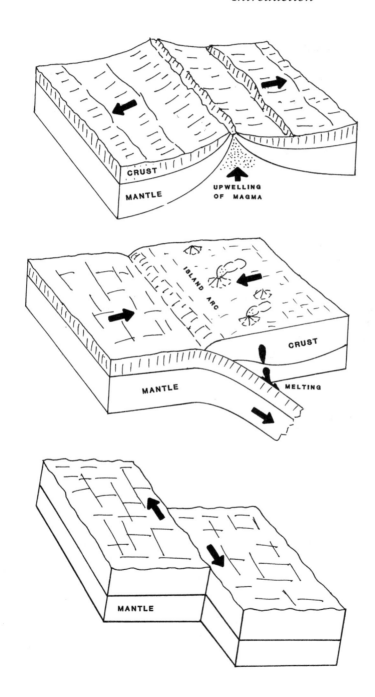

Figure 1-6: The three possible kinds of plate motion. Possibility A, where the plates move away from each other is called a divergent plate margin. New oceanic crust is generated at divergent plate margins. Possibility B, where the plates move toward each other is called a convergent plate margin. The process of subduction consumes oceanic crust at convergent plate boundaries. Possibility C, where the plates slide past each other in contact without either approaching or diverging significantly, is called a transform boundary. Transform faulting is the corresponding process.

CRUST

MANTLE

UPWELLING OF MAGMA

ISLAND ARC

CRUST

MANTLE

MELTING

MANTLE

plates rises to the surface. The material melted from the descending plate is a mixture of chemical ingredients with the lowest melting temperature. If the magma is extruded onto the surface it forms the explosive andesitic to rhyolitic volcanic rocks. If it crystallizes below the surface, it forms large areas of granitic rocks called *batholiths*. Therefore, the presence of andesitic to rhyolitic volcanic rocks and associated granitic batholiths is taken to indicate a former subduction environment. Subduction zones may also be the site of down-warping of crust to form basins or troughs in which sedimentary rocks accumulate. Finally, they are the site of much deformation due to the great compressive forces produced by the converging plates. A zone of folds and faults perhaps a hundred miles wide is produced along the convergent plate boundaries. Heat from rising magmas results in much recrystallization (or metamorphism) of the rocks in the zone of deformation. Convergent plate boundaries are therefore characterized by andesitic to rhyolitic volcanic rocks, associated sedimentary rocks, intrusion of granitic batholiths, long "belts" of metamorphism, and intense deformation. These features are characteristic of what we refer to as *continental crust*, and it may well be that much of the continental materials had their origin in convergent plate boundaries. A present-day example of the features in a convergent plate margin is the Andes Mountains along the west coast of South America, where oceanic crust of the Pacific plate is being subducted beneath the west coast of South America. The long belt of andesite and rhyolite volcanoes and associated granitic batholiths and deformation and metamorphism is a consequence of subduction in the area. Recognition of vestiges of these features in areas of older rocks may indicate the presence of a subduction zone sometime in the geologic past. Figure 1–7 is an idealized sketch of the general plate relationships.

CRUSTAL TYPES

It was mentioned that ocean basins are underlain mainly by basalts that form along spreading plate boundaries, are relatively short-lived, and are consumed in subduction zones. This relatively thin layer is called *oceanic crust*. In contrast, *continental crust* is composed mainly of granitic materials that have a lower density than basaltic crust. Because it has a lower density, continental crust tends not to be carried down in subduction zones. Instead, it is "scraped off" the descending plate and remains at the surface. Therefore, once continental crust has formed, it tends to persist at the earth's surface. This accounts for the fact that the rocks on the continents are, in general, much older than those forming the ocean floors.

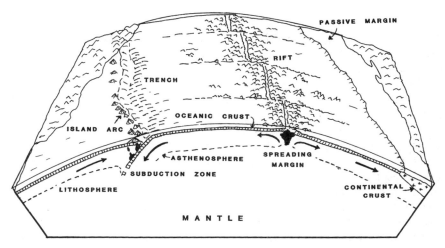

Figure 1-7: Major tectonic features of the earth and their relationship to plate boundaries.

MANTLE PLUMES

Recently, it has been recognized that certain areas on earth not related to plate boundaries have long records of igneous activity. One of these is the Hawaiian Islands which are thousands of miles from a plate boundary. These features are interpreted to be relatively local "hot spots" or "plumes" deep in the earth's mantle where molten rocks are produced and rise to the surface. These "plumes" evidently persist for tens of millions of years as sites of magma generation. Long chains of volcanic islands are produced in oceans when oceanic plates move over the plume. The present volcanic activity on the island of Hawaii indicates that this island is currently over a mantle plume in the Pacific Ocean. Within the Hawaiian Island chain the islands are progressively older northwest of the island of Hawaii. The other islands are extinct volcanoes that formed when they were over the mantle plume. This and other evidence indicates that the floor of the Pacific Ocean is moving northwestward, while the mantle plume appears to remain fixed. When continental plates move over a mantle plume, igneous activity commonly occurs. The continental rocks may be domed upward or even split apart by the upward and outward flow of material from the mantle plume. This rifting may have happened more than once in the Lake Superior region during the Precambrian.

Although plate tectonics does not provide answers to all of the problems in geology, it is a unifying principle that shows that many seemingly unrelated things are, in fact, part of the same process. We do not know what causes the plates to move, although the movement must be due to some type of convection currents in the earth's mantle. Furthermore, it seems likely that if the conditions within the earth have changed considerably over the last 4,000 million years, we cannot apply the pre-sent features of plates (such as their thickness) directly to the early (Archean) history of the earth.

Nevertheless, the basic premise of geology that "the present is the key to the past" should hold. Although the thickness of plates may have caused some differences in style of deformation, the overall process has likely been operative over most or all of geologic time.

With this brief discussion as background, let us look at the sequence of geologic events that has produced the rocks that make up the Lake Superior region. Interested readers may wish to pursue the topic of plate tectonics further and will find a more thorough coverage in most physical geology textbooks written since the middle 1970s.

SUGGESTED ADDITIONAL READINGS

Birkeland, P. W., and Larson, E. E., 1989, Putnam's Geology, 5th ed., Oxford University Press, New York.

Dott, R. H., Jr., and Batten, R. L., 1988, Evolution of the Earth, 4th Ed., McGraw-Hill Book Co. Inc., New York.

Judson, S., and Kauffman, M. E., 1990, Physical Geology, 8th Ed., Prentice Hall, Englewood Cliffs, N.J.

Levin, H. L., 1992, The Earth Through Time, 4th Ed., Saunders College Publishing, Harcourt Brace College Publishers.

Ojakangas, R. W., and Matsch, C. L., 1982, Minnesota's Geology, University of Minnesota Press, Minneapolis.

Stanley, S. M., 1989, Earth and Life Through Time, 2nd ed., W. H. Freeman and Company, New York.

Tarbuck, E. J., and Lutgens, F. K., 1989, The Earth: An Introduction to Physical Geology: Third Edition, Merrill Publishing Co., Columbus, Ohio.

2

THE ARCHEAN

Archean pillow basalts with pillows about three feet wide. Exposure is about four miles west of Marquette, Michigan.

Basically the Archean was an extensive time of generation and assembly of continental crust in subduction environments. In addition to this generation of continental crust, vast amounts of oceanic crust also must have been generated at spreading margins. As is the case in the modern earth system, however, almost all of the oceanic crust produced was consumed as a result of subduction. Although each subduction zone may have generated a relatively small amount of continental crust, the cumulative effect of numerous subduction zones over hundreds of millions of years was the production of substantial quantities of new continental crust. Recall that continental crust is less dense than oceanic crust and therefore tends not to be consumed by subduction. Instead, the masses of continental crust moved about on the lithospheric plates and eventually collided with other blocks of continental crust. This process, known as *accretion*, results in the gradual increase in the size of continental masses, for each collision increases the size of continents.

There is a growing body of evidence that indicates that a large percentage of continental crust present at the end of the Archean was assembled into a large "supercontinent" (or perhaps several supercontinents). This supercontinent was subsequently broken up and reassembled again as a result of plate tectonic activity during later geologic time. In fact, it appears that most continental crust was assembled into supercontinents several times during earth history. The most recent supercontinent, called *Pangaea*, began breaking up about 150 million years ago.

The Archean, then, is the record of the generation of the first continental crust and the assembly of this crust into large blocks of continental size. Let us examine the features of Archean parts of Precambrian shields and see how they support these ideas of the early history of the earth.

It is now widely recognized that Archean parts of all Precambrian shields consist of two major types of rocks that form extensive "belts" or "blocks" within the shields. One of the major features of Archean shields is "greenstone belts," which consist of long, linear units of tightly folded volcanic and associated sedimentary rocks that are typically surrounded by large areas of granitic rocks that intrude and separate adjacent greenstone belts. Greenstone belts, in turn, are bounded and separated from one another by comparable-sized "gneiss belts" comprised of highly metamorphosed and deformed rocks of generally granitic composition. Indeed, Archean parts of the Canadian shield are composed of a number of elongate belts of greenstone–granite crust alternating with gneiss belts (Figure 2–1). Since Archean continental crust is <u>composed</u> of greenstone belts and gneiss belts, it follows that an understanding of the nature and origin of these rock types is, in essence, an understanding of <u>the origin of the continents</u>.

Figure 2-1: Map showing major subdivisions of the Archean Superior Province of the Canadian Shield. Note the "belts" of greenstone and granite alternating with gneiss belts over much of the area. (Adapted from Card, 1990.)

Greenstone belts and gneiss belts are well represented in the Lake Superior region, and their nature, distribution, and origin are discussed in the following pages. Greenstone–granite belts are discussed first because they have been more extensively studied, and because this background should help in understanding the far more complex rocks of the gneiss belts.

GREENSTONE-GRANITE
▲ TERRANES ▲

GREENSTONE BELTS

Greenstones are one of the most important rock types in Archean terranes. They consist dominantly of basaltic volcanic rocks with subordinate amounts of andesitic and rhyolitic volcanics and sedimentary rocks. Small but important concentrations of iron, zinc, copper, gold, and occasionally nickel also occur. These volcanic and sedimentary rocks exist as long narrow "belts" that are tens to hundreds of kilometers long and up to a few tens of kilometers wide. These "greenstone belts" are bounded and intruded by granitic rocks on both sides. Although the rocks are intensely deformed in detail, the overall belt has a U-shaped (synclinal) cross section (Figure 2–2) due to down-folding of the central part of the elongate belt. Thus, the oldest basaltic rocks form the outer margins of the belts, with the younger rhyolites and sedimentary rocks forming the central parts.

The term *greenstone* is derived from the light to dark green color so typical of most of the volcanic rocks. The green color is produced by the presence of large percentages of green minerals, particularly chlorite, actinolite, and epidote. These minerals formed from the original augite

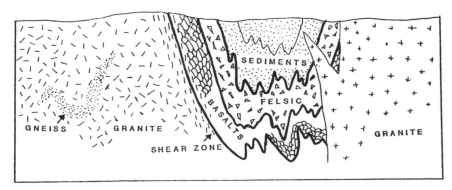

Figure 2-2: Diagrammatic cross-section of a greenstone belt showing the synclinal structure, surrounding granites, and sheared contact zones. The granitic batholiths may contain large areas of gneisses.

and plagioclase in the basalt by chemical reorganization and the addition of water to the volcanic rock. The reorganization occurred under conditions of low-intensity metamorphism after the rocks were erupted. The metamorphism resulted in a chemical reconstitution of the rock but, in many instances, has not obliterated the primary volcanic textures and structures. Greenstones, then, are a somewhat metamorphosed basaltic volcanic rock.

Basaltic Rocks. Probably the most distinctive feature of the basaltic rocks is the widespread occurrence of pillow structures. Pillow structures are balloon-shaped features that range in size from about one foot to more than 10 feet across. The outer margin of the pillows is very fine grained and is called a *selvage*; the interior is somewhat coarser grained, generally lighter in color, and is sometimes dotted with vesicles formed from gas bubbles escaping from the lava. Typically, the vesicles become filled with other minerals and are then called *amygdules*. Figure 2–3

Figure 2-3: Cross-section of a typical basaltic pillow showing the dome-shaped top and the v-shaped bottom. Archean greenstone about five miles west of Marquette, Michigan.

shows the typical shape of an eroded cross section of a pillow. Pillow lavas form when a lava flow is extruded onto the sea floor, or when lava flows into the sea or some other body of water. The pillow is formed when pressure from within a lava flow cracks the cooler "rind" that is in contact with the water (Figure 2–4). When the crack forms, lava is extruded from it. Although the water chills the outer portion, it remains soft and plastic. Continued extrusion inflates the pillow much like blowing up a balloon. Pressure within the lava flow may determine the size of the pillow because it controls the amount that it is "inflated."

Although buried by a thin layer of sediment, pillow lavas cover most of the present-day ocean floor and thus are the most common kind of volcanic rocks in the world. The dome-shaped top and downward V between the tops of the underlying pillows are helpful in determining the top of lava flows in areas where the rocks have been folded. This is particularly important in greenstone belts where the rocks have been intensely and complexly deformed. Pillows tend to be rather plastic features and their form may be greatly altered by deformation. Geologists must therefore use caution and look for a consistent orientation among many pillows when using them for top-determination.

Although pillow structures are extensively formed as a result of hot basaltic lava interacting with sea water, in some cases lava is chilled and "spalls" off, producing angular fragments. These angular fragments may fill the spaces between pillows, or may form layers of fragmental basalt. The fragments were originally glassy fragments that typically have a highly altered outer margin (rind). These fragmental units are called *hyaloclastite* (from the Greek word *hyalo* = glass plus *clasts* = fragments) (Figure 2–5). Some sequences of pillow lavas may be hundreds of feet thick and extend for miles. However, many lava flows interbedded with pillow lavas are massive (structureless). These massive basalts may represent the interior portions of lava flows "insulated" from the water necessary to form the pillows. The interior portions of some lava flows may cool very slowly and thus may develop a coarser crystalline texture. Excellent samples of Archean pillow lavas can be seen in roadcuts along Minnesota Highway 169 just west of Ely, Minnesota; in roadcuts along U.S. Highway 2 just east of Wakefield, Michigan; and along U.S. Highway 41 approximately 5 miles west of Marquette, Michigan.

Basaltic and andesitic tuffs, breccias, and other fragmental materials may form extensive units in the volcanic sequences of greenstone belts. The fragmental units are produced by a more explosive type of eruption where the expanding gases in the magma break up the lava as it is erupted from the vents. If the fragments cool somewhat and harden before they fall back to earth (or before they spread out on the sea floor),

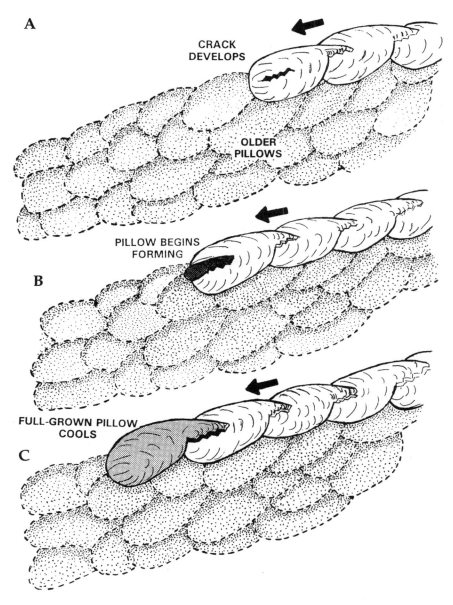

A

CRACK DEVELOPS

OLDER PILLOWS

B

PILLOW BEGINS FORMING

C

FULL-GROWN PILLOW COOLS

Figure 2-4: A series of diagrams illustrating the formation of pillow lavas. A. A crack develops in the rind of a newly formed pillow, exposing the molten basaltic interior. B. Basalt emerges from the crack, and a new pillow grows as lava continues to drain from the older pillow. C. The full-grown pillow cools from contact with the surrounding water.

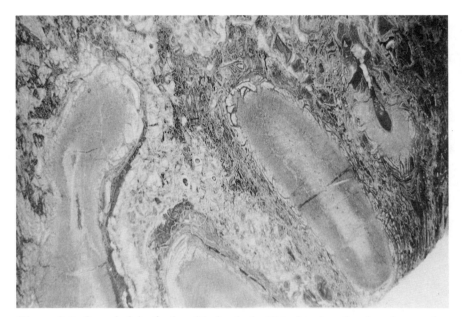

Figure 2-5: Sawed slab of a basaltic hyaloclastite, showing the sharply angular fragments produced by spalling of lava when it is chilled by contact with water. Ely greenstone, near Robinson Lake, Minnesota.

a layer of volcanic fragments accumulates. Some of these fragmental units may have a distinctive character and can serve as "marker horizons" in mapping volcanic rocks. The fragmental texture is best revealed on weathered or glacially polished outcrops. The fragmental volcanic rocks are typically rather altered, with considerable development of carbonate materials. These carbonates are dissolved out by weathering when the rocks are exposed at the surface. On freshly broken surfaces the fragments may be nearly invisible due to the lack of contrast between fragments and matrix.

Where the rocks have been deformed, the fragments may be drawn out into rods, as along the Gile flowage at Montreal, Wisconsin. Where the basalts have been intensely sheared (faulted), the primary textures and structures may be completely obliterated, and the rock is converted to a slabby, schistose rock.

Near granitic intrusions (generally near the margins of the greenstone belts), the greenstones are usually more highly metamorphosed and become darker colored and harder. Hornblende, plagioclase, and quartz become the dominant minerals, forming from the chlorite, actinolite, epidote, and albite of less metamorphosed varieties. In places, pillows and other relatively large features may persist at this level of metamorphism, while the finer tuffaceous textures are usually destroyed by recrystallization.

Chemical studies of the volcanic rocks in greenstone belts show that there are a number of origins and environments in which the rocks formed. For example, substantial amounts of the basaltic pillow lavas are chemically almost identical to modern ocean-floor basalts, and evidently represent Archean ocean floor. Much more limited amounts of greenstone belts have chemical similarities to modern calc-alkaline volcanics formed in subduction zones. Other basalts are chemically similar to plateau basalts or to basalts formed from "hot spots" (similar to the Hawaiian Islands).

In addition to these "standard" volcanic rocks, basalts that are unusually magnesium-rich have been discovered. The rocks are called *komatiites*, acquiring their name from exposures along the Komati River in South Africa where they were first described. They are classified chemically as ultramafic rocks because of their high magnesium content. The presence of pillow structures and distinctive quench textures (Figure 2–6) of olivine and pyroxene demonstrate that these were actually

Figure 2-6: Quench textures in komatiite showing the long slender skeletal olivine crystals. From Munroe Township, Quebec. Photo by M. P. Schaubs.

liquid flows extruded on the ocean floor with resultant rapid chilling of the lava. The long, slender crystals are referred to as "spinifex" after the spinifex grass in the desert regions of Australia. Some ultramafic units are believed to be sills intruded between basaltic flows near the surface of the volcanic pile.

Generally, the ultramafic rocks occur in the lower portion of the volcanic sequence, indicating that the early magmas were unusually magnesium-rich and became progressively more silica-rich during the course of time.

Chemically the komatiites form a distinct group of volcanic rocks different from those higher in the volcanic pile. This poses questions regarding the sources of the different volcanic groups, their relationship to one another, and the significance of these volcanic types to the geologic setting in which greenstone belts are formed. A commonly held interpretation is that the magnesium rich komatiites were produced when the earth's mantle from which these rocks originated was significantly hotter than it is today. Magnesium-rich volcanic rocks form fairly extensive units within the volcanic sequence of the Ely greenstone belt.

Rhyolitic Volcanics. At scattered intervals along greenstone belts the basaltic rocks are overlain by several thousand feet of andesitic and rhyolitic volcanic rocks (Figure 2–7). The andesitic and rhyolitic rocks generally have a much more local distribution than the basalts and usually are separated from them by a marked compositional break. These felsic volcanic rocks are usually tan to gray in color with a creamy white or gray weathered surface. Some varieties are nearly black on freshly broken surfaces. In most cases these rocks are harder than the basalts owing to the higher silica content and the resultant presence of quartz.

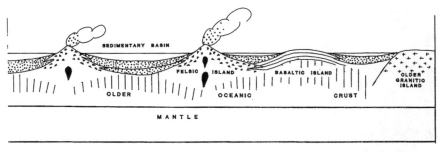

Figure 2-7: Schematic longitudinal diagram of a greenstone belt showing the relationships of basaltic volcanic activity to felsic volcanic centers and granitic intrusions.

Since rhyolitic volcanoes are far more explosive than their basaltic counterparts, most felsic volcanic rocks are fragmental. Various-sized fragments from microscopic shards to blocks more than a foot across are common (Figure 2–8). The finer fragments are much more common and widespread than larger ones. Various-sized shards, pumice, and fragments of other types of volcanic rocks, along with a variable amount of phenocrysts, are common. The larger fragments may be readily visible on outcrops, while the smaller fragments are seen only after careful scrutiny, often in thin sections under a microscope. Most felsic volcanics contain larger crystals (phenocrysts) of quartz and feldspar, which serve as a basis for field classification, but chemical analyses are usually necessary for precise classification and comparison with volcanic rocks elsewhere.

The tuffs are commonly bedded or layered and may be interbedded with normal water-transported materials. Thick, massive lava flows, some of which may contain small pillows and/or massive mudflow deposits, may be present locally. Tuffs can be recognized in the field by the presence of very angular fragments of volcanic material embedded in a matrix of the same rock type. There is usually an almost complete

Figure 2-8: Exposure of andesite showing the typical fragmental texture that results from the more explosive type of eruption. From Deer Lake, north of Ishpeming, Michigan.

lack of sorting of the fragments. Fine-grained tuffs (ash deposits) appear cherty on fresh surfaces, but have a "chalky" kaolinitic appearance on weathered surfaces. Broken crystal fragments are far more common than well-formed phenocrysts.

Rhyolitic volcanic rocks are well-developed and exposed in the Tower–Soudan area of northern Minnesota, where roadside cuts can be seen just west of Tower on Minnesota Highway 169. Fragmental rocks near in composition to rhyolite are also well exposed at Deer Lake, north of Ishpeming, Michigan (see Figure 2–8).

Graywackes. The third major component of greenstone belts is made up of thick accumulations of detrital sedimentary rocks, conglomerate, graywacke, and slate. These sediments overlie and grade laterally into the volcanic sequences. They occur in thick accumulations of 10,000 feet or more. The most abundant and characteristic rock type is graywacke. The graywackes contain more or less angular sand-size grains of quartz and feldspar in a matrix of chlorite- or sericite-rich clay. Fragments of volcanic rocks are also common.

Graywackes are poorly sorted sedimentary rocks that typically form in deep water at the base of relatively steep slopes. They result when large volumes of sand and mud deposited near the top of a slope break loose and rush downward as huge underwater landslides. The sediment-laden currents are very heavy, and as a result, they flow along the ocean floor as muddy (turbid) water called *turbidity currents.* When the currents reach the base of the slope, they spread out and slow down on the flatter deep ocean floor. As the currents slacken the larger (heavier) particles settle out first, forming a sandy or gravelly base. With continued slowing of the current, finer and finer particles settle out of the turbid water. This results in a sorting (or *grading*) in the size of particles deposited on the ocean floor. Larger particles accumulate at the bottom and finer particles form at the top of the sediment layer produced from each turbidity current. The finer particles are also carried farther from the source area than larger particles (Figure 2–9). Therefore, deposits formed near the origin of the slide would be more sandy, whereas deposits formed father from the source would be composed mainly of silt and mud. Thus, the layers produced by turbidity currents possess a lateral as well as vertical gradation in the size of particles that make up the layers of graywackes. These features are very helpful in reconstructing the geological environments in which the rocks formed.

Bedding is usually well developed in the graywackes, with good graded bedding being rather common, as shown in Figures 2–10 and 2–11. The graded beds consist of layers with a sandy lower part grading

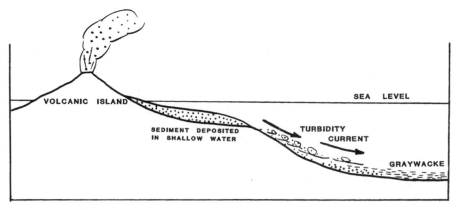

Figure 2-9: Diagram showing the geologic setting in which graywackes form in basins surrounding volcanic islands.

Figure 2-10: Rhythmic layering typical of graywackes. White layers are sand-rich, gray layers are mud-rich. Top of layers is to the left. From Lake Vermilion Formation at the Pike River, west of Tower, Minnesota.

Figure 2-11: Coarse conglomerate with boulders composed mainly of volcanic rocks. From near Rainy Lake, Minnesota.

upward to a much finer grained "muddy" upper portion. Individual graded beds range from less than one inch to nearly 20 inches in thickness, but most are in the 3- to 10- inch range. Thicker units may contain very coarse sand and pebbles at the base and show scouring or erosional channels in the underlying units. These graded units are very useful to determine the top of beds in deformed rock sequences. Fine-grained slaty graywackes are commonly quite rich in carbon and may contain abundant pyrite. They are typically black and easily eroded.

Ojakangas (1972) has shown that graywackes near Lake Vermilion, Minnesota, are interlayered with the surrounding volcanic rocks. He further showed that the graywackes are composed of materials derived mainly from erosion of the rhyolitic volcanic rocks. Volcanic tuffs and tuffaceous graywackes are also present in the sequence.

Therefore, the graywackes in the Lake Vermilion area were apparently deposited at the same time as the volcanic islands were formed. The sediments probably accumulated in basins along and between the islands. The center of volcanic activity may have shifted from one area to another. When an island no longer being replenished with volcanic rock was eroded down, it was buried by sediment derived from erosion on a nearby island still actively volcanic. In short, the relationships between the sediments and volcanics differ from place to place and no single "rule" will be applicable everywhere. Examples of Archean graywackes and slates are especially well developed and exposed around Lake Vermilion, west of Tower, Minnesota, with abundant roadcut exposures.

Iron-formations. In addition to the graywackes, iron-formations form distinctive sedimentary rocks in greenstone belts in Archean sequences. Iron-formations consist mainly of chert (chemically precipitated quartz) and iron-rich minerals. In some units the rock may be mainly chert; in others it may be chert-hematite or it may be jasper-hematite, which is a spectacular rock with alternating red and metallic gray layers, each about one-fourth to one inch thick. This is especially impressive when the rock has been intricately folded, as shown in Figure 2–12. Siderite may be present locally, and even pyrite may occur with the chert in places. However, chert and magnetite are by far the most common minerals in the iron-formations. The Soudan iron-formation, extending from

Figure 2-12: Complexly folded Archean Soudan Iron-Formation at Soudan, Minnesota. Hammer handle points in the direction the folds are plunging.

Tower, Minnesota, eastward to near Ely, Minnesota, is an especially good example of an Archean iron-formation and can be seen at Soudan State Park in Soudan, Minnesota, and at several localities between Soudan and Ely.

Generally, but not always, the iron-formations are associated with the more rhyolitic phase of volcanism. Tuffaceous material is interbedded with many of the iron-formation lenses, and some iron-formation lenses may grade laterally into magnetitic (or pyritic) tuff without chert. The iron-formations in this volcanic association seem almost certainly to have formed by volcanic hot springs contributing iron and silica to the sea water. There is little evidence of chemical weathering, and there may well have been little rock (except islands) exposed to weather. The iron-formations probably formed in basins between volcanic islands.

The silica and iron was probably precipitated by biochemical processes. The specific mechanisms are discussed in a later section in connection with the much more extensive Early Proterozoic iron-formations. Suffice it to say here that the oldest reported fossils in the world have come from cherts in the more than 3,000 million-year-old Fig Tree series in South Africa.

Some iron-formations, including the Soudan, have highly carbonaceous layers (now mainly graphite) associated with them. Indeed, carbonaceous shales and graphitic layers are common in both the sedimentary and volcanic rocks of greenstone belts. Studies of these carbonaceous layers indicate that they are composed mainly of organic carbon. This would attest to the presence of primitive organisms (probably blue-green algae and bacteria) in amounts great enough to accumulate in layers many feet thick in the waters in which the greenstone belts formed. It also points to the antiquity of life on earth, for the oldest greenstone belts yet studied (at least 3,300 million years old in South Africa) have evidence that primitive life was abundant enough to leave a record.

Deformation and Metamorphism. All Archean volcanic and sedimentary rocks have been involved in at least one episode of folding and faulting. Most have been metamorphosed at least slightly; some have been so intensely metamorphosed that the original rock type is scarcely recognizable. Since the deformation and the heating for recrystallization (metamorphism) are separate processes and may or may not occur at the same time, they are discussed separately.

Most greenstone belts with all their components have been folded into a troughlike syncline. Thus, the basaltic rock originally on the bottom occurs on the outer margins of the trough. The overlying (younger) rock units, which are rhyolites and graywackes, occur closer to the center or axis of the syncline. The rocks are so intensely folded that most have been tilted nearly 90º, with the tops of layers on one side of the synclinal belt facing those on the other side. Figure 2–2 shows the relationship diagrammatically. The rock sequences are in effect lying on their sides, so that a geological map of a greenstone belt is really a cross-sectional view (Figure 2–13).

The belts are not simply folded into a syncline. There is typically very complex smaller scale folding that is a small scale model of the larger fold patterns. These small-scale folds, which can be seen on some outcrops, are invaluable in working out the larger fold features. The folding is so complex that a single layer may be brought to the surface several times.

Faulting on both a small and large scale is also typical of the deformation in greenstone belts. Very large-scale faults typically occur along the

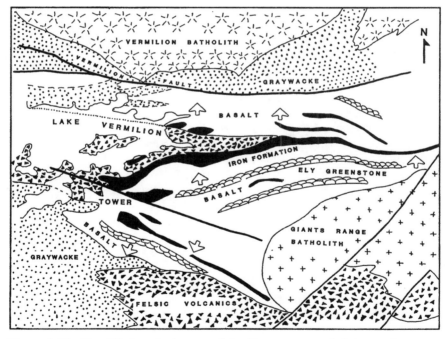

Figure 2-13: Simplified geologic map of the Ely greenstone belt in northeastern Minnesota showing the general geologic relationships. Broad arrows indicate facing direction in the volcanic sequence. Note that the felsic volcanics overlie the basalts, and that the graywackes in the western part of the map overlie basalts and are laterally gradational from felsic volcanics. (Modified from maps by the Minnesota Geological Survey.)

margins of the greenstone belts where they are in contact with the enclosing granitic rocks. Vertical movement on these faults may be thousands of feet, but horizontal movements of many miles occurs along some fault zones. Faults may produce offset of layers, or may result in some layers being repeated on outcrop surfaces.

Most rocks in greenstone belts have undergone at least slight metamorphism, suggesting some heating and recrystallization of the rocks after they formed. Greenstone belts over many large areas are only slightly recrystallized, however, leaving a remarkable preservation of primary features. This is truly remarkable when we consider that most of these rocks are nearly 2,700 million years old, for it indicates that little has happened in those areas since the rocks formed. An example of this is an area of eastern Ontario and western Quebec where a number of greenstone belts are exceptionally well preserved.

In other equally large areas the rocks have been much more highly recrystallized with few, if any, primary features preserved. In these areas the basaltic rocks are converted to amphibolites, hornblende schists, or gneisses. The rhyolitic rocks may be converted to biotite or muscovite schists, and under intense metamorphism may also become gneisses. When these rocks are also intensely deformed and fragmented by granitic intrusions and faulting, it is extremely difficult to ascertain the nature of the original rock. Many of the graywackes have an average composition near that of granodiorite. When these sediments are deeply buried they are converted to schists or banded gneisses, which may cover large areas. It is also possible to partially or completely melt them. Thus, some of the granitic intrusions cutting through the intensely metamorphosed gneisses and schists could actually be the melted portions of more deeply buried parts of greenstone belts.

These intensely metamorphosed areas may have been involved in a mountain-building episode, whereas their less metamorphosed counterparts probably have not. We will refer to these rock types again in the section on gneiss belts.

The Mineral Wealth. From the early days of prospecting in Canada and other countries it was recognized that most of the mineral wealth in the Precambrian rocks was found in the greenstone belts. The deposits include most gold, silver, copper, zinc, lead, nickel, cobalt, and iron. These deposits are quite different from one another, but they have one important feature in common: they occur in the volcanic rocks. We have already briefly considered the nature of the iron-formations in the volcanic sequences. Let us examine briefly the other types of deposits.

One of the major types of ore deposits is an elongated lens-shaped body composed almost entirely of sulfide minerals. These deposits are called *massive sulfides*, and they are the source of much of the copper, zinc, lead, silver, nickel, and cobalt in Canada. The ore bodies are composed mainly of pyrite and its relative, pyrrhotite, but contain variable amounts of chalcopyrite ($CuFeS_2$), sphalerite (ZnS), and galena (PbS). Some may contain nickel- and cobalt-bearing arsenic minerals. Massive sulfide deposits of pyrite and/or pyrrhotite are relatively common in volcanic rocks; those containing worthwhile accumulations of the copper, zinc, lead, and other valuable minerals are much less common—a discouraging feature for many companies prospecting for deposits. Figure 2–14 shows an idealized cross-sectional profile of these massive sulfide deposits. They characteristically occur in rhyolitic volcanic rocks. Underlying them are highly altered rocks believed to be an "alteration pipe" formed by the hot-spring activity that brought the sulfide minerals up to the ocean floor. The various metals were dissolved in the hot waters ("hydrothermal" solutions). When these solutions came out onto the ocean floor they were cooled and mixed with the chemicals in the seawater.

As a result, there occurred a rapid precipitation of the metals as sulfides directly above the hot springs. A modern-day, on-land occurrence somewhat analogous to this can be seen in Yellowstone Park where vast

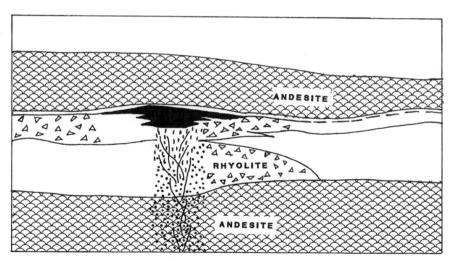

Figure 2-14: Schematic cross-section of a massive sulfide ore body showing the altered zone below the ore body, the associated iron-formation, and the unaltered volcanics above the ore body.

quantities of pyrite have been formed as some of the hot springs have brought iron (and some copper, silver, and gold) to the surface. Most of the Precambrian occurrences are overlain by and grade laterally into iron-formations. Thus the hot springs that formed the sulfide deposits also appear to have contributed much iron and silica for the formation of iron-formations. Overlying the massive sulfides and iron-formations are almost completely unaltered andesitic lava flows that buried the sulfide deposits and preserved them. The fact that the overlying lava flows are unaltered indicates that the hot springs activity had ceased before they were formed. Therefore, the sulfide deposits must have formed during a lull in the volcanic activity; however, it is likely that the hot water, along with the metals dissolved in it, came from the same reservoir of molten rock at the depth that formed the volcanic rocks.

The occurrence of gold in the volcanic rocks is commonly within or intimately associated with the iron-formation. The gold was probably also brought to the surface in the hot spring waters and deposited in some of the siderite-rich or pyrite-rich iron-formations, perhaps becoming "fixed" in these rocks by the presence of minor amounts of arsenic, as suggested by Hutchinson (1970). The gold deposits at the famed Homestake mine in the Black Hills were probably formed in this way.

Much of the mineral wealth in Archean rocks therefore appears to be related directly in time to the volcanic activity. Our understanding of this relationship, however, is a recent development.

Great strides toward understanding the genetic relationships between volcanic rocks, iron-formations, and various sulfide mineral deposits have been made during the past twenty years. One of the first to recognize a genetic relationship between mineral deposits and volcanic activity was a Norwegian, Christopher Oftedahl, who published a truly landmark paper on his theory in 1958. Since the concept seemed to explain many previously puzzling aspects of the deposits, it was adopted by many geologists. In the years since it was proposed, the idea has been rigorously tested and found to be correct. It has been greatly expanded upon by many geologists and is now widely accepted. This concept has been extremely helpful to exploration geologists in their never-ending search for new mineral deposits.

Not all mineral deposits in Archean rocks are related to volcanic or sedimentary process. Many of the large gold deposits in Archean parts of the shield are in large fault zones, some in the boundary faults between gneiss belts and greenstone belts. Fluids generated by the faulting evidently carry gold to higher levels in the crust where it is deposited. The faults also act as channelways for the fluids. Therefore, recognition of large fault zones becomes an important exploration guide in the search for gold.

GRANITIC BATHOLITHS

Background. While greenstone belts are economically important, they constitute only about 15 percent of shield areas; the remaining 85 percent is composed of granitic rocks. The shield areas are therefore composed dominantly of granitic rocks. Thus, an understanding of the nature and origin of the granitic rocks is essential to an understanding of the origin and growth of the shields. Since granitic areas contain little in the way of economic minerals, however, they have been largely neglected until quite recently. In an attempt to unravel some of the problems of shield areas, government surveys and research teams at several major universities in Canada, the United States, and in several other countries have established long-term research programs to obtain basic geological data on the Precambrian shields. The programs consist of systematic field mapping of large areas (thousands of square miles) along with regional geophysical studies, such as aeromagnetic and gravity surveys. Age dating and local detailed studies on geochemistry and structure have also been conducted. Data from these diverse studies have helped greatly in understanding the general framework of Precambrian shields, but they have also brought to light a number of previously unrecognized problems. The following discussion is taken from a number of reports on various aspects of Archean geology with the aim of summarizing some of the major aspects of the granitic rocks.

Types of Granitic Rocks. Large areas of granitic rocks separate the greenstone belts, and these granitic parts of Archean shields show a great deal of diversity. At the contacts the granitic rocks almost always intrude (and therefore postdate) the greenstones. This has led to the widely held belief that the granitic parts of shields are universally younger than the greenstones. For example, many textbooks still refer to "Keewatin greenstones" as the oldest rocks that are intruded by "Algoman granites." Mapping within granitic terranes, however, has shown large areas of gneissic rocks that do not fit this simple model. The gneisses record a deformational and metamorphic history that is not present in the greenstone belts. Many geologists believe that these "gneiss belts" are remnants of crustal materials that predate the greenstone belts. If this is correct, then the Keewatin greenstones are not the oldest rocks in shield areas; the gneisses are. In any event, the granitic rocks reveal that the Archean shields have a long and complex history.

Radiometric dating has shown that most of the greenstone belts in the southern Canadian shield formed between 2,750 and 2,600 million years ago. Dating of the rocks in the gneiss belts is much more difficult, but suggests that at least some of these rocks are more than 3,000 million years old, and therefore significantly older than the greenstones. The precursors of the gneisses appear to be older volcanic, sedimentary, and intrusive rocks that have been intensely metamorphosed and deformed. We will return to these gneissic rocks later; first let us examine the granitic rocks adjacent to the greenstone belts and attempt to resolve the problem of the origin of the granitic parts of Archean shields.

The granitic batholiths that surround and intrude greenstone belts are not everywhere the same, and the structural relationships between the granites and greenstones vary from place to place. Sims (1976) provides an excellent discussion of the major granitic rocks flanking the greenstone belt in the Vermilion district of northeastern Minnesota. The volcanic–sedimentary rocks were intruded almost simultaneously by an immense volume of granitic magma both north and south of the greenstone belt. As the granite magma rose through the earth's crust, flanking the greenstone belt, it caused much deformation in the volcanic–sedimentary rocks. The magmas appear to have risen almost to the surface where confining pressures were very low, allowing the magma to "mushroom" or spread horizontally as more magma was injected from below. The resultant folds and flattened pillows are roughly parallel to the margin of the invading granite bodies. These granites therefore forcibly intruded the rocks, shouldering them aside, but they do not appear to "cut out" much of the pile nor did they digest large volumes of volcanics. Intensity of folding and flattening is greatest among the granitic contacts where the rocks have also been more extensively recrystallized. The continued rise of the granites (due to their lower density) also caused much vertical movement in the greenstone belt; pillows and volcanic fragments were "stretched" out or elongated from four to more than ten times their original length, as shown in Figure 2–15. This elongation indicates that the rocks in the greenstone belt were moving down into the crust, while the flanking granites were rising. Figure 2–16 is a photograph of typical granitic rocks in an Archean batholith.

Another type of granitic intrusion into the greenstone belts is exemplified by the eastern end of the Giants Range Batholith on the south side of the Ely Greenstone near Ely, Minnesota (refer to Figure 2–13). This intrusion has engulfed a large part of the Ely Greenstone, cutting across folds and faults and, in effect, "cutting out" a considerable amount of the greenstones. This intrusion is younger than the western part of the Giants Range Batholith, which deformed the greenstone belt

Figure 2-15: Pillows in the Ely greenstone. The view is approximately at right angles to that shown in Figure 2-3 and in the fronticepiece for the chapter. Note that the pillows are elongated vertically due to deformation within the green-stone belt. Exposure is at the western outskirts of Ely, Minnesota.

as described earlier. Why the late granites tend to engulf and cut out large parts of the volcanic pile whereas the earlier granites do not is not clear. Perhaps the later granite formed after the crust had become more stable, and the mechanism of intrusion was to engulf the older rocks rather than to shoulder them aside.

The entire volcanic–sedimentary–intrusive history of a greenstone belt and the enclosing of granites lasted for 50–100 million years, from about 2,750 to 2,650 million years ago, according to Goldich (1972). Sims and Viswanathan (1972) and Hanson (1972) conclude from chemical studies that the granitic magmas were formed either by partial melting of the mantle or by the melting of volcanics and graywackes formed earlier during the volcanic phase of the greenstone belts. These studies show that the granitic rock did <u>not</u> form by the melting of <u>older</u> granitic crust. This suggests that the granitic batholith may have formed in approximately the same manner as did the associated green-stone belt.

Figure 2-16: Typical massive to slightly foliated granitic rock intruded into Archean greenstone. Puritan Quartz monzonite about six miles south of Hurley, Wisconsin.

THE ORIGIN OF GREENSTONE BELTS AND ASSOCIATED GRANITES

The origin of greenstone belts has been debated by geologists for many years. In spite of the thousands of man-years of investigation there is no generally accepted explanation for their origin. We now briefly summarize the characteristics of the rocks and then present the current ideas on their origin.

Greenstone belts consist of an elongate belt of basaltic rocks that formed mainly under water. Many belts contain ultramafic rocks in the basal part of the volcanic succession indicating contributions of magma from the mantle. Rhyolitic rocks are relatively common in the upper parts of the volcanic sequence, representing rhyolitic volcanic islands at scattered intervals along the volcanic belt. The volcanic chain was flanked by subsiding troughs, as indicated by the widespread development of deep-water graywackes in the upper parts of the succession.

The graywackes were derived largely by erosion of the volcanic rocks, especially the rhyolites.

The belts continued to subside into the earth's crust, and the sinking was accompanied by the upwelling of huge volumes of granitic magma on both sides of the volcanic belt. Intrusion of the granitic magma intensely deformed the volcanic-sedimentary sequence shortly after it formed. Radiometric ages indicate that the greenstones and granitic batholiths developed in an interval of about 50–100 million years and thus probably are both related to the same geological event.

Chemical studies of the enclosing granites show that they were not derived by the melting of older granitic crust. Rather they represent "new" magma derived either by partial melting of the mantle or by melting volcanic rocks and graywackes that had not been at the earth's surface for more than 100 million years. The immense volume of granitic magma in the batholiths also requires that it must have originated in an environment capable of generating this amount of granite.

Extensive studies of Archean areas have shown that greenstone belts have rock sequences, deformation styles, and chemical similarities to rocks formed in modern-day convergent boundaries. It is probable greenstone belts represent island arcs produced by the convergence of two plates of oceanic (basaltic) crust or where oceanic crust was subducted beneath continental crust. In other words, it appears that the subduction zones that formed greenstone belts were near or at the margin of a continent. Although it is probably not possible to make a direct comparison between greenstone belts and present plate boundaries, they appear to have formed in an ancient counterpart of an island arc environment.

▲ GNEISS BELTS ▲

Extensive areas of high-grade gneisses are also major components of Archean shields. The gneiss belts differ from greenstone belts in both the chemical composition of the rocks and the intensity of metamorphism to which they have been subjected. Card (1990) provides an excellent summary of the nature and origins of the Archean Superior craton of the Canadian shield. He shows that the gneisses may be produced by high-temperature metamorphism of a variety of different precursor rocks. The gneisses have been produced from: (1) original sedimentary rocks (mainly graywackes), (2) original granitic intrusions, and (3) intense metamorphism in deep levels of greenstone belts.

Examples of several different types of gneiss belts are present in the Lake Superior region. The Quetico gneiss belt (also referred to as the Quetico subprovince in Canada) extends some 600 miles across Ontario and parts of Minnesota in the Rainy Lake, Lake Kabetogama area (Figure 2–1). The dominant rocks within the belt are schists and gneisses produced by intense metamorphism of graywackes and minor amounts of other sedimentary rocks. The belt is characterized by relatively low-grade metamorphism on the margins with high-grade metamorphism in the central part. Studies of low-grade metamorphic components indicate that the graywackes were derived primarily from volcanic rocks, presumably volcanic islands along a trench. At higher intensities of metamorphism the mineralogy of the rocks changes, with the production of

Figure 2-17: Gneissic rocks formed by intricate intrusion of granite (white) in and around darker layers of metamorphosed sedimentary rocks. About five miles east of Fort Francis, Ontario.

more coarse-grained rocks and metamorphic minerals that reflect the higher temperatures. Granitic intrusions within the high-grade metasediments are produced by subduction of oceanic crust and, in part, by partial melting of metasedimentary rocks (Figure 2–17). The partial melting of metagraywackes results in innumerable granitic veins intricately invading the older rocks. These mixtures of igneous and metamorphic rocks are called *migmatites* (Figure 2–18), which may comprise large areas of gneiss belts.

Structures in gneiss belts are very complex, like the structures in greenstone belts. Large areas may be characterized by intense folding, whereas other areas contain relatively straight-banded gneisses. The current interpretation of the Quetico gneiss belt is that it represents an "accretionary wedge" that formed in a trench during collision of several island arcs (greenstone belts) (Percival and Williams, 1989) (Figure 2–19). Boundaries between the gneiss belt and flanking greenstone belts to the north and south are major fault zones.

The gneiss belt in the Minnesota River valley in southwestern Minnesota is an example of gneisses that formed in a rather different environment. Although the rocks have undergone very high-grade metamorphism, geochemical studies suggest that they are mainly volcanic and

Figure 2-18: Contorted migmatitic Archean gneiss from an abandoned quarry near Pittsville, Wisconsin.

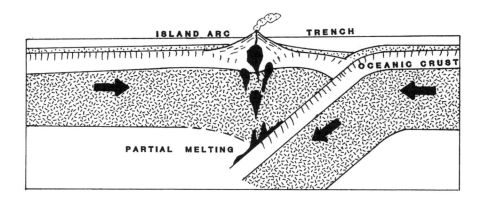

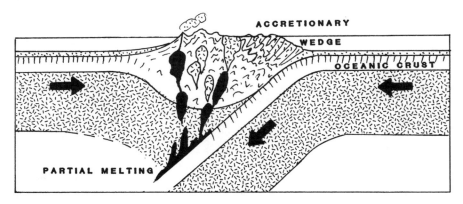

Figure 2-19: Diagram showing the development of an accretionary wedge along a convergent plate margin. The accretionary wedge is formed as sedimentary rocks are "scraped-off" the down-going plate at a subduction zone. The accretionary wedge continues to grow until subduction ceases.

granitic intrusives. Therefore these rocks apparently represent a highly metamorphosed and deformed greenstone belt. In effect, the area may represent the deeply eroded "roots" of a greenstone belt. Radiometric dating of the rocks indicates that some rocks of the Minnesota River valley gneiss belt are at least 3,600 million years old, and therefore are nearly 1,000 million years older than rocks in the Ely greenstone belt to the north.

The boundary between the gneisses of the Minnesota River valley and the greenstone–granite terrane to the north is a major fault zone called the Great Lakes Tectonic Zone. The Great Lakes Tectonic Zone extends some 600 miles to the east and is interpreted to be the "suture" between an older block (an exotic terrane) of continental crust that collided with the Superior craton as part of the accretion process that resulted in the supercontinent that was produced at the end of Archean time.

It would be incorrect to give the impression that the Archean continent consisted of nothing but volcanic and plutonic rocks and graywackes. Rather clean quartz sandstones and stromatolitic carbonate (dolomite) sediments formed in shallow water (platform) environments and are present in a number of areas (Card 1990). These sequences evidently formed in stable parts of earlier formed continental masses. Comparable rock units are also present in Archean shields of Western Australia and southern Africa. These rock types become more abundant in the succeeding Early Proterozoic successions that overlie the Archean, and are discussed further in later sections.

In summary, the record of events in the Archean documents that continental crust was generated throughout most of this vast period of earth history. Studies of Archean rocks demonstrate that the rocks formed during the Archean are in environments and by processes in every way analogous to modern-day plate tectonics. The numerous greenstone and gneiss belts were deformed, metamorphosed, and intruded by voluminous granitic batholiths during convergent tectonics, and became "welded" together to form large continental masses by 2,500 million years ago—the end of the Archean. As Card (1990) points out, the Archean parts of the Canadian shield are remnants of a larger continental mass (a supercontinent) that was assembled during Late Archean time. It was subsequently broken up and assembled again to form another supercontinent during the Early Proterozoic.

SUGGESTED ADDITIONAL READINGS

Card, K. D., 1990, A review of the Superior Province of the Canadian Shield, a product of Archean accretion, Precambrian Research, vol. 48, pp. 99–156.

Franklin, J. M., Lydon, J. W., and Sangster, D. F., 1981, Volcanic associated massive sulfide deposits, Economic Geology, 75th Anniv. volume, pp. 485-627.

Nisbet, Euan, 1987, <u>The Young Earth, an Introduction to Archaean Geology</u>, Unwin Hyman.

Ojakangas, R. W., and Matsch, C. L., 1982, <u>Minnesota's Geology</u>, University of Minnesota Press, Minneapolis, MN, 255 p.

Percival, J. A., and Williams, H. R., 1989, Late Archean Quetico accretionary complex, Superior Province, Canada, <u>Geology</u>, vol. 17, pp. 23–25.

Sims, P. K., 1976, Early Precambrian tectonic-igneous evolution in the Vermilion District, northern Minnesota, <u>Geol. Society of Amer. Bull.</u>, vol. 87, pp. 379–389.

Sims, P. K., and Morey, G. B. (Editors), 1972, <u>The Geology of Minnesota: Centennial Volume</u>, Minnesota Geological Survey.

Sims, P. K., and others (Editors), 1993, The Lake Superior Region and Trans-Hudson orogen, <u>The Geology of North America, v. C-2, Precambrian: Conterminous U.S.</u> The Geological Society of America.

Thurston, P. C., Williams, H. R., Sutcliff, R. H., and Stott, G. M., 1991, Eds, <u>Geology of Ontario</u>, Parts 1 and 2, Ontario Geological Survey, Toronto.

3

THE EARLY
PROTEROZOIC

The Early Proterozoic is noted for the vast sedimentary iron-formations that are the source of huge quantities of iron ore. This photo, taken in 1957, shows one of the large open pit mines on the Mesabi Range in northeastern Minnesota.

Early Proterozoic time in the Lake Superior region witnessed several major events. First was a long period of erosion of the large "supercontinent" that had been assembled during the Archean. The second major event was the gradual break up of the Archean continent into a number of smaller "fragments" that moved off to various places on the earth. Several hundred million years after the breakup there was a reassembly of some of the continental fragments to form another supercontinent. A major mountain range (the Penokean Mountains) was formed in the Lake Superior region as a result of the reassembly of the continental fragments.

▲ THE "EPARCHEAN INTERVAL" ▲

The "granitic" continental crust generated during the immense span of Archean time was assembled into one or more large continental masses. Like modern-day continents, these ancient masses stood mainly above sea level, and as a result, were subjected to erosion by streams flowing across the landscape. Because there were no land plants to protect the decomposed rocks, however, erosion may have been very severe. The sand, mud, and materials dissolved from the rocks were carried to the seas on the margins of the continents. Once in the seas the transported materials were sorted by waves and currents and deposited much like modern deposition in oceans.

The relatively large size of these new-formed continents produced extensive areas that were subjected to erosion. The numerous mountain ranges produced by volcanic activity and collision of smaller continental masses were cut down to a gently rolling surface. The landscape must have been very bleak, indeed, with no plants (or animals) to cover the naked soil. Modern deserts might be somewhat analogous to the continents at the end of Archean time. However, Archean landscapes lacked vegetation even in areas of heavy rainfall.

This extensive period of erosion has long been recognized, and is referred to in older geological literature as the "Eparchean Interval." The Archean rocks were deeply eroded during this time, as shown by the vast expanses of granites and gneisses exposed at this ancient erosion surface.

Because gneisses are formed at depths of perhaps 10 miles or more, gneiss belts indicate areas of especially deep erosion. The duration of the period of erosion represented in the Lake Superior region is uncertain. Archean rock-forming events appear to have ended about 2,650 million years ago. The oldest overlying rocks of Early Proterozoic age are difficult to date, but appear to be about 2,200-2,300 million years old. Therefore, the erosion interval may have lasted for several hundred million years.

The Early Proterozoic, as used in this book, is the period of time from 2,500 million to about 1,600 million years ago and thus represents another very long chapter in the history of the Lake Superior region. As one might expect in such a long span of time, a number of very different geological events occurred.

In simple terms two major events occurred in the Lake Superior region during Early Proterozoic time. The first event was the breakup of the supercontinent formed near the end of Archean time. One of the major breaks extended across northern Wisconsin, Michigan, and eastward into Ontario, Canada. Therefore, the break up of the Archean supercontinent had a major impact on the Lake Superior region. The continental masses that broke off from the Superior craton were carried away by plate tectonic processes to unknown localities.

The second major event was the reassembly of the continental crust into another "supercontinent" (or supercontinents) later in Early Proterozoic time. Rocks formed during this reassembly were produced by convergent plate tectonics, and are similar in many respects to rocks in Archean greenstone belts. The history of these two major events is well represented in the Lake Superior region.

Let us examine the rocks formed and geological features produced to learn why we have arrived at this interpretation. As is shown, both events are rather complex, and have resulted in a wide variety of rock types and structures.

RIFTING AND
▲ CONTINENTAL BREAKUP ▲

Approximately 2,300 million years ago an elongate east-trending zone from western Minnesota across northern Wisconsin and Michigan and extending eastward to the Lake Huron area of Ontario began to slowly

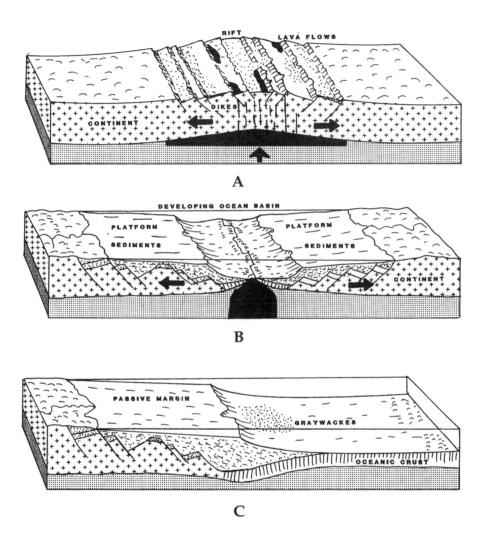

A

B

C

Figure 3-1: Series of diagrams illustrating stages in the break-up of the Archean continent in the Early Proterozoic. (A) Upwelling of magma beneath the continental crust produces an elongated rift with associated volcanic rocks. (B) Early stages of continental separation with step-like blocks along continental margins and initial formation of oceanic crust along a spreading ridge. (C) Complete separation with well developed platform on continental margin, graywacke deposition on the margins of the platform and a broad expanse of oceanic crust.

subside (Figure 3–1). The sea gradually advanced over the relatively flat surface of eroded Archean greenstones, granites, and gneisses. The record of this early subsidence and invasion of the sea is especially well preserved along the north shore of Lake Huron. The sequence of rocks is referred to as the *Huronian Supergroup*, a term used for a group of similar rock formations that are related in origin.

Young (1983) presented evidence that the subsiding trough (or basin) formed as a major rift (or fracture) developed across the Archean continent. In Canada the Huronian Supergroup is a thick sequence of rocks, mainly sandstones (now quartzites), some shales (now slates), and dolomites that were deposited in shallow water. In addition there are minor volcanic rocks and several distinctive units that are probably of *glacial origin*. The sequence of rocks is believed to have formed in what is called a *passive margin* formed by the pulling apart (rifting) of the Archean continent.

Passive margins are formed as a result of the development of a divergent plate margin beneath a continent. The initial phase is a doming of the crust, presumably due to addition of basaltic magma to the base of the continental crust. Doming is associated with extensive fracturing of the crust that produces large crustal blocks that may be tilted to produce elongate basins (called *grabens*) and ridges (called *horsts*). The horsts were subjected to erosion, and sediments were deposited in the grabens. Some of the basaltic magma escaped to the surface to form basaltic lavaflows and basaltic dikes.

With continued rifting the zone tends to subside and an arm of the sea covers the spreading region. This results in a change from nonmarine to marine sedimentation as shown diagrammatically in Figure 3–2. Note the development of steplike blocks in the continental crust formed by extension of the crust during the rifting process. Eventually one side of the rift is carried away by plate motion. What remains is a submerged margin of a continent on which sediment is deposited across the steplike faulted continental crust, which gradually changes to oceanic crust (Figure 3–1). Sediments are carried to the continental margin by streams flowing from the interior of the continent. These margins are typically the site of deposition of sandstone, shale, and limestone. After the initial block-tilting and basaltic volcanisms the margins are characterized by the lack of deformation and volcanic activity. The term *passive margin* is applied to signify the stability and lack of deformation in these areas.

In the Lake Superior region the rifting stage is represented by the deposition of a sequence of sandstones, shale, and carbonate rocks on the Archean basement. According to Larue (1981) and Larue and Sloss (1980) deposition was mainly in down-dropped grabenlike basins on a continental margin.

Figure 3-2: Glacial tillite from the Bruce conglomerate near Whitefish River, Ontario. Note the large cobbles and pebbles in an unsorted matrix.

Before we discuss the marine sediments in the Lake Superior region it might be useful to discuss the glacial deposits in the Lake Huron area. Several thick, extensive units of probable glacial origin are well exposed in that area. Some contain grooved, polished surfaces of Archean rocks overlain by rocks composed of mixtures of boulders, sand, and mud. Although the mixtures are now thoroughly lithified into rocks, they are remarkably similar to the much younger glacial deposits that cover most of the Lake Superior region. In places, the glacial deposits represent lake deposits, where the dominant deposits were silt and clay. Scattered through the thinly layered silt and clay are boulders up to several feet in diameter. These boulders apparently were frozen into the ice, carried out into the lakes, and then dropped into the fine sediments when the icebergs melted (Figure 3–2 contains an example). Some of the deposits appear to have formed where the glacial ice moved out to sea, again much like recent glacial deposits, where glacial deposits are interbedded with marine sediments.

The wide distribution of these deposits indicates that they were the result of *continental glaciation*. At approximately 2,300 million years old, they may be the oldest record of continental glaciation on earth.

Similar deposits, probably also of glacial origin, are present north of Negaunee and Marquette in northern Michigan (Figure 3–3). This early continental glaciation also appears to have occurred in the Lake Superior region, where these glacial deposits underlie the typical marine sediments.

The basal sedimentary units are quartzites (originally deposited as sandstone and conglomerate) derived from the weathering and erosion of granites and gneisses. In general the quartzites are composed mainly of quartz sand, suggesting intense chemical weathering in the Archean source area. The quartzite is commonly thick-bedded with good sorting and well-rounded grains, and contains abundant cross-bedding and ripple marks. These features suggest deposition on a shallow, stable ocean floor where waves frequently stirred up the sediments and currents were active. Studies of cross-bedding indicate that major current direction and sand transport was to the southeast (Trow, 1948; Pettijohn, 1957).

The sand accumulated to thicknesses of about 700 feet in the Marquette area of Michigan, although it was thinner in most other areas. Remnants of this quartzite unit are preserved at a number of localities in the Lake Superior region. These occurrences are given local names, such as the Mesnard Quartzite near Marquette, Michigan; the Sunday Quartzite in the Gogebic district of northern Michigan and Wisconsin, and the

Figure 3-3: Reany Creek Formation north of Negaunee, Michigan. Note the large cobbles in a finer matrix. This unit has been interpreted to be of glacial origin.

Sturgeon Quartzite near Iron Mountain, Michigan. The sandy unit may originally have extended from northwestern Wisconsin to Sault Ste. Marie or beyond, a distance of more than 300 miles. If so, it was far more extensive than any Archean sedimentary unit (most of which are a few tens of miles or less in extent). This greater extent of sedimentary units reflects the larger size of continental masses, and consequent longer coastlines during Early Proterozoic time. Extensive sandy beaches undoubtedly existed along the coast of the Early Proterozoic sea.

A dolomite unit several hundred feet thick overlies the quartzite in the Lake Superior region. In some areas the quartzite grades upward into dolomite. The transition is marked by interbedded dolomite and quartzite; the dolomite beds become thicker and more abundant with quartzite beds becoming thinner and less abundant upward. In the Marquette, Michigan, area a shaly unit (the Wewe slate) occurs between the quartzite and the overlying dolomite.

Like the quartzite, only scattered erosional remnants of the dolomite are preserved, and these are given local formation names. Perhaps best preserved is the Kona Dolomite near Marquette, Michigan. Exposures in the Iron Mountain area are called the Randville Dolomite, and exposures in the Gogebic district are called the Bad River Dolomite. Dolomite in these various localities is almost universally believed to be essentially the same age and to have formed in the same type of geological environment. Interestingly, similar dolomite has been encountered in drill holes in central Minnesota (the Trout Lake Formation), and this unit may also be correlative with other dolomites in the Lake Superior region.

Dolomite is a chemically precipitated sedimentary rock composed of calcium-magnesium carbonate. The ingredients were carried in solution in sea water and were precipitated mainly by primitive microscopic organisms such as algae and bacteria. The dolomite probably formed offshore somewhat from the sandy beaches, but still in very shallow water. Although thin, discontinuous dolomites are present in some Archean greenstone belts (Card, 1990), they became a major sediment type in Early Proterozoic time.

The most distinctive feature of the dolomites is the widespread occurrence of laminated dome-shaped structures called *stromatolites* (Figure 3–4). Stromatolites are formed by microbial mats of algae and bacteria that live in very shallow water, and result in the deposition of carbonate rocks with the distinctive mound shape. Most reported stromatolites are several inches to several feet in size, like those shown in Figure 3–4. However, locally the dolomites contain tiny stromatolites about one-half an inch in size in flat layers. These small stromatolites appear to have developed in essentially flat microbial mats (Figure 3–5). Furthermore,

Figure 3-4: Stromatolites in the Bad River Dolomite, near Cable, Wisconsin. Mounds are about one foot wide.

Figure 3-5: Small stromatolites about 1 cm tall in flat layers in the Kona Dolomite from near Marquette, Michigan.

some larger (1- to 2-foot) domal stromatolites contain the small, half-inch stromatolites within the layers. The stromatolites therefore appear to be rather complex features. Variations in the size of stromatolites is believed to reflect the depth of water in which they formed; tiny stromatolites in flat layers may form in water only a few inches deep, whereas the giant 6- to 8-foot stromatolites indicate deeper water. A modern-day environment in Shark Bay, Western Australia, exhibits the development of stromatolites similar to those in Early Proterozoic carbonate rocks, and illustrates these features very well. Many of the stromatolites in Shark Bay are basically in very shallow water, and are thus exposed at low tide, while covered at high tide.

Additional evidence of shallow water deposition of the Early Proterozoic dolomites is the presence of remnants of anhydrite and casts of gypsum in some layers of the dolomite. These calcium sulfate minerals typically form in extremely arid environments due to evaporation of very briny water within the surface sediments. Spectacular casts of gypsum crystals to 2 inches long in reddish brown dolomite layers are present in the Kona Dolomite near Marquette, Michigan (Figure 3-6). Taken together, the presence of abundant stromatolites, gypsum crystals, and

Figure 3-6: Casts of gypsum crystals in brown, laminated Kona Dolomite near Marquette, Michigan.

thin sandy layers in the dolomite suggest that the dolomites in the Lake Superior region formed in an environment much like the present day Persian Gulf. The flat, arid environment along the Persian Gulf is called a *sabkha*, the Arabic name for this type of geologic setting. This suggests that the Lake Superior region was in a tropical setting during deposition of the dolomites some 2,200 million years ago.

Following deposition of the dolomite, further rifting caused a tilting of crustal blocks on the continental margin. Uplifted areas were subjected to erosion and down-dropped areas were sites of deposition. Thus, much of the dolomite and sandstone on the Early Proterozoic continental margin was removed by erosion "shortly" after it was deposited. The region was again leveled by erosion, then submerged beneath the sea a second time and buried by another sequence of rocks. This tilting and erosional event is shown by a gentle angular unconformity of regional extent between the quartzite-dolomite and the next overlying sequence of rocks.

The basal quartzite and dolomite of the Early Proterozoic are referred to in the geologic literature as the *Chocolay Group*. The name comes from exposures in the Chocolay Hills southwest of Marquette, Michigan. The Chocolay Group is overlain by another sequence of sedimentary rocks called the *Menominee Group*. As we will see, the Menominee Group is significantly different from the Chocolay Group.

THE ANIMIKIE BASIN

Following the period of tilting and erosion of the Chocolay Group sediments, most of Wisconsin, Minnesota, northern Michigan, and parts of Ontario began to subside beneath the sea. The development of a large east–west basin, and the events associated with it, have provided one of the most important and interesting chapters in the geological history of the Lake Superior region. The approximate size and shape of the basin are shown on the map in Figure 3–7. The sequence of rocks deposited is different from those of the Chocolay Group, especially in that dolomite is absent and a thick, extensive layer of iron-rich rock called iron-formation is present. This sequence of rocks is called the Menominee Group from exposures on the Menominee iron range near Iron Mountain, Michigan. The basin in which these and associated rocks accumulated is generally referred to as the Animikie Basin, from the Indian name for the area around Thunder Bay, Ontario, where the rocks are well exposed.

As is usually the case when the sea advances over a land surface, the basal unit to be deposited was quartz sand and gravel derived from the

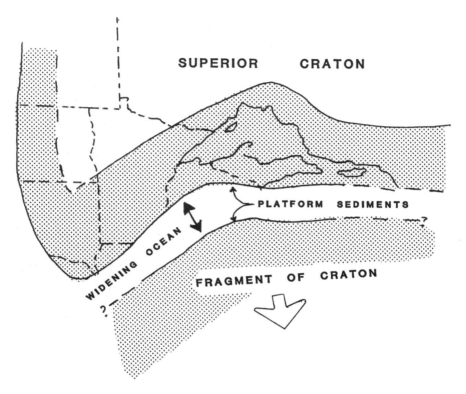

Figure 3-7: Sketch map of the Lake Superior region, showing the possible location of the developing continental margin and opening ocean basin about 2,100 million years ago.

land surface over which the sea advanced. Cementation of these units produced sandstone and conglomerate, which were later metamorphosed to quartzite. In much of the Animikie Basin the basal sandstone (now quartzite) was deposited directly on an eroded surface of Archean granite and greenstone. Locally the Menominee Group sediments were deposited on the remnants of the dolomite and quartzite of the Chocolay Group. On the northern edge of the Animikie Basin, in the Thunder Bay, Ontario, area, the basal conglomerate and quartzite the Kakabeka Formation (Figure 3–8) is only a few feet thick. In Minnesota, northern Wisconsin, and northern Michigan, the unit is several hundred feet thick. Like the formations of the Chocolay Group the basal quartzite was given local names in various parts of the Lake Superior region. Called the

Figure 3-8: Massive stromatolitic chert at the base of the Gunflint Iron-formation. Only a thin conglomerate of greenstone boulders separates the chemical sediment from the underlying Archean greenstone on the north shore of Lake Superior. From Schreiber, Ontario.

Ajibic Quartzite in the Marquette district of Northern Michigan, it overlies the older Mesnard Quartzite and Kona Dolomite near Negaunee. However, it rests directly on Archean greenstones and granites farther west near Champion. In the Gogebic district the basal unit is called the Palms Formation (Figure 3–9). It overlies the Bad River Dolomite on the eastern and western ends of the range, but rests on Archean rocks throughout the central part of the district. Farther west, in the Cuyuana range in central Minnesota, the Mahnomen Formation overlies a dolomite (the Trout Lake Formation). On the Mesabi range to the northeast, however, the Pokegama Quartzite directly overlies Archean granite and greenstone. Finally, on the Gunflint range in Ontario, the Kakabeka Formation rests on Archean rocks.

Perhaps the reason for the various names for the same rock unit should be explained. The original geologic mapping, done in the late 1800s and early 1900s, was done by a number of different geologists with the U.S. Geological Survey. They assigned names to the rock formations in the various areas they mapped. It was not until many years later

Figure 3-9: Palms Formation, the basal unit of the Menominee Group showing the irregular bedding and channel-and-fill structures. From Radio Tower Hill, Wakefield, Michigan.

that it was realized that the various districts are really part of one extensive sequence of sedimentary rocks. Therefore, we <u>correlate</u> the rocks from one area to another (Figure 3–10). However, the original, local names are still used for the rocks.

Following the deposition of up to several hundred feet of sandstone in shallow water, the environment changed to one of biochemical sedimentation. Instead of carbonate (dolomite) deposition, however, the Menominee Group was characterized by the widespread deposition of very iron-rich sedimentary rock called iron-formation. Isotopic studies indicate that the iron-formations in the Lake Superior region were deposited between 2,100 million and 2,200 million years ago.

Iron-formation is perhaps the most enigmatic and controversial rock type ever formed. It was deposited in many parts of the world during the Early Proterozoic in formations that are 500 to 2,000 feet or more thick and that extend for hundreds of miles. Therefore, thousands of cubic miles of iron-rich sediments were deposited in a number of basins. After the Early Proterozoic (about 2,000 million years ago) deposition of iron-formation ceased, and this distinctive rock type is essentially absent from younger geological sequences. Thus, we are left to puzzle over where the vast quantities of iron came from during the Early Protero-zoic, and why iron was not available in younger sedimentary sequences. Recall that iron-formations are also common sedimentary rocks in Archean greenstone belts. This indicates that iron-formations are com-mon sedimentary rocks in Archean and Early Proterozoic sequences, and are absent in younger sequences. This suggests that a major change in the chemistry of the surface environment of the earth must have occurred around 2,000 million years ago to prevent iron-formation depo-sition in younger sedimentary sequences. Most geologists now believe that the major change was the development of an oxygen-bearing atmos-phere on earth. Iron is relatively soluble in an oxygen-deficient environ-ment and therefore would be present in large amounts in ocean waters. In oxygen-rich environments, like the present atmosphere, iron is incred-ibly insoluble, and therefore is not present in quantity in ocean waters.

Iron-formations have played an important part in the settlement and economic development of the Lake Superior region, for these rocks are the source and host for a vast majority of the iron ore produced in North

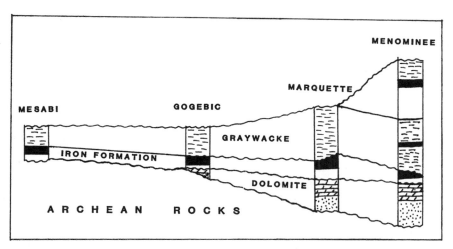

Figure 3-10: Generalized correlation of Precambrian rock units within the Lake Superior region.

America. The ores were first "discovered" by European settlers when the early land surveyor, William Burt, was shown iron ore by the Indian chieftain, Marji Gesick, at what is now Negaunee, Michigan, in 1844. Mining commenced in 1846, grew steadily, and has continued to the present time. Discovery of iron ore in other parts of the Lake Superior region (the Menominee district near Iron Mountain, 1867; the Vermilion district, Minnesota, 1875; the Iron River–Crystal Falls district, 1880; the Gogebic district, 1883; the Mesabi district, 1892; and finally the Cuyuna district in 1904) constitutes one of the most colorful chapters in the history of the Great Lakes area. Mining was second only to logging in bringing in new people and in opening the area to settlement. Its importance, however, has far outlasted that of logging, for it is still a major contributor to the economy of the region.

Iron-formation was first studied in the Lake Superior region in the late 1800s. In fact, iron-formations in this region are the "standard" to which iron-formations throughout the world are compared. The various mining districts (Figure 3–11) were described by a series of comprehensive reports by the U.S. Geological Survey between 1892 and 1911. Interested readers should refer to these monographs for details of the geology. Hundreds of articles have been published by numerous authors on the various aspects of iron-formations and iron ores. While there is now a general agreement on the nature and origin of iron-formations, some unresolved problems still remain. The following paragraphs summarize some of the major features of these unique rocks.

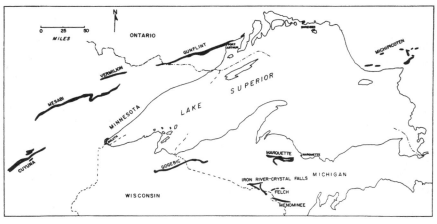

Figure 3-11: Location map of iron districts of the Lake Superior region.

Although iron-formation has a simple composition—it is composed of chert (biochemically precipitated quartz) and iron minerals—it is extremely variable in appearance. Both the chert and iron minerals are varied in color. Despite these variations, iron-formations have distinctive features that provide a basis for identification. As the name implies, it is rich in iron minerals, with one or more iron-bearing minerals constituting nearly half of the volume of the rock. The chert-rich layers range in color from white to gray, black, or green to brown, red, or maroon depending upon the type and amount of iron minerals present as pigment. The iron-rich layers also vary in color: magnetite layers are black; hematite layers are often metallic gray; siderite layers are light to dark brown; and iron silicate layers are green to black. Thus, no single color is diagnostic.

Iron-formations are characterized by one of two basic types of layering. *Banded* or laminated iron-formation is composed of uniform layers of chert generally less than 1 centimeter thick alternating with similar thin layers of iron minerals (Figure 3–12). This variety of iron-formation is believed to have formed in quiet (deep?) water. *Granular* or cherty iron-formation consists of chert-rich layers that are highly variable in

Figure 3-12: Even-bedded iron-formation consisting of thin, uniform layers of chert alternating with iron-rich layers. Note the folds in the rock. From Jasper Knob, Ishpeming, Michigan.

thickness (up to 15 centimeters) alternating iron-rich layers to produce an irregular (or wavy) bedded rock (Figures 3–13 and 3–14). The chert-rich layers are characterized by round "granules" about the size of sand grains set in a matrix of chert. Larger angular and rounded fragments of chert are also present. The iron-rich layers are typically thinner than the lens-shaped granular layers, and consist of siderite, magnetite, or hematite. Granular iron-formations have bedding features similar to sandstones or shallow-water carbonates (limestones). Therefore, they are believed to have been deposited in shallow water.

Iron-formations in the Lake Superior region have units of granular-type iron-formation alternating with units of banded (laminated) iron-formation. In fact the iron-formations are subdivided into "members" on the basis of these bedding features. These variations in bedding indicate that iron-formations were deposited in both shallow and deep water. The variations also indicate that water depth in the basin changed from time to time.

Iron-formations also contain stromatolites similar to those in the older dolomites. Well-preserved stromatolites are found on the Mesabi, Gunflint, and Gogebic ranges. The stromatolites consist of somewhat irregular pillars

Figure 3-13: Granular iron-formation showing the typical thick, massive, granule-bearing chert layers alternating with thinner, more continuous iron-rich layers. Ironwood Iron-formation, Mt. Whittlesey, near Mellen, Wisconsin.

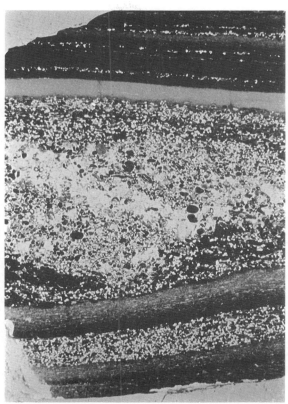

Figure 3-14:
Granular iron-formation
showing thick granule-
bearing chert layers
separated by thinner
layers of fine-grained
siderite. Biwabik
Iron-formation, near
Aurora, Minnesota.
Sample is about
one inch wide.

0.5–2.0 centimeters wide and 1.0–10.0 centimeters high. Interpillar areas are generally filled with granule-bearing or oolitic chert (Figures 3–15 and 3–16). In some cases the pillars are highly irregular; the stromatolites produce a wavy, laminated chert. Like modern varieties, these stromatolites are believed to have formed in *microbial mats*, which consist of a diverse group of microscopic organisms.

The late Professor Stanley Tyler of the University of Wisconsin examined stromatolitic chert from the Schreiber, Ontario, area of the Gunflint district under high magnification in the mid-1950s. He found that the dark black color of the chert was produced by innumerable microscopic organic structures in the chert. This was the first discovery of well-preserved fossils in rocks of this great age (about 2,100 million years old). Results of this study were published in 1965. Prior to this time it was generally believed that well-preserved fossils did not exist in Precambrian rocks.

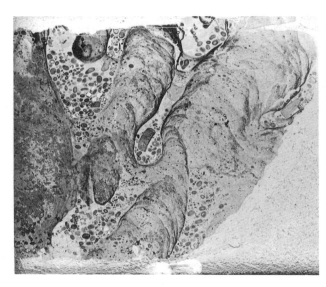

Figure 3-15:
Profile of irregular
stromatolites about
1 cm. across with
sand-size granules
between columns in
black chert.
Schreiber, Ontario.
Area shown is about
one inch wide.

Figure 3-16:
Cross-section of pillars
in stromatolites
showing concentric
layers and sand-size
clasts between pillars.
Biwabik, Minnesota.
Area shown is about
one inch wide.

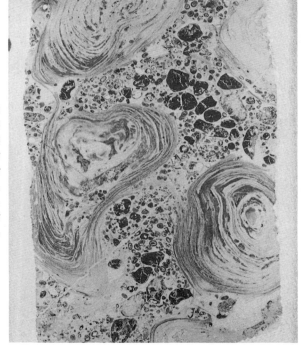

A number of different types of microfossils are present in the chert of the Gunflint Iron-formation. As might be expected in rocks more than 2,000 million years old, fossils are all of primitive life forms, primarily bacteria and algae (Figures 3–17 and 3–18). The most abundant forms are minute filaments that are probably ancestors to modern cyanobacteria. These forms may be present by the thousands in a single thin section. Also common are several spherical sporelike bodies that may be ancestors of blue-green algae. Some forms, such as *Kakabekia* and *Eosphaera* are much less common, however, and the biographical groups to which they belong are uncertain. As we will see later, structures similar to *Eosphaera* are abundant in some types of iron-formation, and may be significant regarding the precipitation of the iron and silica. In summary, the variety of microfossils in iron-formation cherts demonstrates that a number of diverse types of organisms had evolved by Early Proterozoic time.

Well-preserved macroscopic fossils have recently been described from the Negaunee Iron-formation near Negaunee, Michigan (Han and Runnegar, 1992). The fossils are preserved as coiled carbonaceous filaments up to nearly 2 feet long on bedding surfaces in the iron-formation (Figure 3–19). They were discovered by Tsu-Ming Han during mining operations in the Empire taconite mine southeast of Negaunee, Michigan. The fossils are similar to *Grypania spiralis*, which was found in rocks about 1,000 million years old in Montana. Their presence in the 2,100 million year old Negaunee Iron-formation is the oldest known occurrence of organisms of this size and complexity. The fossils are believed to be large, filamentous, photosynthetic algae. The discovery by Han is a significant addition to the rich heritage of fossils found in Precambrian Iron-formations.

Many of the types of organisms present were *photosynthetic*; that is, they produced oxygen. It is now widely accepted that the oxygen in the earth's atmosphere was generated in large part by great "blooms" of these primitive organisms. Luxuriant growth of photosynthetic bacteria and algae in the Early Proterozoic seas is believed to have resulted in the deposition of iron-formation and to the production of an oxygen-bearing atmosphere. Thus, iron-formations are believed to have been precipitated by biological processes; the production of oxygen that rendered the iron very insoluble and perhaps by organisms that had siliceous skeletons (like modern-day diatoms and radiolaria).

Iron-formations are associated with a wide variety of other rock types—conglomerate, sandstone, shale, graywacke, dolomite, and volcanic rocks—yet one of their most notable features is the lack of other rock types. There are two possible explanations. It may be that iron-formations accumulated slowly in an extremely stable basin into which

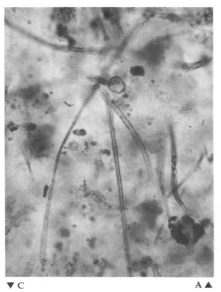

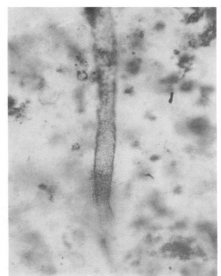

▼ C   A ▲   B ▲

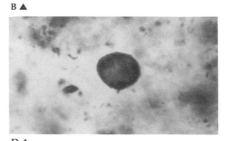

D ▲

Figure 3-17: Microfossils in iron-formation. A. Gunflintia Minuta, blue-green algae filaments about 1 micron across. Schreiber, Ontario. B. Gunflintia grandis, blue-green algae filaments about 6 microns across. Schreiber, Ontario. C. Animikea septata, portion of a segmented filament of glue-green algae about 5 microns across. Schreiber, Ontario. D. Huronispora microreticulata (?), spore-like body about 12 microns across. Probably blue-green algae. Schreiber, Ontario. E. and F. Huronispora microreticulata, Spheroidal spore-like bodies with a finely crenulated surface. They range from 10-12 microns in diameter. Schreiber, Ontario.

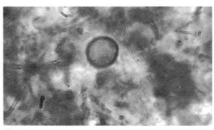

E ▲

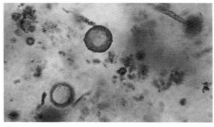

F ▲

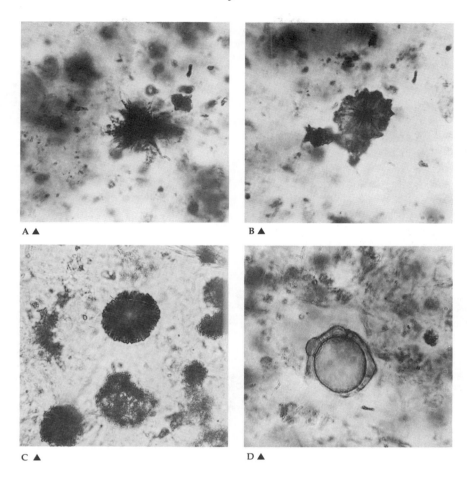

Figure 3-18: Microfossils in iron-formations.

Eoastrion simplex, a probable iron bacteria with thin radiating arms. Structure is about 20 microns across. Schreiber, Ontario. B. Kakabekia umbellata, a microfossil shaped something like a tiny parachute. The biological affinity of this form is uncertain. The organism is about 25 microns across. Schreiber, Ontario. C. Microfossil of unknown affinity with minute hair-like surface. About 30 microns in diameter. Eveleth, Minnesota. D. Eosphaera tyleria, a microfossil consisting of a spherical organic sheath about 20 microns in diameter surrounded by a number of smaller spherical bodies and an outer organic sheath about 30 microns in diameter. From Schreiber, Ontario.

little or no sedimentary materials were being added. Alternatively, iron-formations may have been deposited very rapidly, with the biochemical sediment overwhelming the "normal" sedimentary contribution to the basin. Considering the wide variety of environments in which iron-formations were deposited, it seems most likely that they accumulated very rapidly in an otherwise "normal" basin. The rapid deposition occurred as a result of special chemical (or biochemical) conditions that developed in the basin.

The deposition of iron-formations is very complex, but may have occurred approximately as follows. Iron was fairly abundant in Archean and Early Proterozoic seas because the earth's atmosphere lacked oxygen. In some basins there were great blooms of microorganisms. Many were photosynthetic and produced oxygen, which combined with the iron to form an insoluble iron-oxide. Most, or all, of the iron was probably precipitated as iron-oxide. Some organisms had siliceous skeletons. Periodic blooms of these organisms produced alternating iron-rich and silica-rich layers on the basin floor along with variable amounts of other organic debris. Although photosynthetic oxygen caused the surface waters to be oxidizing, deeper parts of the basin (below the depth of light penetration necessary for photosynthesis) would remain chemically reducing. Iron-oxide that settled into the deeper water may have

Figure 3-19: Grypania spiralis, the oldest known macrofossil. They are coiled carbonaceous filaments on bedding surfaces in the 2,100 million year old Negaunee Iron-formation, near Negaunee, Michigan. Photo courtesy Tsu-Ming Han.

been converted to siderite, or may have gone back into solution (Figure 3–20). Detailed examination of siderite in some iron-formations (Figures 3–21 to 3–23) suggests that it formed by replacement of earlier features like *Eosphaera*.

In shallow parts of the basin the iron may have remained as hematite with alternating layers of chert. The chert-rich layers contain spheroidal structures outlined by fine "dusty" hematite (Figure 3–24). In deeper parts of the basin, the iron would be converted to siderite, again with alternating layers. This picture is further complicated by waves and currents in the basin. Storms (perhaps even hurricanes!) would stir up and transport the sediment just as they do today. The transport and redistribution of material in a chemical sediment like iron-formation produced very complex results. The presence of granular iron-formation units and conglomerate layers tend to confirm the hypothesis that there were storms. These chemical and physical complications result in some of the variations in the appearance of iron-formations. In addition, nearly all iron-formations have undergone some degree of metamorphism and this, too, has imposed some mineral and textural changes in the rock.

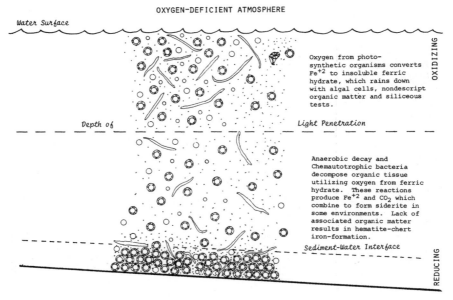

OXYGEN-DEFICIENT ATMOSPHERE

Water Surface

OXIDIZING

Oxygen from photo-synthetic organisms converts Fe^{+2} to insoluble ferric hydrate, which rains down with algal cells, nondescript organic matter and siliceous tests.

Depth of   Light Penetration

Anaerobic decay and Chemautotrophic bacteria decompose organic tissue utilizing oxygen from ferric hydrate. These reactions produce Fe^{+2} and CO_2 which combine to form siderite in some environments. Lack of associated organic matter results in hematite-chert iron-formation.

Sediment-Water Interface

REDUCING

Figure 3-20: Diagram illustrating the several different microbial communities and different geochemical environments in the water column in which Precambrian iron-formations were precipitated.

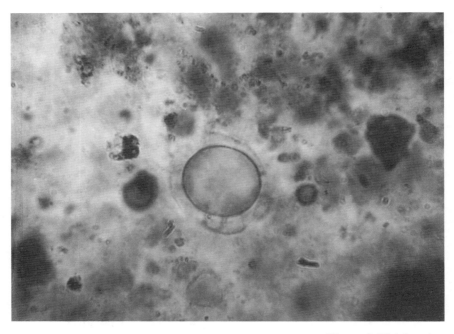

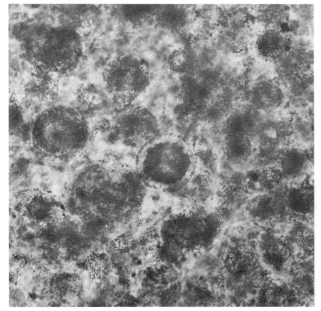

Figure 3-21 (above): Eosphaera tyleri in chert from the Schreiber, Ontario, area, showing the inner spherical organic sheath surrounded by smaller spherical bodies. Overall diameter is about 30 microns.

Figure 3-22 (left): Siderite in chert. Note the spherical shape and the "halo" around the 30 micron siderite grain, and the similarity to Eosphaera. From the Kakabeka Falls area, Gunflint district.

*Figure 3-23:
Electron micrograph
of spherical siderite
in chert. Siderite is
gray, chert is black.
Note that the siderite
is in double-walled
spheres similar to
Eosphaera tyleri.
Outer sphere is 30
microns in diameter.
From Pass Lake,
Ontario.*

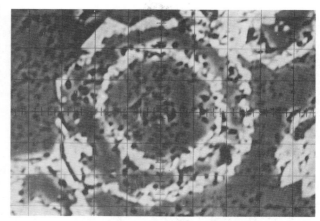

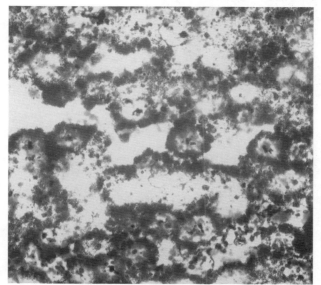

Figure 3-24:
*Photomicrograph of jasper showing the distribution of
fine hematite (black). Note that the hematite dust
defines spheroidal structures about 30 microns in diameter and that there are smaller "satellite" spheres of
densely pigmented areas producing a structure similar
in size and shape to Eosphaera. These structures are
common in jasper from many areas, and suggest that
Eosphaera initially may have been abundant in the
rocks. Wakefield, Michigan.*

Formation of the Iron Ores. One of the most important events in the economic development of the Lake Superior region was the conversion of parts of the iron-formations into naturally formed iron ore bodies. Although the formation of the iron ores took place long after the iron-formations were deposited, they will be discussed here for the sake of continuity. The alteration of the original rock to iron ore involved two processes that probably occurred at essentially the same time: (1) oxidation of the iron minerals, especially the siderite and iron silicates, caused by waters circulating through the rocks. The relatively soluble ferrous iron in the minerals was converted to extremely insoluble hematite, geothite, or limonite. In the process the iron carbonates and iron silicates were rendered very unstable, and (2) continued circulation of water through the rocks gradually dissolved the silica from the iron silicates and the chert and carried it out of the rock. This leaching of silica amounted to removal of nearly 50 percent of the original volume of the rock. As a result, the ore was very porous and unable to support the weight of overlying rock layers, which slumped into the ore bodies (Figure 3–25). Some iron was carried downward into the porous ores from higher levels in the zone of weathering. The removal of silica thus

Figure 3-25: Natural iron ore body on the Mesabi range. Note the down-warping of the layers near the center of the photo due to solution of silica. Photo taken in 1959 of the Auburn Mine at Virginia, Minnesota.

allowed an increase in the iron content from an initial 25 to 35 percent to about 55 to 60 percent in the ore bodies.

Although many hundreds of millions of tons of silica were dissolved out of the original iron-formation to form the ore bodies, it has left virtually no trace. The rocks beneath, around, and overlying the ore bodies do not show evidence of silica being added. The only alternative explanation is that as it was dissolved out of the rocks, the silica was carried away in the groundwater to the rivers and ultimately to the oceans. The areas converted to natural ores comprised only a small percentage of the total volume of the iron-formations, since only the iron-formations adjacent to the channelways along which the ore-forming solutions moved were preferentially converted to ore. For example, waters were channeled along local folds and fracture zones in the Biwabic Formation to produce the ores on the Mesabi range. The large areal extent of the ore bodies and their close relationship to the present erosion surface indicates that they probably formed by the circulation of groundwater through the rocks (Figure 3–26). The largest of the natural ore bodies was mined as a large open pit called the Hull Rust-Mahoning Mine at Hibbing, Minnesota (see Fronticepiece of this chapter). It has an irregular outline but is nearly 3 miles long, 2 miles wide, and up to 500 feet

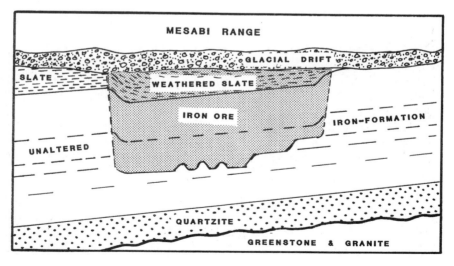

Figure 3-26: Diagram showing the development of iron ore bodies on the Mesabi Range in Minnesota. Note the proximity of the ore bodies to the present erosion surface, suggesting that the ore was formed by surface weathering.

deep. Nearly 200 million tons of iron ore were removed from this mine over a period of about fifty years. Observation sites at a number of large open-pit mines on the Mesabi range afford an excellent opportunity to see the extent and nature of these huge natural ore bodies. The ore bodies are immense in size, but we must remember that a roughly equal volume of material (silica) was leached out of these areas, in most cases without leaving a trace. While we tend to consider quartz as an insoluble material, these mines dramatically demonstrate that it is far more soluble than iron oxides.

Ore bodies in the more deformed iron-formations of the iron ranges on the south shore of Lake Superior have no obvious connection to the surface, and must have been formed by a different mechanism. On the Gogebic range, the channelways for the ore-forming solutions were formed by the intersections of shaly layers in the steeply dipping iron-formation and cross-cutting basaltic dikes (Figure 3–27). On the Menominee range, ore bodies formed in troughs created by folded sedimentary layers. Impervious shales again formed the bottom of the ore bodies.

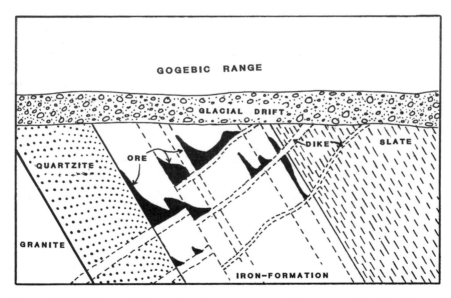

Figure 3-27: Diagram illustrating the occurrence of iron ore on the Gogebic and other ranges on the south shore of Lake Superior. Note that most ore bodies do not extend to the surface. This fact may indicate that the ore was not formed solely by surface weathering.

Similar controls for ore bodies existed in the Marquette, Cuyuna, and Iron River–Crystal Falls ranges. Many of these ore bodies do not extend to the surface and thus they may not have formed solely from surface weathering. These ore bodies may have formed at least in part by hot ascending solutions that oxidized the iron and dissolved the silica. The source of these hot solutions is not known, but may have been deeply circulating groundwaters. In all of these areas the iron-formations are sufficiently deformed so that it was necessary to utilize underground mining methods rather than the large open-pit operations as on the Mesabi range. Since underground mines cannot be mechanized as can surface mines, they have been unable to compete economically, and all have closed. The numerous underground mines, however, provided a source of employment for early settlers in the region. Figures 3–28 and 3–29 show examples of underground mines.

The ore consists primarily of goethite [FeO(OH)], hematite [Fe_2O_3], limonite [microcrystalline goethite with additional water], and some magnetite. In open spaces produced by the removal of silica, however,

Figure 3-28: Scene at the Sunday Lake Mine in Wakefield, Michigan, in 1960, typical of the underground mining operations. The head frame of the mine (near the center of the photo) and the stockpile are surrounded by the town in which the miners live.

Figure 3-29: Head frame and stockpiles of ore at the Champion Mine at Champion, Michigan, in 1965. This mine and other underground mines are now closed.

large botryoidal masses of crystalline hematite or goethite (Figure 3–30) were found, as well as local concentrations of manganite [MnO(OH)], pyrolusite [MnO_2], psilomelane (romancheite) [a complex barium–manganese oxide], barite [$BaSO_4$] (Figure 3–31), calcite [$CaCO_3$], gypsum [$CaSO_4 \cdot 2H_2O$], rhodochrosite [$MnCO_3$], and others.

It is almost impossible to establish with any degree of certainty when the natural ore bodies formed. Some may have formed during the Early Proterozoic when the iron-formations were first elevated above sea level and subjected to erosion. Some, such as those on the Marquette range appear to have formed shortly after the iron-formation was deposited. The Early Proterozoic Goodrich Quartzite that overlies the Negaunee Iron-formation, locally, has a matrix of iron-ore as well as cobbles of iron-ore. To the west at Republic and Champion, the iron ore at the Negaunee–Goodrich contact was metamorphosed about 1,800 million years ago and must be at least that old. On the Gogebic range, the approximately 1,200 million-year-old Bessemer Quartzite that was deposited on an erosion surface on the Ironwood Iron-formation contains pebbles and cobbles of iron ore, suggesting that the ore was formed at least 1,200 million years ago. At the Quinnesec mine near Quinnesec, Michigan, on the Menominee range, pebbles and cobbles of iron ore are present in the basal part of the roughly 500 million-year-old upper Cambrian sandstone. On the Mesabi range there are areas where Cretaceous

Figure 3-30: Botryoidal mass of hematite and goethite showing the typical radiating fibrous crystals within the masses. Sample is from the Sherwood Mine, Crystal Falls, Michigan.

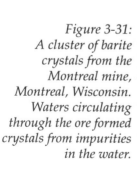

Figure 3-31:
A cluster of barite
crystals from the
Montreal mine,
Montreal, Wisconsin.
Waters circulating
through the ore formed
crystals from impurities
in the water.

sediments contain cobbles of iron ore along with 80 million-year-old shark teeth, fish vertebrae, wood, and various marine invertebrate fossils. In other areas the ore is overlain by glacial drift that is about 10,000 years old. It is entirely possible that the ores were formed at different times in different areas. The ore in a particular ore body may have formed when that volume of rock was subjected to weathering or other ore-forming processes. The occurrence of an ore body overlain by, for example, Cambrian sandstone does not necessarily mean that the ore formed in Cambrian time. It simply means that the ore is older than the sedimentary rock overlying it. It may be 1,000 million years older!

Taconite.   In almost all of the Lake Superior region the mining of natural ores has been phased out in favor of mining and mechanical concentration of taconite. Taconite is iron-formation that has not been oxidized and enriched by natural processes; in a sense, it is the original iron-formation generally variably metamorphosed. Two factors have contributed to the demise of the mining of natural ores: (1) natural ore bodies have been largely mined out; and (2) it has been found that blast furnaces are more efficient when using processed ores. The tremendous consumption of iron ore during World War II, when the Lake Superior region was the major producer of iron ore for the Allied forces, was the zenith of production of natural ores. A rapid decline in the mining of natural ores was accompanied by major technological advances that led to the development of the taconite industry. Natural ore bodies varied considerably in composition from place to place, and these differences had to be dealt with in the smelting by adding various ingredients to remove the undesired constituents. In contrast, processed taconites are mined from large pits covering many square miles and are blended in the mining, crushing and concentrating so as to provide the smelters with a uniform product. In effect much of the metallurgy in iron and steel production is now done in the mines.

The taconite process of concentrating iron from low-grade iron-formation has been made possible by very large-scale operation and mechanization. Because of the low value per ton of iron ore, it is necessary to handle many millions of tons of rock as economically as possible. Specialized techniques for drilling the ore, special blasting techniques, huge equipment to haul and crush the ore, and equally large concentrators to extract the iron from the waste rock are some of the developments. Problems then arise concerning the disposal of the huge quantities of waste materials. The costs to undertake this type of mining are monumental. Therefore, to initiate a taconite operation, many hundreds of millions of tons of ore must be accessible to mining. On the Mesabi range where the rocks are almost flat-lying, broad areas are available to mining. Some of the ore is transported to Lake Superior where it is treated (Figure 3–32), other ore is concentrated at the mine site, and only the concentrate is shipped. Where the rocks are steeply dipping, such as on the Gogebic range, a much narrower width of rock is available to mining, even though the iron-formation is as thick as on the Mesabi range.

Basically the taconite process involves crushing the rock to a fine-grain size, then mechanically removing the iron minerals from the waste material. It is important that the iron in the taconite is present mainly as magnetite or hematite that can be readily separated and concentrated. If the iron is combined in the form of silicates, it cannot be used as a taconite ore. Magnetite can be removed from the siliceous waste materials by large electromagnets. Hematite requires a more sophisticated process for concentration. It may be selectively removed from the waste by a process called *flotation*. After the iron minerals are concentrated, they are washed to remove the fine dust adhering to the grains. Because the remaining fine powder of iron minerals cannot be handled readily, it is necessary to form it into larger sized "pellets" that can be transported

Figure 3-32: Aerial view of the taconite plant at Silver Bay, Minnesota, on the shore of Lake Superior, where the ore from Babbitt, Minnesota, is processed to form pellets for shipping to blast furnaces in the lower Great Lakes states. Photo taken in 1977.

to and handled at the blast furnaces. The pellets are formed by adding a small amount of bentonite clay and water to the iron concentrate to bind the iron particles together. Tumbling this mixture in large cylinders of inclined drums produces marble-sized balls that are then hardened by firing to enable them to withstand handling and shipping. The reserves of taconite are immense, and will provide the basis of an iron industry that should far outlast that of the natural ores.

The Overlying Graywacke-Slate. Let us return again to our general discussion of the development of the Animikie Basin. Overlying the major iron-formation in all of the Lake Superior region is a thick blanket of graywacke and slate that extends from central Minnesota east at least to Marquette, Michigan, and from Thunder Bay on the North Shore southward at least to the Iron Mountain, Michigan area. In some areas, as on the Marquette range and the Gogebic range in Michigan, an erosion surface and a quartzite unit (the Goodrich Quartzite) are present between the iron-formation and the overlying graywackes. In other areas, however, the graywacke directly overlies the iron formation. Thus, an area of at least 40,000 square miles was covered by a layer of sediments that ranges in thickness from a few thousand to perhaps 10,000 feet. The graywacke-slate sequence has different names in various parts of the region. For example, it is called the Michigamme Formation in most of northern Michigan; the Tyler Formation in the Gogebic district of Wisconsin; the Thomson, Rabbit Lake, Virginia, and Rove formations in Minnesota. Few geologists, however, doubt that all of these formations were deposited in the same basin at approximately the same time. Collectively these various formations constitute the Baraga Group of the Marquette Range Supergroup.

The deposition of tens of thousands of cubic miles of poorly sorted sediments marks a major change in the history of the Animikie Basin. This abrupt change in sediment type posed a difficult problem in interpreting the geological events necessary to produce such a rapid change. Recent age dating (Barovich, et al., 1989), however, indicates that the graywackes were deposited about 1,860 million years ago, whereas the underlying iron-formations were deposited more than 2,100 million years ago. Therefore, the graywackes are perhaps 300 million years younger than the underlying iron-formations, and were the result of very different processes.

As might be expected in a basin covering such a large area, the nature of the rocks overlying the iron-formation is variable from place to place. The dominant rock types are graywackes and slate (Figure 3–33), however, volcanic tuffs and lava flows are present locally (such as the

Figure 3-33: North-dipping Tyler Formation at Hurley, Wisconsin, showing the typical alternating layers of graywacke and slate.

Clarksburg and Hemlock volcanics in northern Michigan and unnamed units in the Cuyuna district of Minnesota). At various levels in the overall graywacke sequence, layers and lenses of iron-formation are present, as are lenses of limestone or dolomite. In places the rocks contain high concentrations of organic material that evidently accumulated in deeper, stagnant parts of the basin. The organic material has subsequently been largely converted to graphite. In fact, graphite mining has been attempted (unsuccessfully) in some of the thicker accumulation near L'Anse, Michigan. Near Iron River, Michigan, the organic matter, which accumulated in layers many feet thick, was less metamorphosed and is still preserved as a rather low grade coal (Tyler et al., 1954) (Figure 3–34). This may represent the oldest coal on earth; certainly, it is one of the oldest deposits. Minor amounts of uranium are widespread in the Michigamme Formation, mainly associated with the organic-rich layers; however, no commercial deposits are known. Another common feature of the sequence is the presence of numerous disc-shaped concretions of calcite or dolomite that range from a few inches to several feet across

Figure 3-34: Precambrian coal formed in the Michigamme Formation near Iron River, Michigan, as a result of the accumulation of abundant algae in a stagnant part of the Animikie Basin. Sample is about nine inches long.

and several inches thick. Although they appear to have formed at the same time as the enclosing sediments, the factors controlling the formation of the concretions is not known.

The thousands of cubic miles of graywackes and slates over this vast basin were derived from several different source areas. The Rove and Thomson Formations in Minnesota were derived mainly from a granitic terrane to the north, and the Tyler Formation in Wisconsin was derived largely from a granitic terrane to the south. The Rabbit Lake Formation in central Minnesota and the Michigamme Formation in northern Michigan have significant volcanic contributions, probably from volcanic islands to the south. The source areas for the sediments may have been landmasses of older rocks outside the basin. This seems likely for the sediments derived from granitic terranes to the north. However, some of the granitic landmasses to the south, such as the source area for the sediments in the Tyler Formation, are more difficult to explain. They appear to represent large blocks of older rocks uplifted by faulting or folding while at the same time they were rapidly being eroded.

The tectonic lands might have broken the Animikie Basin into a number of smaller basins. More or less cut off from the main basin, some of these smaller basins could have developed chemical conditions quite different from that of the overall basin. For example, due to the accumulation of much organic matter in the muds of its floor, a rather deep, fault-bounded basin might have developed very stagnant waters. During later metamorphism and deformation, the organic matter, converted to graphite, would form graphitic slates. A remnant of such a basin evidently extends from near Mercer in Iron County, Wisconsin, southwestward about 100 miles to Couderay in southern Sawyer County. Since the area is covered with a thick layer of glacial drift there are almost no exposures of these rocks. Its discovery took place during testing of the earth's conductivity in an attempt to locate a transmitter site for Project Sanguin (later called Seafarer and ELF). Since graphite is a good conductor of electricity, the zone is highly conductive, and its occurrence along the Flambeau River has given rise to the name Flambeau Anomaly. Core drilling for mineral exploration by various mining companies has provided samples of the rocks that comprise the zone.

The discovery of sedimentary phosphate deposits in parts of the Marquette district suggests another local basin with unusual chemistry. These occurrences constitute one of the oldest known sedimentary phosphate deposits. Occurring as phosphatic pebbles in conglomerates near the base of the Goodrich Quartzite and as phosphatic (apatite-rich) layers in an iron-formation lens near the base of the Michigamme Formation, these phosphate deposits are also uranium-bearing and have been investigated for possible phosphate and uranium ores.

Rift-related Igneous Rocks. Basalt dikes and lava flows characteristically form during continental breakup. Recall that continental breakup results from the addition of basaltic magma to the base of the continental crust. Doming and fracturing of the crust provides channelways for the molten basalt to rise toward the surface. Material that cooled in the cracks formed dikes, and magma that reached the surface formed lava flows.

Basaltic dikes and sills are widespread in Early Proterozoic and Archean rocks in the Lake Superior region. In addition, in the Marquette district, dikes and sills are abundant in the Negaunee Iron-formation near Ishpeming, Michigan, and basaltic dikes also cut older Archean

Figure 3-35: Early Proterozoic basaltic dikes cutting Archean granite south of Republic, Michigan.

rocks (Figure 3–35). Basaltic dikes are also well known in the Gogebic district of Michigan and Wisconsin.

Volcanic rocks that formed during the continental breakup are also widespread. The Clarksburg volcanics are basaltic lava flows and tuffs interbedded with the Michigamme Slate in the western part of the Marquette district. The Hemlock volcanics are basaltic and rhyolitic lava flows and tuffs within the Michigamme Slate in the Iron River–Crystal Falls district. The Emperor Volcanics constitute a thick pile of volcanic rocks and sills in the eastern Gogebic district. Except for a number of basaltic dikes and sills, igneous rocks are scarce in the western part of the Gogebic range. Igneous rocks are abundant, however, east of Wakefield, Michigan, where they reach a thickness of more than 5,000 feet. Both basaltic and rhyolitic rocks are present. They are mainly interbedded with the Ironwood Iron-formation. Textural features in the volcanic rocks indicate that they were extruded under water. The basaltic rocks include pillow lavas and fragmental rocks produced by the interaction of lava and water (Figures 3–36 and 3–37). When hot rock fragments and pillows came in contact with the cooler water, fragments spall off due to the rapid cooling (and contraction) of the volcanic debris. These conditions produce spectacular textures in the rocks. Many fragments had chilled rims, and might have chemically reacted with the water. The reaction rinds can still be seen on many fragments. These types of rocks are spectacularly developed north of Mareniso, Michigan.

Although the volcanic rocks do not look different, their <u>chemical</u> <u>composition</u> shows that they formed during a rifting event (Schulz, 1990) associated with a continental breakup. Therefore, the volcanic rocks support the geologic interpretation of continental breakup somewhere around 2,100 million years ago.

Schulz (1990) suggests that the onset of graywacke deposition may represent the time of actual breakup of the continental margin, and the development of oceanic crust offshore. At this stage volcanic activity on the continental margin ceased. Instead, basaltic magma emerged at the surface in a spreading margin and produced basaltic oceanic crust in an everwidening ocean basin offshore from the Lake Superior region.

Although a fragment of the Archean continent was carried away with the spreading crust, we have no record of how large it was or where it went. Since continental crust is not destroyed, it must still be present somewhere. Some day that missing crustal fragment may be identified.

The sequence of rocks described previously is the record of geological events that occurred over a period of 200 million to 250 million years during Early Proterozoic time. They are interpreted to be the record of

Figure 3-36: Pillow breccia in the Emperor volcanics, consisting of a highly fractured pillow in a matrix of pillow fragments. Knife is on a fractured pillow. Exposure is 6 miles north of Marenisco, Michigan.

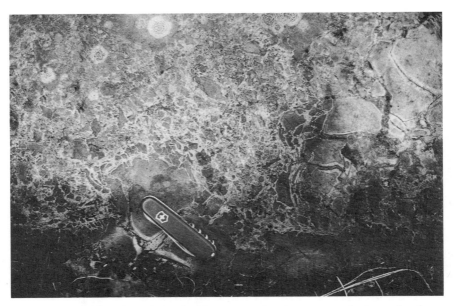

Figure 3-37: Pillow breccia in the Emperor volcanics composed of angular fragments of basalt with prominent alteration rims. Exposure is 6 miles north of Marenisco, Michigan.

the rifting event described earlier. At the conclusion of the rifting the Lake Superior region was probably somewhat like the present east coast of North America. This concludes the first major phase of the Early Proterozoic history of the region.

▲ CONVERGENT (ACTIVE) ▲
MARGIN

The divergent (spreading) tectonics along the margin of the Superior craton continued for approximately 150 million years. The result was the development of a large ocean basin off the passive continental margin. Presumably a wedge of graywackes continued to accumulate in the deeper waters off the continental margin (Figure 3–38). As we shall see, the existence of these rocks became evident during later geologic events.

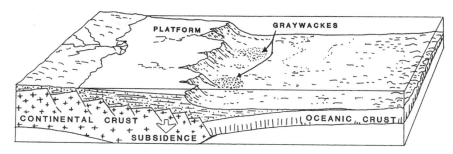

Figure 3-38: Diagram of a passive continental margin similar to what may have existed in the Lake Superior region about 2,000 million years ago. A platform (or continental shelf) and a steeper slope of the continental rise form offshore from the continent.

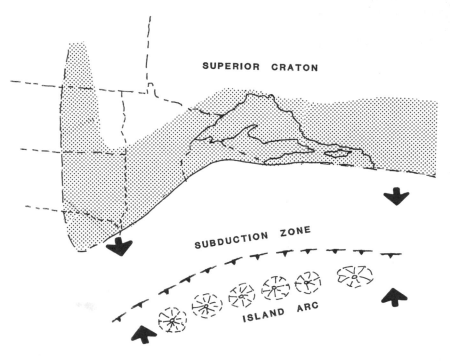

Figure 3-39: Sketch map showing the general tectonic relations about 1,880 million years ago. The Superior craton was moving toward a volcanic island arc. Oceanic crust between the craton and the subduction zone was gradually consumed during convergence.

Then, about 1,900 million years ago the direction of plate motion changed and a period of convergent plate tectonic activity replaced the divergent tectonic environment. This reversal in plate motion resulted in a dramatic change in the rock types produced in the Lake Superior region.

Current interpretations of the distribution of rock types, geologic structure, geochemistry, and geochronology (the age of the rocks) (Sims et al., 1990) indicates that a south-dipping subduction zone developed well offshore from the Superior Province. The subduction resulted in the generation of an oceanic volcanic island arc. As shown in Figure 3–39, the volcanic islands were built up on basaltic oceanic crust. This basaltic crust had been generated earlier at the spreading margin that had migrated offshore from the margin of the Superior craton during the spreading stage (refer to Figure 3–1). Initially the volcanic islands were very small. However, with continued subduction the islands continued to grow in size due to the addition of volcanic materials at the surface as well as the addition of batches of magma that cooled below the surface. As the island chain grew in size, an increasing amount of material was eroded from it and deposited in the surrounding seas. In this way the volcanic island arc became broader and deeper in the crust (Figure 3–40). Geologically we say the island arc becomes more "evolved" or more "mature" with time.

OCEAN-FLOOR CRUST

The ocean-floor crust consisted of pillow basalts along with numerous gabbro dikes and sills as well as scattered blocks or intrusions of "ultramafic" rocks. The ultramafic rocks were initially of olivine or pyroxene (or both). These minerals are rich in magnesium. On the sea floor the ultramafic rocks are typically converted to the minerals *serpentine* and *talc* by the addition of water to the original rock. The basalts and gabbros are also altered (metamorphosed) by the addition of water to the hot lava flows. The basalts are converted to "greenstones" very similar to those in Archean greenstone belts. The mixture of altered basalt, gabbro, and ultramafic rocks is a major component of modern ocean floors (along with relatively thin sedimentary cover) and is almost identical in rock type and chemistry to the crust of the Early Proterozoic ocean floor.

Pillowed basalts are widely distributed in the volcanic belt across northern Wisconsin. Excellent exposures are present at Quiver Falls along the Menominee River that forms the border between Wisconsin and Michigan. Somewhat deformed pillows are exposed in various

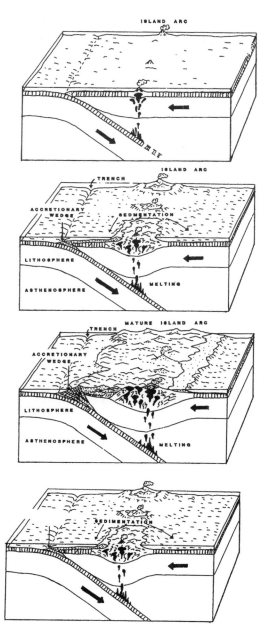

Figure 3-40: Diagrams showing development of a volcanic island arc that increases in size as subduction continues.

places in Marinette and Florence counties. Pillow lavas are also well exposed farther west, in the Monico, Wisconsin, area, to the north, in the Mercer, Wisconsin, area, and to the south, in the Wausau area (Figure 3–41). Featureless, massive basalts and broken fragments of basalt that probably slid down the front of submarine lava flows as <u>debris</u> flows form accumulations of odd-shaped fragments of basalt in a matrix of fine basaltic ash.

In addition to the basalts, at least thirty occurrences of ultramafic rocks are present. Although some bodies of ultramafic rocks are well out within the volcanic belt, a vast majority of the known occurrences are along the southern and northern margins. For example, about twenty ultramafic occurrences are present in Portage, Wood, and Jackson counties along the southern margin of the volcanic belt. The serpentine and talc may take on spectacular colors, such as a vivid yellow-green or pale blue, as well as the common variegated olive green and black. Some of the ultramafic bodies have been explored over the years as possible commercial sources of asbestos, building stone (*verde antique*), or talc. However, none of the occurrences has been the site of any significant mining.

As subduction continued the Superior craton slowly moved toward the trench and the line of growing volcanic islands offshore. The oceanic

Figure 3-41: Basaltic pillow lava exposed along Artus Creek west of Wausau, Wisconsin. Top of the flow is to the upper right hand side of the photo.

crust that had been generated offshore was slowly consumed in the sub-duction zone. Scattered along the length of the subduction zone a num-ber of andesite or rhyolite volcanic centers built up islands in the sea (Figure 3–42).

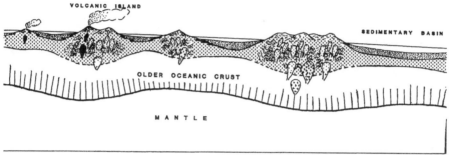

Figure 3-42: Diagram showing probable relationships along the subduction zone. Volcanic islands of andesite and rhyolite built on older basaltic crust alter-nate with sedimentary basins in which graywackes accumulate.

ANDESITIC ISLANDS

Andesitic lava, produced by the partial melting of basaltic crust, typi-cally contains about 60 percent silica (SiO_2). By contrast, basalts usually have about 50 percent silica. This difference in chemical composition results in a different mineral composition in andesites. The increased sil-ica content also makes andesitic lava much less fluid than basaltic lava. Because andesitic lava does not flow readily, the resulting volcanic fea-tures are very different from basaltic landforms. Andesitic volcanoes typically have rather steep sides; basically they have the "classical" shape we associate with volcanoes. Thus, the andesitic volcanoes built up on the sea floor with curved sides rising to a peak with steep slopes that may have extended above the water surface to form an island.

Andesites contain several features that provide a basis for identifying them in outcrops. They are commonly very *porphyritic*, that is, they con-tain abundant 0.5- to 1.0-centimeter crystals of feldspar and black ferro-magnesian minerals in a very fine-grained gray to black matrix. The large crystals (the *phenocrysts*) formed before the lava was extruded, and the fine matrix formed by rapid cooling at the earth's surface. The abun-dance of crystals also indicates that the lavas were cooled to the point that they were crystallizing before extrusion.

In addition to containing abundant crystals, andesites are commonly fragmental. The stiff lava tends to break up into blocks upon extrusion, and gases (mainly water vapor) contained in the lava expand to produce fragmentation of the lava by "lava fountaining" when the lava reaches the surface. The result is a mixture of fragments ranging in size from dust to large blocks that accumulate on the slopes of the volcano. Periodically these materials become saturated with water and form large mud (or debris) flows that move rapidly down the valleys on the flanks of the volcano. Debris flows result in chaotic mixtures of blocks and mud, and may form on land or under water (Figure 3–43).

Andesites may also produce ordinary lava flows on land or under water. Submarine lava flows commonly contain pillow structures and look very much like basaltic pillow lavas. In fact, the most reliable way to distinguish andesites from basalts is by chemical analyses.

The andesitic islands would, of course, be subject to erosion as rain fell on the slopes of the volcanoes. The lack of any land plants to protect slopes during Early Proterozoic time probably resulted in rapid erosion of the islands.

Figure 3-43: Coarsely fragmental andesite exposed along Hamann Creek north of Stratford, Wisconsin. The fragments have been flattened and deformed during a later period of deformation.

Materials eroded from the islands would be deposited in the waters surrounding the volcanic islands. The frequent earthquakes associated with the subduction zones would periodically shake the sediment loose and cause turbidity currents that carried the sediment out into deep water surrounding the islands, where the deposits formed were graywackes. Some graywackes filled in basins between volcanic islands, some were carried into the trench of the subduction zone, and some accumulated behind islands—away from the subduction zone. Therefore, the volcanic islands were surrounded by graywackes (Figure 3–44) derived from the erosion of the islands. Thus the sediments have a composition essentially the same as the islands from which they were derived.

Figure 3-44: Graywacke interbedded with volcanic rocks, and composed mainly of fragments of volcanic rocks, Wausau, Wisconsin.

RHYOLITIC CENTERS

In some areas along the subduction zone the basaltic crust, and perhaps substantial amounts of graywackes in the trench, were carried down into the earth's interior and melted to form magmas that were

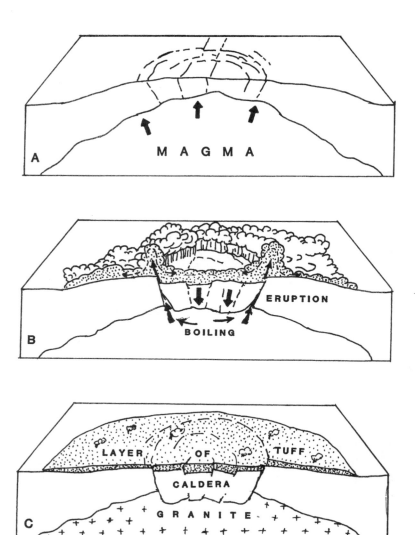

Figure 3-45: Schematic diagrams illustrating the formation of ash-flow tuffs. Pre-eruption stage in A shows the hot, viscous granitic magma with some dissolved water toward the surface, doming the surface and producing an elliptical ring of fractures. The eruption stage, B, shows the violent blast of gas-charged lava that results from boiling in the magma chamber. The dense, white-hot, bubble-rich lava explodes as it erupts, forming a dense, hot cloud that spreads out from the eruptive center. Subsidence of a circular block above the magma forms a depression called a caldera (C), which may be partially filled by the volcanic fragments. Many of the fragments are pieces of stiff liquid lava blown apart by the force of the eruption. These fragments "weld" together after the eruptive cloud settles.

very rich in silica. These high-silica (about 70 percent SiO_2) volcanic rocks are called *rhyolites*. They typically form extremely violent eruptions (Mt. St. Helens' eruption in 1980 was a small example). The reason for their explosive nature is twofold. First, the high silica content produces very stiff lavas. Second, and most important, the lavas contain superheated water, probably derived from the melting of sediments containing hydrous minerals. Whatever its source, the water is heated to about 700°C, but it is held in the magma by the tremendous pressures of the overlying rocks. As the magma works its way toward the surface however, the confining pressure becomes less and less. At some point near the surface the water in the magma begins to boil violently. This boiling produces huge quantities of steam that rise rapidly through the stiff, pasty magma, producing innumerable gas-filled bubbles. The gas-filled magma, still under great pressure, is carried rapidly up toward the surface. When the magma breaks out at the surface the confining pressure is suddenly released and the bubbles explode, tearing apart the stiff, still-molten lava. Since the lava is like a froth, the rapid expansion of the gas explodes the bubbles, producing angular fragments of still-molten lava. Many of these fragments cool quickly in the air to form glass shards.

The fragments may be blown miles into the air, forming immense, heavy clouds of hot ash (Figure 3–45). When the fragments fall to the earth they can accumulate to form layers several hundred feet thick that can be compacted and cemented to form a rock we call *tuff*. The tuff may contain crystals that had formed before eruption, and sometimes contain fragments of older rocks broken up by the violent eruption (Figure 3–46).

Sometimes the fragments are still molten when they settle to the earth. When this happens, they may be hot enough to partially liquify and "weld" together to form rocks we call *welded tuffs*. They can be recognized because the fragments of bubble walls were "soft" and are draped around crystals or fragments in the tuffs (Figure 3–47). Tuffs and welded tuffs are exposed in and around Wausau, southwest of Monico, east of Pembine, and near Athens, Wisconsin.

Rhyolite lava flows, probably lava domes of glassy obsidian, are also found with the tuffs. In more recent volcanic centers, the obsidian domes form after the explosive phase of eruption. The stiff lava domes slowly flatten out due to their own weight and produce a distinctive "layering" in the rocks that tells us that they were once lava flows. The layering in the rhyolites is referred to as *flow-banding*. Excellent flow-banding is present in rhyolite exposed along the Rib River east of Athens, Wisconsin (Figure 3–48). Microscopic features still preserved in some rhyolites show the rhyolites were originally glassy obsidian.

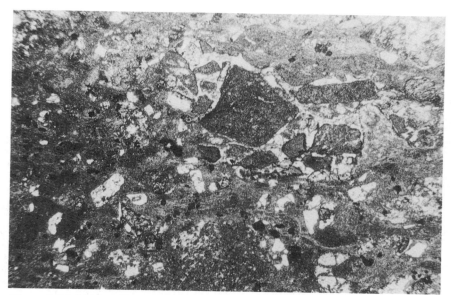

Figure 3-46: Lithic tuff composed of abundant fragments of older volcanic rock (dark) in a matrix of fine ash. Area shown is about 8 x 10 mm. From Brokaw, Wisconsin.

Figure 3-47: Welded rhyolitic tuff, showing the rounded ends of the elongate shards. Round, white grains are quartz crystals, gray textured grains in the lower part of the photo are feldspar crystals. Area shown is about 8 x 10 mm. From Wausau, Wisconsin.

Rhyolitic volcanic islands were also subjected to erosion to form graywackes in the surrounding basins. Graywackes derived from rhyolitic islands are more quartz-rich and similar to rhyolite in composition. Additionally, the violent rhyolitic eruptions result in volcanic ash falling directly into the sea, which produces layers of rhyolitic tuff interbedded with the graywackes. Some of the graywackes accumulated in deep, stagnant water, where organic debris was not decomposed by oxygen. The result was carbon-rich sediments, sometimes also containing abundant iron sulfide (pyrite).

Figure 3-48: Flow-banded rhyolite lava flow showing the typical laminated nature of the rock. They form as a very viscous lava flow spreads out from the vent. From along the Rib River east of Athens, Wisconsin.

INTRUSIVE ROCKS

In all volcanic areas a substantial amount of the magma solidifies before it reaches the surface to form a myriad of dikes and irregular intrusive rocks in the channelways where the magma was rising toward the surface. Large intrusive bodies may form in some areas, such as the one along the Flambeau River valley in northeastern Rusk County and adjacent Price County. Most of the intrusions are relatively small bodies that may have formed the "core" of volcanic islands.

Some of the intrusions have been quarried as a source of building and monument stone (Figure 3–49 and 3–50). For example, the St. Cloud granite in central Minnesota, the red granite near Wausau, Wisconsin, and the Athelstane and Amberg granites in northeastern Wisconsin have been extensively used for industrial purposes.

Dating of rocks in the volcanic belt indicates that igneous activity continued for about 50 million years, from 1,890 million to 1,840 million years ago. During this long span of time major changes took place along the island arc. The arc gradually became wider and extended deeper into the crust as a result of additional volcanic materials being added above and by addition of magmas from below that cooled within the crust. Furthermore, as the islands became larger, greater and greater quantities of sediments accumulated along the flanks of the island arc.

Figure 3-49: Basaltic rocks cut by numerous "veins" of granite. This represents an early stage of magmatic stoping. From near Niagara, Wisconsin.

Figure 3-50: Granite quarry north of Wausau showing the method of quarrying using long wire saws to saw the blocks in the quarry. Blocks are then lifted out with the cranes.

Because island arcs form in areas of intense compression (subduction zones), the rocks are subjected to almost continuous folding and faulting—and heating due to additions of molten rocks from below. The deformation and heating produces metamorphism within the island arc. Rocks deeper in the belt (those that formed earlier) are subjected to the most intense and prolonged metamorphism. Therefore, it is not surprising that large areas within the volcanic belt in Wisconsin consist of rather highly metamorphosed rocks. They consist mainly of gneisses and schists (Figure 3–51 to 3–53). Mineral composition of the rocks indicates that some were derived from volcanic rocks and others were derived from sedimentary rocks (graywackes). Faulting subsequent to metamorphism caused large blocks to move vertically or horizontally or both, to bring gneissic rocks against relatively unmetamorphosed rocks along large fault zones. Some of these faults, such as the Athens Fault Zone (Figure 3–54) extend for at least

Figure 3-51: Amphibolitic gneisses produced by intense deformation and meta-morphism of basaltic rocks. Note the complex folding due to multiple deforma-tions. From Jim Falls on the Chippewa River. Photo by Paul E. Myers.

150 miles across Wisconsin. Gneissic rocks are exposed north of the fault and relatively unmetamorphosed volcanic rocks are found south of the fault.

Another type of complication in island arcs occurs when volcanic activity ceases on an island and a new island begins to form elsewhere along the arc. The older island is gradually eroded away, whereas the new one grows. In places the newer volcanic rocks may be deposited on the eroded remains of an older island. Older volcanic rocks overlain by younger, less altered rocks are present in the Monico area and in Marathon County, Wisconsin.

Like the volcanic rocks, intrusions that were emplaced before or during major deformation are deformed and converted to gneissic rocks. By contrast, intrusions that invaded the volcanic pile after deformation had ceased are not deformed. Therefore, by examining a granite to see if it is deformed we can determine when it was emplaced relative to the major deformation.

In addition to the igneous and sedimentary rocks, important zinc-copper-gold deposits formed in association with the rhyolitic centers. The deposits located thus far include those at Ladysmith (found in 1968), the "Reef" deposit in eastern Marathon County (found in 1970), near Monico (found in 1974), near Crandon (found in 1976), in Taylor County (found in 1987), and the Lynn deposit west of Rhinelander (found in 1989). For each of these favorable sites mining companies have explored dozens of false leads, many of which proved to be mainly carbonaceous (graphitic) sediments. Only one of these sites (Ladysmith) has been brought into production, although all have been thoroughly studied. Exhaustive environmental studies have been undertaken at the most favorable sites to ensure that no environmental degradation will occur if, in fact, the deposits are ever mined.

Figure 3-52: Gneiss exposed along the Rib River near Goodrich, Wisconsin. The rock has the appearance of an intrusion breccia, but both intrusive material and the blocks of older rocks have been deformed and highly metamorphosed.

Like their Archean counterparts in greenstone belts, the deposits are lenses perhaps 30–50 feet thick and about 1,000 feet long. The ore is composed mainly of pyrite with important concentrations of the zinc mineral, sphalerite, the copper mineral, chalcopyrite, and minor amounts of gold, silver, and lead. The enclosing rocks are typically volcanic ash and breccias. A "pipe" of highly altered volcanic rocks beneath the deposits was produced as the hot, metal-bearing fluids rose toward the sea floor on the flanks of the volcanic islands. The deposits evidently formed where hot springs emanated onto the sea floor. The dramatic change in chemistry where the metal-bearing hot waters mixed with seawater caused wholesale deposition of the metals. Although hot springs are common features in volcanic areas, only a few carry enough metals and last long enough to produce significant concentrations of the metals we use in our economy.

Figure 3-53: Garnet-mica schist produced by metamorphism of a graywacke. The wavy nature of the mica layers indicates that the rock has been subjected to at least two episodes of deformation. Area shown is about 2 feet by 3 feet. From eastern Eau Claire County, Wisconsin.

Figure 3-54: Mylonite along the Athens Fault zone about one mile west of Athens, Wisconsin. These highly crushed and recrystallized rocks were produced along the boundary between gneissic rocks to the north and less metamorphosed volcanic rocks to the south.

▲ THE PENOKEAN MOUNTAINS ▲

THE NIAGARA FAULT ZONE

The plate convergence that produced the volcanic island arc we have described was the result of movement of the older Superior craton toward the subduction zone. Subduction stopped when the continent collided with the island arc along its northern margin (Figure 3–55). This collision resulted in extensive deformation of the island arc as well as deformation of the sedimentary rocks on the continental margin described

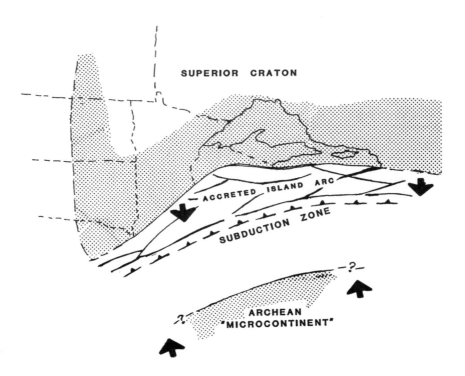

Figure 3-55: Sketch map of the Lake Superior region as it might have been about 1,850 million years ago. The earlier island arc was accreted to the Superior craton. A north-dipping subduction zone developed as an Archean microcontinent approached from the south.

earlier. The collision produced a mountain range across northern Wisconsin. This ancient mountain range is called the *Penokean Mountains*. The eroded remnants of these mountains constitute much of the bedrock in Wisconsin, Minnesota, and Michigan.

The actual collision zone is generally believed to be the *Niagara Fault Zone*, which extends in an arcuate line across northern Wisconsin (Figure 3–56).

Figure 3-56: Generalized geologic map of Wisconsin showing the distribution of major rock units. Note the Niagara Fault zone in northern Wisconsin which separates Early Proterozoic volcanic and plutonic rocks in Wisconsin from older Early Proterozoic sedimentary rocks that had accumulated on the passive margin of the Archean Superior craton

The fault passes through Niagara, Wisconsin, on the Michigan border, from which it takes its name. In the area near Niagara the fault zone forms the boundary between Wisconsin and Michigan. The Menominee River flows generally along the fault zone for approximately 20 miles, from near Florence southeastward beyond Niagara. Rocks along the fault zone are typically strongly foliated, may show a lineation, and locally contain *folded foliation* (or "kink-folds") indicating multiple, or complex deformation.

Note that the feature is referred to as a *fault zone*. The Niagara Fault is not a single fault; rather it consists of numerous faults that branch and recombine along the zone. Furthermore, since the Niagara Fault Zone is an "extinct" subduction zone, there are numerous small and large wedges or lens-shaped rock masses along the fault zone. In fact, the collision zone is a long, narrow strip of very complex geology.

Collision also resulted in large-scale *thrusting* of rocks onto the margin of the Superior craton. The zone of thrusting extends at least 50 miles north of the Niagara Fault Zone to the village of L'Anse, Michigan, on Lake Superior. Numerous folds and thrust slices have been recognized in northern Michigan in the area from Iron Mountain north to Lake Superior, producing a very complex pattern in the geology (Klasner et al., 1991) (Figure 3–57). Similar north-directed fold patterns have been recognized in east-central Minnesota. Therefore, deformation was very widespread along the collision zone.

Collision between the island arc and the continent is believed to have occurred about 1,860 million years ago. This date is indicated by the presence of *undeformed* granitic intrusions near the Niagara Fault Zone that are about 1,860 million years old.

A zone of highly metamorphosed sedimentary rocks occurs along the collision zone in parts of northern Wisconsin. The sediments probably accumulated along the continental margin long before the onset of convergent tectonics. During the collision the rocks were subject to intense deformation and heating to produce metamorphic minerals like kyanite and sillimanite. These minerals formed from original clay minerals such as kaolinite in the graywacke sediments. Rocks containing these minerals are widespread in northern Price County, where they were encountered in cores drilled for mineral exploration. They are also exposed at various places in the upper reaches of the Flambeau River in southern Ashland and Iron counties. Excellent exposures of kyanite (and sillimanite)-bearing schists and gneisses are exposed near Powell, between Manitowish and Park Falls. These high-grade metamorphic rocks were formed at great depths within the collision zone and were uplifted along large faults so that they are now exposed at the surface.

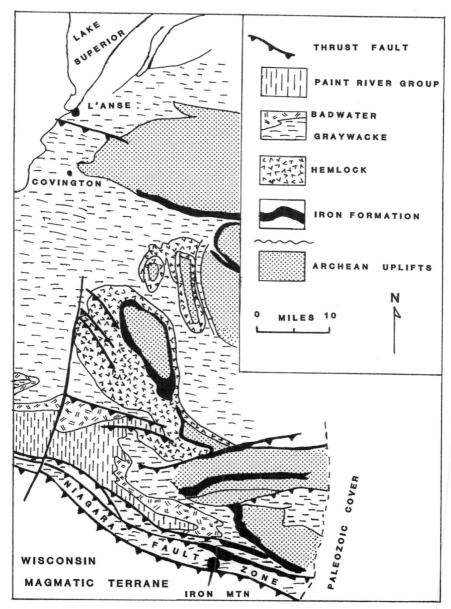

Figure 3-57: Sketch map of a portion of northern Michigan showing the complex fold and fault pattern produced by collision of the Wisconsin Magmatic terranes with the older continent to the north (from Klasner and others, 1991).

CENTRAL AND SOUTHERN WISCONSIN

Exotic Terranes. When the island arc and the Superior craton collided about 1,860 million years ago consumption of oceanic crust along the south-dipping subduction zone ended. However, convergent forces continued. The Superior craton with its newly accreted island arc continued moving against an oceanic plate offshore. The continued convergence resulted in the development of a new subduction zone along the southern margin of the island arc. The new subduction zone appears to have been dipping to the north (opposite the direction of the older subduction) (Figure 3–58).

This subduction resulted in a second generation of volcanic rocks in central Wisconsin. Like the earlier volcanic rocks, pillow basalts, andesites, and rhyolites were produced as a result of subduction. Some of these volcanic rocks were deposited on the eroded remnants of the older volcanic rocks, others may have accumulated as new volcanic islands. As might be expected, it is very difficult to distinguish second-cycle from first-cycle volcanics.

The plate moving toward the Superior craton, and being consumed in the north-dipping subduction zone, was not an endless expanse of oceanic crust. It was a "block" of Archean continental crust of unknown size that moved slowly toward the Superior craton (Figure 3–59). This block of Archean crustal rocks is referred to as an *exotic terrane* because it originated somewhere else and was carried to its present site by plate motions. The Archean exotic terrane eventually collided with the southern edge of the volcanic island arc. The collision zone is approximately along the Eau Pleine River valley in southern Marathon County. Archean rocks are relatively widely exposed south of the Eau Pleine valley, but are unknown for nearly 100 miles to the north. Only Early Proterozoic volcanic and intrusive rocks are found in the area north of the Eau Pleine River valley.

Like the Niagara Fault Zone on the northern edge of the island arc, the margin along the Eau Pleine valley is extremely complex. The rocks are extremely compressed and flattened to produce a prominent northwest-trending zone of schists. A number of talc-serpentine bodies are present within and south of the Eau Pleine Fault Zone.

The Archean rocks that make up the exotic terrane are mainly gneisses near the collision zone. These gneisses are well exposed in the Black River valley near Lake Arbutus, near Neillsville, in a quarry near Pittsville (see Figure 2–18), and in several exposures along the southern edge of Marathon County. Gneisses at the quarry west of Pittsville have been dated at a minimum of 2,800 million years, and may be as much as 3,200 million years old.

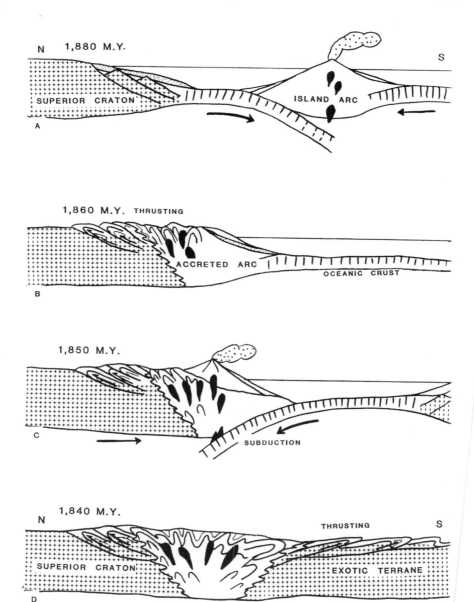

Figure 3-58: Cross-sectional sketch showing the change from south-dipping to north-dipping subduction during the convergent phase of the Early Proterozoic events in the Lake Superior region.

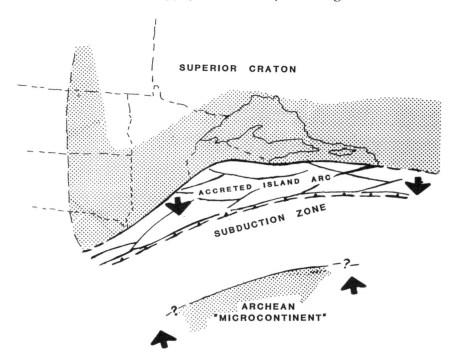

Figure 3-59: Sketch map showing general tectonic relationships as an Archean microcontinent converged on the Superior craton with the accreted Early Proterozoic island arc. Oceanic crust between the converging cratons was consumed in the subduction zone dipping beneath the accreted island arc.

The gneisses evidently form a zone about 20 miles wide, because extensive drilling in the area from Babcock west to Black River Falls shows that the rocks are typical greenstones, granite, and iron-formation. In other words, a typical Archean greenstone belt is present south of the gneisses. The Jackson County iron mine near Black River Falls recovered ore from iron-formations within this belt.

The extent of Archean rocks in central Wisconsin is not known because a blanketlike cover of Paleozoic sedimentary rocks (about 500 million years old) has buried nearly all of the older rocks. Although the northern edge of the Archean is well documented along the Eau Pleine Fault Zone, the southern margin is almost completely unknown. Therefore, the size of the exotic terrane is open to speculation.

Quartzites in Southern Wisconsin. Proterozoic quartzite protrudes through the cover of Paleozoic sedimentary rocks at a number of localities in central and southern Wisconsin (Figure 3–56). Because the quartzites occur in a number of isolated localities, and only a few of the localities reveal relationships to any other Precambrian rocks, the origin, age, and relationship of the various quartzites to one another is problematical. Cuttings from drilling of deepwater wells show that quartzite is widely distributed beneath the Paleozoic cover in southeastern Wisconsin.

The best-known of the quartzite occurrences is an oval-shaped ring of prominent hills in southern Wisconsin known as the Baraboo Quartzite. In the 1970s the quartzite and associated rocks in the Baraboo area were interpreted by Dott (1983) to be significantly younger than the Early Proterozoic tectonic events in the volcanic belt to the north. Geological mapping of the various occurrences of Proterozoic quartzite in Wisconsin by LaBerge et al. (1991) suggests, however, that the quartzites throughout southern Wisconsin have undergone a similar deformation history. The more recent studies suggest that the quartzites in southern Wisconsin were deformed during a major event of folding and thrusting. The rocks are folded and thrust from north to south, away from the Eau Pleine collision zone. These relationships are shown diagrammatically in Figure 3–60. We now review some of these features.

The Baraboo Quartzite has been folded into a syncline in which the north limb is vertical and the south limb dips gently to the north (Figure

QUARTZITES OF SOUTHERN WISCONSIN

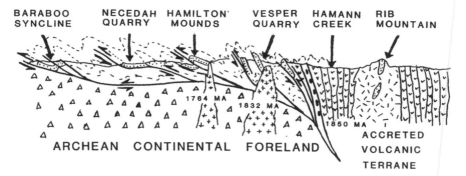

Figure 3-60: Diagram showing structural interpretation of quartzite occurrences in southern Wisconsin.

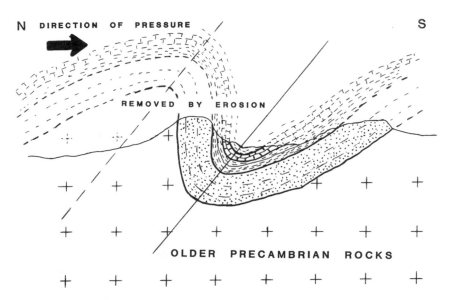

Figure 3-61: Diagram showing the general structure in the Baraboo area of southern Wisconsin. The fold is overturned to the south, indicating movement from the north.

3–61). Rocks on the north limb are well exposed just north of Rock Springs, where Van Hise Rock shows well the relationships (Figure 3–62). The north limb is also exposed at "lower narrows" between Baraboo and Portage, where the contact between the quartzite and underlying rhyolite can be seen. The gently dipping south limb is spectacularly exposed in the cliffs along Devil's Lake (Figure 3–63). The steep north limb and gentle south limb indicate that the syncline is "overturned" (or tilted) to the south. This suggests that the major forces that produced the fold were from north to south.

Approximately 45 miles north of Baraboo seven small knobs of quartzite called Hamilton Mounds rise above the blanket of Paleozoic sandstone. A quarry in one of the hills produces crushed rock for use on Adams County roads. Highly deformed quartzite is exposed in the quarry. Studies conducted in the quarry in the late 1980s reveal a complex structural pattern (Figure 3–64) in the quartzite. Like the Baraboo area the structural relationships suggest that the rocks moved from north to south. A relatively undeformed granitic dike intrudes the highly deformed quartzite. This suggests that the deformation was

Figure 3-62:
Van Hise Rock
Vertically dipping
layers of Baraboo
Quartzite and slate
on the north limb of
the Baraboo basin.

largely completed before intrusion of the granite. Had the intrusion occurred before deformation it, too, would be highly deformed. The granite has been dated at 1,764 million years old. This indicates that deformation occurred before 1,764 million years ago. This is an example of how geological events are dated. Large zones of brecciated quartzite cemented by quartz are present in many of the quartzite exposures. Cavities lined with quartz crystals can be found in several of the occurrences (Figure 3–65).

Elsewhere in central Wisconsin quartzite is intruded by granites as much as 1,832 million years old, suggesting that the quartzite is older than that. Quartzite boulders in a conglomerate interbedded with 1,840 million-year-old volcanic rocks are exposed along Hamann Creek west of Stratford, Wisconsin. Therefore, a quartzite must have been undergoing erosion during volcanic activity 1,840 million years ago in central Wisconsin.

Figure 3-63: Gently north-dipping Baraboo Quartzite at Devil's Lake State Park on the south limb of the Baraboo syncline.

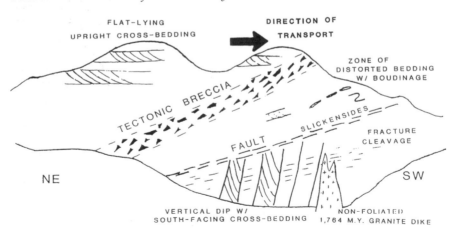

Figure 3-64: Diagram of structural relationships in the quartzite at Hamilton Mounds. The deformed quartzite was intruded by a granite dike 1,764 million years ago. This shows that deformation occurred before 1,764 million years ago.

In the Baraboo area the quartzite is some 4,000 feet thick. It is overlain by a thick sequence of shaly rock (the Seely Slate), a dolomite, and, locally, an iron-formation, In fact, iron ore was mined from the iron-formation southwest of Baraboo in the early part of the twentieth century. These sedimentary rocks are very similar to the platform sedimentary rocks farther north in the Lake Superior region. Recall that the sedimentary rocks to the north are believed to have formed on a passive margin during rifting and break up of the Archean continent during the early part of the Early Proterozoic.

It is likely that the rocks in central and southern Wisconsin also formed on the passive margin of an Archean continent. Remnants of the Archean continent are present in central Wisconsin. The quartzites and other sedimentary rocks in central and southern Wisconsin seem best explained as the deeply eroded remnants of a passive margin sequence that was deposited on an Archean "microcontinent." The rocks were deformed by a major south-directed event of folding and thrusting that probably was the collision of the microcontinent with the southern margin of the island arc. Deformation revealed in the remnants of quartzites suggests that a substantial mountain range extended across central and

Figure 3-65: Quartz crystal group about two inches wide from a breccia zone in the McCaslin quartzite near Townsend, Wisconsin.

southern Wisconsin. Thus, the Penokean Mountains appear to have been a major feature during Early Proterozoic time.

Final collision of the microcontinent with the volcanic island arc occurred about 1,830 million years ago. Melting continued, however, for many millions of years after collision. Magmas produced were largely granites that intruded the overlying crust long after deformation had ceased.

Rhyolites of Southern Wisconsin. During the late stages or after the main deformation of the Penokean Orogeny, a different type of volcanic event occurred in southern Wisconsin. Remnants of rhyolitic rocks formed on land by extremely explosive eruptions are found over an area at least as large as shown in Figure 3–66. The rhyolites appear to have been extruded onto a surface of mixed Archean and Proterozoic rocks similar to those now exposed in the Stevens Point area to the north. Accompanying extrusion of the rhyolites, a large composite granitic

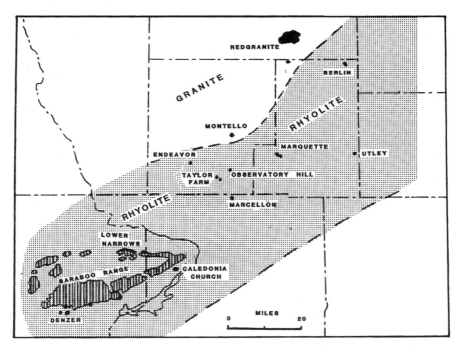

Figure 3-66: Map of the Fox River Valley - Baraboo area showing the location of Early Proterozoic rocks in the area. Dashed lines show possible limits of the different igneous rock types (modified from Smith, 1978).

batholith was intruded into the older rocks, and many of the rhyolite exposures are interpreted to be roof pendants within this batholith. Since most of southern Wisconsin has a blanket of Paleozoic sedimentary rocks covering the Precambrian, however, we know very little about the nature of the rocks on which the rhyolites were extruded.

The rhyolite is exposed in a number of isolated hills that protrude through the blanket of Paleozoic sandstones at Berlin, Utley, Marquette, Observatory Hill, Taylor farm, Marcellon, Endeavor, and west of Portage in the Baraboo range. Some of the rhyolite knobs, which stand several hundred feet above the surrounding Precambrian rocks, were small, steep-sided islands in the Paleozoic seas. The rhyolite forms hills because the dense, fine-grained rock is more resistant to erosion than the surrounding granites that intruded the rhyolites. The rhyolite exposures form a belt extending from near Baraboo northeasterly toward Oshkosh, and genetically related granite is exposed northwest of the rhyolites at Redgranite and Montello (Figure 3–66). Isolated exposures of similar rhyolite at Cary Mound in Wood County, however, suggest that the rhyolites may originally have been much more extensive.

A number of these rhyolites, called *black granite*, have been quarried in the past. Granites were also quarried at several localities. This quarried material was used locally for building stone; for example, a number of buildings in Berlin are made of Berlin rhyolite. Granite quarried at Montello has been used for monument stone, as in the tomb of U.S. Grant. Large quantities of granite and rhyolite were quarried for cobblestones for paving the streets in Milwaukee, Racine, Chicago, among other cities, before the turn of the century. An interesting account of the building and ornamental stone industry in Wisconsin has been presented by E. R. Buckley (1898).

The rhyolite in most of the exposures is dark brown to black and at first glance appears to be nearly featureless. Close examination of the rhyolite on weathered surfaces however reveals that the various rhyolite knobs actually consist of a series of different rock units. Some are composed of coarsely fragmental material; others are extremely fine grained, with pumice and glass shard fragments visible only under the microscope; while other units consist of a mixture of fragments and crystals up to nearly 1 centimeter in size (Figure 3–67). The variations in the rocks reflect differences in the magma at the time of extrusion. In some cases, the magma was entirely liquid and, upon extrusion, may have formed a glassy fragmental rock, probably obsidian. In other instances, crystals may have begun forming in the magma before extrusion, producing porphyritic rhyolite. In general, rhyolitic eruptions are extremely explosive, and the resulting rocks are usually fragmental.

Figure 3-67: Extremely flattened pumice fragments (white streaks) deformed around a rock fragment in an ash-flow tuff from Marcellon, Wisconsin.

The violence of the eruption is so great and the volcanic materials so hot that many of the glassy fragments are still a plastic <u>liquid</u> when the ash-flow sheets accumulate. The fragments are commonly flattened and may stick (weld) together to form very hard rocks called <u>welded</u> <u>tuffs</u>. Usually the bottom of an ash-flow unit is not welded because of the rapid cooling against the underlying land surface. The top also tends to be unwelded due to rapid loss of heat to the atmosphere. The central part of ash-flow tuffs may be so densely welded, however, that it becomes a solid, glassy, obsidian. As described earlier in the section on the volcanic island arc, a wide variety of volcanic materials are produced during a rhyolitic eruption.

The magma that cooled and crystallized below the surface formed bodies of granite such as those now exposed at Redgranite and Montello. In places the granite intruded the rhyolite. Indeed, the rhyolite and granite are nearly identical in chemical composition, suggesting that they were derived from the same magma. Smith (1978) concluded that rhyolites probably formed a cover for the underlying granites that intruded them. The few scattered exposures and cuttings and cores from deepwater wells show that this distinctive type of granite underlies a large area in southern Wisconsin. As pointed out by Bickford et al. (1981), this distinctive rhyolite–granite association is the oldest and northernmost of a series of similar rocks that forms the Precambrian basement in the midcontinent region from northern Ohio to the Texas panhandle. The rocks are present in a series of linear belts that are successively younger to the south, and appear to be a major feature of continental growth during the latter part of the Precambrian in North America. The rhyolitic and plutonic rocks in Wisconsin were formed about 1,760 million years ago, which is 50 to 60 million years after the main Penokean Orogeny farther north. A number of post-tectonic granites were intruded at this time in central Wisconsin. These granites are conspicuous in that they are undeformed and contrast sharply with the older foliated granites of the Penokean Orogeny. Granites of this type are exposed just south of Monico, at Radisson, east and south of Marshfield, and south of Owen.

A more recent example of this explosive volcanic event in Wisconsin's geologic history is the development of Yellowstone Park. The rocks in southern Wisconsin are mainly rhyolites and have almost certainly formed in the same way as those in Yellowstone Park. In fact, much of our understanding of the nature of the volcanic eruptions that produce these rhyolitic rocks has come from studies in and around Yellowstone and elsewhere in the American Southwest and in New Zealand. The violent eruption of Mount St. Helens in May, 1981, was a relatively small example of the type of eruption that must have been prevalent in southern Wisconsin 1,760 million years ago.

SUMMARY OF EARLY ▲ PROTEROZOIC EVENTS IN ▲ THE LAKE SUPERIOR REGION

The Early Proterozoic events in the Lake Superior region include a very diverse series of geological events that occurred over a span of nearly 800 million years. The events produced different rock types at different times, and some events happened in widely separated places. As a consequence of plate tectonics however, the rocks have been brought together to form a major part of the Lake Superior region. The following is a brief summary of the events.

1. Gradual rifting and break up of a large continent assembled during Archean time.
2. Development of a passive margin with widespread accumulation of clean sandstone, dolomite, iron-formation, and graywacke between 2,300 and 2,000 million years ago.
3. Formation of an ocean basin off the rifted continental margin by continued divergent plate motion.
4. A change to convergent plate motion and development of a volcanic island arc over a south-dipping subduction zone somewhere offshore from the Superior continent about 1,900 million years ago.
5. Collision of the island arc with the Superior continent about 1,860 million years ago, accompanied by extensive thrusting to the north onto the Superior continent.
6. Continued convergence and change to a north-dipping subduction zone beneath the island arc.
7. Collision between the island arc and a northward-moving Archean microcontinent on which passive margin sediments had accumulated. Major south-directed folding and thrusting occurred. Collision occurred about 1,830 million years ago.
8. Extensive posttectonic caldera-type rhyolites and related granite emplaced in central and southern Wisconsin about 1,760 million years ago.

SUGGESTED ADDITIONAL READINGS

Barghoorn, E. S., and Tyler, S. A., 1965, Micro-organisms from the Gunflint chert, Science, vol. 147, pp. 563–577.

Barovich, K. M., Patchett, P. J., Peterman, Z. E., and Sims, P. K., 1989, Origin of 1.9-1.7 Ga Penokean continental crust of the Lake Superior region, Geological Society of America Bulletin, vol. 101, pp. 333–338.

Cloud, P. E., 1965, Significance of the Gunflint (Precambrian) Microflora, Science, vol. 148, pp. 27–35.

Dalziel, I. W. D., and Dott, R. H., Jr., 1970, Geology of the Baraboo District, Wisconsin, Geological and Natural History Survey Information Circular 14, Madison.

Hoffman, P. E., 1988, United Plates of America, The Birth of a Craton: Early Proterozoic Assembly and Growth of Laurentia, Annual Reviews Earth and Planetary Science, vol. 16, pp. 543–603.

Klasner, J. S., Ojakangas, R. W., Schulz, K. J., and LaBerge, G. L., 1991, Nature and Style of Deformation in the Foreland of the Early Proterozoic Penokean Orogen, Northern Michigan, U.S. Geological Survey Bulletin 1904-K.

LaBerge, G. L., Klasner, J. S., and Myers, P. E., 1990, New observations on the Age and Structure of Proterozoic Quartzites in Wisconsin, U.S. Geological Survey Bulletin 1904-B.

LaBerge, G. L., and Myers, P. E., 1983, Precambrian Geology of Marathon County, Wisconsin, Wisconsin Geological and Natural History Survey Information Circular 45.

LaBerge, G. L., Robbins, E. I., and Han, T-M., 1987, A model for the biological precipitation of Precambrian iron-formations: Geological Evidence, in Precambrian Iron-formations, P. W. Appel and G. L. LaBerge, editors, Theophrastus Publications, Athens, Greece.

Larue, D. K., and Sloss, L. L., 1980, Early Proterozoic sedimentary basins of the Lake Superior region, Geological Society of America Bulletin, vol. 91, pp. 1836–1879.

Medaris, L. G., Jr., 1983, Early Proterozoic Geology of the Great Lakes Region, Geological Society of America Memoir 160.

Ojakangas, R. W., and Matsch, C. L., 1982, Minnesota's Geology, University of Minnesota Press, Minneapolis.

Sims, P. K., Van Schmus, W. R., Schulz, K. J., and Peterman, Z. E., 1989, Tectono-stratigraphic evolution of the Early Proterozoic Wisconsin magmatic terranes of the Penokean orogen, Canadian Journal of Earth Sciences, vol. 25, pp. 2145–2158.

4

THE MIDDLE PROTEROZOIC

Basaltic lava fountains bringing molten rock to the surface along fractures (or rifts) in the earth's crust. Scenes similar to this were probably common during the latter part of the Middle Proterozoic in the Lake Superior region. (Photo from the U.S. Geological Survey Volcano Observatory in Hawaii.)

The events of the Early Proterozoic left an indelible record in the rocks of the Lake Superior region. Several major rock-forming events in the last 1,000 million years of Precambrian time were, however, to add the final chapter to the history of the "basement complex." This period of time includes the Middle and Late Proterozoic. The Middle Proterozoic extends from 1,600 to about 1,000 million years ago, and the preserved record of this interval consists of two major episodes of igneous activity and two periods of deposition of sedimentary rocks. The Late Proterozoic evidently was an extensive period of erosion in this part of North America.

Recall that rocks formed during Early Proterozoic time in the Lake Superior region suggest that a boundary between two crustal plates existed in this part of North America and that these crustal plates were active during much of the Early Proterozoic.

The final phase of convergent tectonics appears to have been the deformation and metamorphism that occurred between 1,890 million and 1,840 million years ago, which produced the Penokean mountain range. Following the development of the Penokean Mountains there is little evidence for compressional forces in the Lake Superior region, or for the presence of plate margins. Instead, the area appears to have been well within a large continental block. Therefore, the geological events that occurred after the Penokean Mountains are significantly different from those of preceding geologic time, and add a totally new dimension to the history of the region.

At the end of Early Proterozoic time the Penokean Mountains were a lofty range comparable to the Appalachian Mountains, but probably as high as the present Rockies. The mountain range extended from northeastern Iowa (or beyond) eastward across Wisconsin, Michigan, and southern Ontario at least to the Lake Ontario area.

This major mountain range was subjected to erosion for most of Middle Proterozoic time. Streams flowed out of the mountains carrying the sand and clay to the sea some hundreds of miles off to the southeast. The site of deposition of the debris eroded from the Penokean Mountains has not been found, mainly because the probable area of deposition is buried by much younger Paleozoic rocks. Evidence that the Penokean Mountains ever existed lies in the folded, faulted, and metamorphosed volcanic and sedimentary rocks now exposed at the surface in Wisconsin, Michigan, and Minnesota.

Thus, a major part of the Middle Proterozoic history of this part of North America was the erosion of the Penokean Mountains. Erosion continued for at least 500 million years, gradually reducing the lofty

Penokean Mountains. Although erosion was an important part of the Middle Proterozoic history, the only record it left is the eroded edges of the older rocks.

In addition to the incredibly long period of erosion, there were several major rock-forming events in the Lake Superior region during the Middle Proterozoic. Each of these events was the result of geological processes that produced distinctive rock types. Let us examine briefly each of these events and the processes that caused them.

▲ THE WOLF RIVER ▲ BATHOLITH

A major rock-forming event in the Lake Superior region occurred about 1,500 million years ago. It consists of the intrusion of a group of granitic masses that are sparsely exposed over an area of some 3,600 square miles in central and northeastern Wisconsin. Although its southwest corner is at Stevens Point, the southeast corner near Waupaca, the northwest corner near Antigo, and the northeast corner near Mountain, the main continuous part of the granitic intrusion is in the valley of the Wolf River, from which it takes its name. Figure 4–1 shows the general distribution of the batholith and the major rock types present.

While granite and quartz monzonite comprise over 80 percent of the batholith, minor amounts of several other rock types are also present. Approximately the northern half of the batholith in the Wolf River valley is composed of a coarse-grained porphyritic quartz monzonite with microcline crystals about one inch long set in a finer grained matrix of quartz, plagioclase, and biotite. The southern part of the batholith (extending from Shawano southwestward to Stevens Point) is somewhat finer grained with crystals about half the size of those in the body to the north. Both units, however, contain scattered microcline phenocrysts enclosed by a shell of plagioclase. Locally, as in the Waupaca–Tigerton area, these "mantled" phenocrysts are very abundant and produce a distinctive texture in the rock known as *rapakivi*, a Finnish term for similar rocks of similar age in Finland. Figure 4–2 shows an exposure of the coarse-grained granite typical of the northern part of the batholith, and Figure 4–3 shows the typical porphyritic texture.

In several major respects the Wolf River Batholith is different from the Early Proterozoic batholiths to the west and north. It truncates many

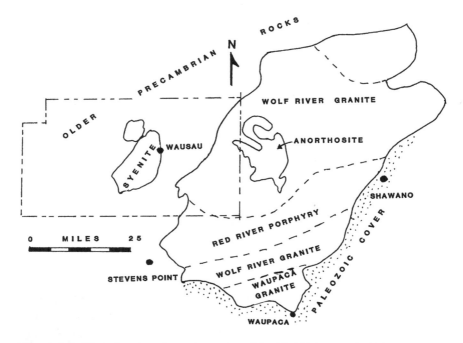

Figure 4-1: Map showing the major units of the Wolf River Batholith.

older structures (rock units and faults) and its area of continuous granite is much larger than the older plutons. Whereas widespread folding, faulting, and deformation occurred in connection with the intrusion of the Early Proterozoic granites, no large-scale deformation was associated with the intrusion of the Wolf River Batholith. It was not formed as part of a mountain-building event; instead it formed well within a continent as a result of intrusion of granitic magma from deep in the crust. The minerals within the various parts of the batholith show no evidence of the crushing so common in the older rocks. Although no significant deformation occurred during intrusion of this immense volume of granite, the surrounding rocks were contact metamorphosed by heat from the intrusion. Pyroxene hornfelses are present within about 100 feet of the batholith; however, the intensity of metamorphism decreases rapidly away from the contact. Virtually no metamorphic effects can be detected in the surrounding rocks that are more than quarter of a mile from the contact. When granitic magmas crystallize at depths of only 1 to 2 miles in the earth, the small amounts of water in the magma are concentrated into small "pockets" in which crystals of quartz, feldspar, and other minerals may form. The presence of numerous, small, crystal-lined (miarolitic) cavities in the batholith indicate that it was emplaced at very shallow depths in the earth. The batholith is surprisingly free of xenoliths of the rocks it intruded. When one considers that the batholith occupies some 3,600 square miles formerly occupied by older rocks, that there was little "shouldering aside" (deformation) of the rocks it intruded, and that the batholith contains few xenoliths of older rocks, it is difficult to explain the intrusion of this batholith. Chemical studies suggest that the magma for the Wolf River Batholith originated by partial melting of the lower crust (some 15 to 22 miles deep) in a tensional environment, possibly related to incipient continental breakup during the Middle Proterozoic.

A similar large granite the same age and composition as the Wolf River Batholith was recently discovered in deep drilling into the Precambrian "basement" along the Illinois–Wisconsin border in southwestern

Figure 4-2: Typical subdued exposure of the Wolf River Batholith with parallel depressions caused by weathering along joints in the outcrop. Southeast of Wausau, Wisconsin.

Figure 4-3: Coarse-grained porphyritic granite with mantled microcline phenocrysts typical of the Rapakivi granite phase of the Wolf River Batholith. From near the southeastern corner of Marathon County.

Wisconsin. This evidently represents another batholith comparable to the Wolf River Batholith. Yet another batholith of remarkably similar appearance and age is the Sherman Granite in the Laramie, Wyoming, area. Similar granites occur in a belt that extends from Labrador to Nevada. Therefore, igneous activity of this age and type was a widespread event in the Middle Proterozoic in North America.

A mass of rock known as the Tigerton Anorthosite is exposed in the central part of the batholith. Outcrops of anorthosite occur over an area of approximately 100 square miles mainly east of Wittenberg and north of Tigerton. At nearly every exposure the anorthosite is cut by numerous granitic dikes that are commonly pegmatitic. In fact, the anorthosite is evidently a number of large blocks of older rock incorporated in the batholith. This interpretation is supported by the fact that much of the anorthosite has been deformed, whereas the granite intruding it has not. The anorthosite is composed mainly of gray plagioclase, near labradorite in composition, with most crystals about one inch long. However, crystals up to 10 inches long are present locally. We do not know the age of the anorthosite except that it is older than the 1,500 million-year-old granite in which it occurs.

THE SYENITE BODIES
▲   NEAR WAUSAU   ▲

Four relatively small syenite bodies, called the Wausau Syenite Complex, were intruded into older rocks of the Penokean Mountains just west of Wausau, Wisconsin (Figure 4–4). Their chemical composition and age indicate that they are genetically related to the Wolf River Batholith, which lies some 6 to 10 miles to the east. The syenite bodies differ from rocks of the Wolf River Batholith in that they contain little quartz.

Field relations and radiometric dating suggest that the Stettin pluton is oldest, and that the Wausau, Rib Mountain, and Ninemile plutons are successively younger to the south, with the Ninemile pluton being the youngest (Figure 4–4). Furthermore, all of these plutons are as much as 20 million years older than the Wolf River Batholith.

The Wausau and Rib Mountain plutons contain numerous blocks (xenoliths) of quartzite incorporated in the syenite intrusions. Xenoliths of quartzite range in size from less than one inch to the huge blocks of the Rib Mountain Quartzite (Figure 4–5), a steeply dipping block of quartzite at least 2 miles long and half a mile wide (this indicates that the quartzite was several thousand feet thick) that forms the top of Rib Mountain. Other large quartzite blocks form the cap of Hardwood Hill near Marathon City, and north and south Mosinee Hills near Wausau. Syenite is exposed on the lower parts of each of these hills, showing that the quartzite really is included within the syenite. Because the quartzite is so much more resistant to erosion than the enclosing syenite, these hills stand up to 600 feet above the surrounding countryside. Rib Mountain is, in fact, the highest *bedrock* exposure in Wisconsin.

These large blocks, as well as thousands of smaller blocks of quartzite, are present in a nearly circular ring nearly 6 miles in diameter in the Rib Mountain pluton. Quartzite xenoliths are also abundant in part of a circular ring about 5 miles in diameter in the Wausau pluton.

We must ask the question, Where did these blocks of quartzite come from? One possibility is that a thick blanket of quartzite was present on

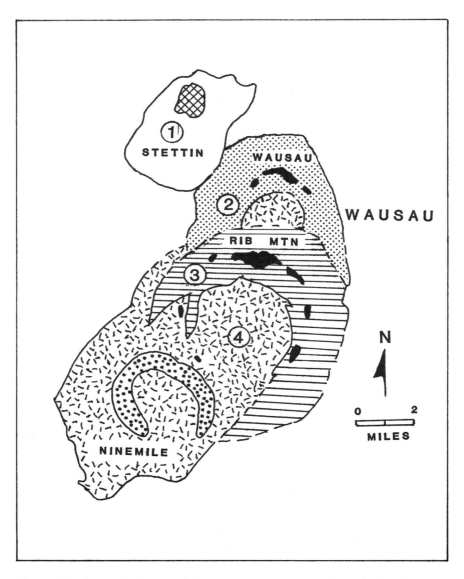

Figure 4-4: Generalized map of the Wausau Syenite complex. The Stettin Pluton is the oldest and most deficient in silica. The plutons are younger to the south, with the Ninemile Pluton being the youngest. (From Myers, 1984.)

the eroded remnants of the Penokean Mountains in central Wisconsin, and that the syenite magma intruded the blanket of quartzite from below. Alternatively, the quartzite blocks may have been carried upward in the syenite magma. Let us examine the evidence.

First, the quartzite occurs only as blocks within the syenite plutons. Assuming that a 2,000-foot-thick blanket of quartzite covered central Wisconsin, it would be a rare coincidence that the only remnant is xenoliths in the syenite intrusions. The limited distribution of quartzite within the syenite, however, does not completely rule out the possibility of intrusion from below the quartzite. Other evidence, however, limits the choices of interpretation. Some blocks of quartzite contain the fibrous aluminum silicate mineral sillimanite which forms as a result of the high temperature and pressure metamorphism of the clay mineral kaolinite that was deposited with the quartz grains in the sandstone from which the quartzite formed. Sillimanite typically forms at great depths within the earth. The volcanic rocks exposed around the syenite complex have undergone only relatively low temperature and pressure

Figure 4-5: Rib Mountain at Wausau, Wisconsin, looking across the Rib River valley from the north. This prominent landmark can be seen for over 25 miles.

metamorphism, however, suggesting that the volcanic rocks have <u>not</u> been deeply buried. These observations led to the conclusion that the quartzite has been deeply buried, probably <u>beneath</u> the volcanic rocks in the area, and that the quartzite was carried to higher levels in the earth's crust by the syenite magma.

The outer margins of the plutons proved to be easily eroded zones. Intrusion of the syenite magma caused extensive fracturing of the surrounding rocks. Much later, when the area was exposed at the surface, these fractured zones were broken up and carried away by streams flowing over the land. In fact, the outer margins of igneous intrusions, as well as fault zones, commonly form stream valleys or swamps. Only rarely are these types of geologic features exposed, the exceptions being

Figure 4-6: Exposure in a "rotten granite" quarry showing the alteration of solid granite to loose material. Granite on which the hammer handle rests is unaltered whereas the surrounding layers are completely disaggregated. Hammer handle is 18 inches long. From south of Marathon, Wisconsin.

areas where the rocks have been thoroughly cemented together by fluids that deposit quartz in the fractures.

These Middle Proterozoic intrusions have become an important resource in central Wisconsin. Weathering of the Ninemile Pluton and parts of the Wolf River Batholith causes the mineral grains to "fall apart" and become a very crumbly rock that is extensively used in central Wisconsin for road "gravel" and "fill." The disaggregated granite is locally called "rotten granite" and is almost identical to the "grus" developed on the Sherman Granite in southeastern Wyoming. The "rotten granite" is quarried in a ring about a mile wide around the margin of the Ninemile Pluton and near the western margin of the Wolf River Batholith near Hogarty. The disaggregated granite extends to depths of more than 100 feet and constitutes a substantial resource in the area. The conversion of solid granite into "rotten granite" appears to be controlled by joints or fractures in the granite. Intersecting vertical and horizontal fractures produce numerous rectangular blocks. Solutions moving along the fractures cause corners and edges to become rounded, and finally attack the faces of these blocks, gradually converting the angular blocks into spheroidal boulders (Figure 4–6). In time the entire boulder becomes "rotten granite." At deeper levels there are innumerable residual boulders, and one can observe examples of all stages in the transformation of hard, massive granite into a very crumbly material that can be quarried and used without blasting or crushing.

Recently a variety of well-formed crystals has been found in cavities in small pegmatite bodies in the Ninemile Pluton. Smoky quartz

Figure 4-7: Eight-inch-wide slab of iron-stained, blocky feldspar and elongated quartz crystals from a cavity in the Ninemile pluton west of Wausau, Wisconsin.

*Figure 4-8:
Two-inch tall smoky
quartz crystals from
a cavity in the
Ninemile pluton
west of Wausau,
Wisconsin.*

crystals that range up to nearly 2 feet long, and much smaller microcline crystals are most common (Figures 4–7 and 4–8). However, a variety of rare minerals, including aquamarine (a form of beryl) and
phenakite have also been reported. Parts of the Stettin Syenite, an
attractive greenish gray colored stone, have been quarried in the past
for monument and building stone. At a few localities the feldspar in
the syenite has a blue internal color called *schiller*, referred to by lapi-
darists as moonstone. Attractive jewelry can be fashioned by cutting
and polishing properly oriented slabs of this moonstone feldspar. A
wide variety of commercially important minerals can be found in syenite bodies, including phosphate (for fertilizer) and uranium minerals.
Therefore, the syenite bodies and the Wolf River Batholith, which now
yield only "rotten granite," could in the future become important for
other minerals.

▲ QUARTZITES ▲

Red quartzite of Middle Proterozoic age is exposed at several localities in northwestern Wisconsin and in southwestern Minnesota and adjacent parts of South Dakota (Figure 4–9). These quartzites contain several features that indicate they were deposited in the same type of environment. These features also distinguish these Middle Proterozoic quartzites from the older quartzites discussed earlier.

The Barron Quartzite crops out in an area of about 300 square miles in parts of Barron, Rusk, Sawyer, and Washburn Counties in northwestern Wisconsin (Figure 4–9). It is composed mainly of pink to red cross-bedded sandstone with quartz cement in addition to thin layers of red clay-rich material. The rock is evidently <u>not</u> metamorphosed. The quartzite was produced by thorough cementation of the sand grains by quartz cement. The mineralogy of the clay-rich layers also suggests that the

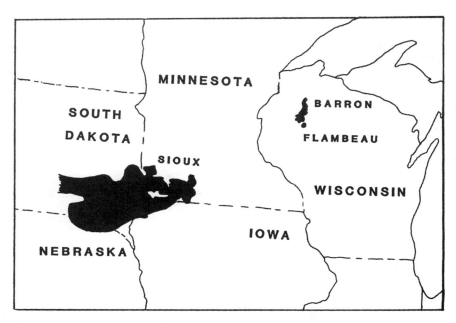

Figure 4-9: Map showing the location and distribution of Middle Proterozoic red quartzites in the Lake Superior region.

rock is not metamorphosed. A conglomerate with pebbles of white quartz, jasper (iron-formation), granite, and volcanic rocks is present at the base of the quartzite. The Barron Quartzite rests unconformably on an erosion surface developed on volcanic and intrusive rocks that were deformed and metamorphosed during the Penokean Orogeny.

The Barron Quartzite is at least 600 feet thick, and may be as much as 1,200 feet thick. The thickness is uncertain because the top of the unit is not exposed. Furthermore, erosion has removed an unknown amount of the formation prior to deposition of the overlying Paleozoic sandstone. The Barron Quartzite remains almost flat-lying with layering dipping only 5°–10°, and therefore it has not been deformed.

The Flambeau Quartzite is exposed on several hills in northern Chippewa County, approximately 16 miles southeast of the Barron Quartzite. The Flambeau Quartzite is reddish in color, and basically is similar to the Barron Quartzite. It differs in that there is far more conglomerate present in the Flambeau Quartzite, and it has been tightly folded. Exposures show approximately 2,200 feet of conglomeratic quartzite. The basal conglomerate unit is about 160 feet thick and contains abundant angular fragments up to about 2 inches across of iron-stained slate. These fragments are probably derived from underlying rocks that were intensely weathered. A maroon-colored quartzite unit approximately 300 feet thick overlies the conglomerate. The quartzite is in turn overlain by a 1,400-foot-thick conglomerate unit containing abundant round pebbles of white quartz, granular iron formation (jasper), yellowish chert, and pale-green volcanic rocks. The uppermost unit is a 330-foot-thick unit of well-cemented reddish orange quartzite with prominent cross-bedding.

Like the Barron Quartzite, metamorphism seems to be lacking in the Flambeau Quartzite. Folding of the Flambeau Quartzite is difficult to explain because deposition occurred after mountain-building events in the area. The fact that the rocks are folded into a tight fold requires that deformation has occurred. The only time during which deformation could have occurred is the Keweenawan, which is described below. Movement along one of the large faults that were active during Keweenawan time may have produced the folding in the Flambeau Quartzite.

Red quartzite interbedded with conglomerate and red clay-rich layers is present in a large area in southwestern Minnesota, southeastern South Dakota, and the northwestern corner of Iowa. The unit is known as the Sioux Quartzite. Although the Sioux Quartzite covers a large area, it is mostly covered with younger (Cretaceous) sedimentary rocks and Pleistocene glacial deposits. Its distribution is known from scattered outcrops and drill holes in the region.

The Sioux Quartzite is exposed in three areas in southwestern Minnesota; in Rock and Pipestone Counties, in Cottonwood, Brown, and Watonwan Counties, and in Nicollet County, along the Minnesota River east of New Ulm.

In each of the outcrop areas layering in the quartzite indicates broad basins with gently dipping layers. The Sioux Quartzite is at least 5,000 feet thick with neither the top nor the bottom of the formation exposed. The most abundant rock type is well-cemented reddish, cross-bedded, ripple-marked quartz sandstone. The sand grains are dominantly well-rounded quartz grains, indicating prolonged weathering in the source area to decompose the feldspars and other rock-forming minerals. The well-rounded grains suggest that they were abraded by long transport in streams moving across a nearly flat landscape, or, alternatively by rolling around in the surf of a shallow sea.

Conglomerate layers in the Sioux Quartzite (Figure 4–10) contain pebbles of white (vein) quartz, jasper, granular iron-formation, and quartzite, and thus, are very similar to conglomerates in the Barron and Flambeau Quartzites in Wisconsin. The abundance of iron-formation pebbles suggests that the conglomerates were produced by erosion of the Early

Figure 4-10: Gently dipping layers of conglomerate layers in the Sioux Quartzite near New Ulm, Minnesota.

Proterozoic iron-formations and surrounding area to the north in Minnesota and Wisconsin. The abundance of quartz-rich pebbles in the conglomerates indicates prolonged weathering in the source area to decompose all the other rock types. Particularly, the absence of feldspar-bearing pebbles is indicative of intense chemical weathering in the source area.

The clay-rich "mudstone" layers consist mainly of kaolinite, fine quartz, hematite, and the aluminum oxide mineral diaspor. Like the other units in the quartzites, these minerals are indicative of a rather flat source area with intense chemical weathering. Furthermore, they indicate that the quartzite has not been metamorphosed, because these constituents would combine to form new (metamorphic) minerals if the rocks had been heated.

The clay-rich layers have been called catinite or "pipestone" because the red clay-rich material was quarried by Native Americans and carved to make ceremonial pipes and other objects. An unusual feature of pipestone is that it is relatively soft and easily carved when first-quarried (and wet). It becomes much harder and more durable when dried. Pipestone, and objects carved from it, were widely traded by Native Americans in the mid-continent area. Pipestone National Monument near Pipestone, Minnesota, was established to preserve this important historical site.

Summarizing the information that these Middle Proterozoic quartzites provide affords some interesting glimpses of what the Lake Superior region might have looked like 1,200 million to 1,500 million years ago. The quartzite, conglomerates, and mudstones were deposited on the eroded remnants of the Penokean Mountains. Therefore, the Penokean Mountains must have been largely eroded to a low rolling plain by the time these quartzite units were deposited. The well-rounded quartz sand and abundance of silica-rich (quartz, jasper, iron-formation) pebbles indicate a relatively flat source area with intense chemical weathering. The red color of the rocks results from the coating of fine hematite that coats the grains. The red color and well-developed cross-bedding suggests that most of the rocks were deposited from streams swinging back and forth over a broad alluvial plain. The clay-rich layers may have formed in shallow lakes or perhaps along stream channels during occasional floods. Features similar to these are widespread in Australia and parts of Africa today.

The age of the quartzites is very poorly constrained because there is almost nothing in the rocks that can be dated. They clearly are younger than the Penokean Mountains formed from 1,840 to 1,890 million years ago. The Barron Quartzite is cut by basaltic dikes that are 1,200 million years old. We do not know just when during the vast span of 640 million years the sediments were deposited. Since considerable time would be required to level the Penokean Mountains, however, we might infer that deposition must have occurred toward the 1,200 million year end of the timespan. Whatever the actual time of deposition, the general lack of any typical metamorphic minerals indicates that these various quartzites have not been involved in any mountain-building events. Or expressed another way, there was no evidence for mountain-building activity in the Lake Superior region after deposition of these sedimentary rocks, and thus it is reasonable to assume that these rocks are younger than those that have been metamorphosed and deformed.

▲ THE KEWEENAWAN ▲

The final chapter of rock-forming events in the Lake Superior region during the immense span of Precambrian time was no less awesome than the preceding events. The last geological episode is referred to as the Keweenawan, and it takes its name from the Keweenaw Peninsula in northern Michigan, where rocks formed during this time interval are especially well-exposed. The Keweenawan was another long event that began about 1,109 million years ago and ended somewhere around 1,000 million years ago.

Following the formation of the Penokean Mountains about 1,840 million years ago, the Lake Superior region (and all of central North America) appears to have been undergoing erosion for most of the next 500 to 600 million years. Evidently the area was far removed from any oceans (and continental margins) for most, or all of this time. Intrusion of the Wolf River Batholith and deposition of the red quartzites are the only rock-forming events recorded during this long interval of erosion. At the beginning of Keweenawan time, therefore, the Penokean Mountains had been leveled by erosion, and the Lake Superior region was evidently a gently rolling surface with a warm climate. This tranquility was to be interrupted by a major sequence of events that left an indelible record on the region.

THE VOLCANIC EPISODE

The events of the Keweenawan began with the development of a "hot spot" beneath the continent in what is now the Lake Superior region. Upwelling of basaltic magma from the mantle accumulated beneath the continent and produced a broad, gentle doming of the continental crust. The dome was several hundred miles across, covering all of the Lake Superior region. The doming produced large-scale tensional forces in the earth which, in effect, split the crust and caused opposite sides of the fracture to move apart. This type of structure, with opposite sides moving apart, is referred to as a rift (Figure 4–11).

The rift that formed was a linear belt of subsidence that cut across the broad dome (Figure 4–12). The belt of subsidence probably consisted of

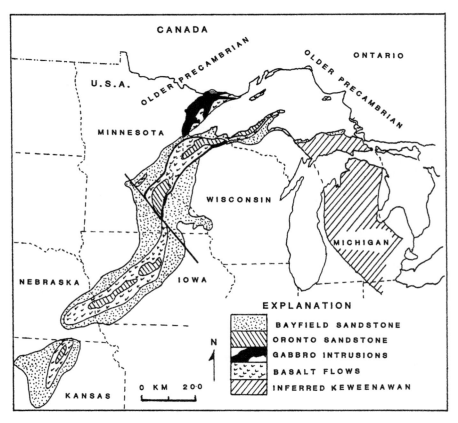

Figure 4-11: Sketch map of the north-central U.S. showing the general distribution of Keweenawan rocks. Keweenawan rocks are widely exposed in the Lake Superior region, but are known only from subsurface work in Kansas, Nebraska, Iowa, and lower Michigan. (Modified from Craddock, 1972.)

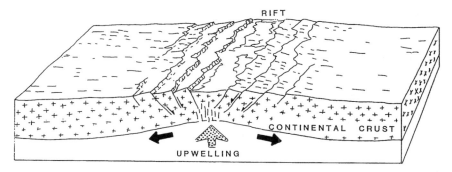

Figure 4-12: Diagram showing geologic relationships during doming and rifting stages of the Keweenawan event in the Lake Superior region.

a number of fault-bounded blocks that tilted in various directions during rifting.

Evidence for early subsidence within the central zone of the belt is the presence of several hundred feet of sediments that underlie the lowest basalt lava flows in the Lake Superior region. The sediments are exposed in only a few places around Lake Superior: the Bessemer Quartzite underlies the lava flows in northern Michigan and Wisconsin (Figure 4–13); the Nopeming Formation and overlying lava flows are exposed just west of Duluth; the Puckwunge formation underlies the flows in far northeastern Minnesota; and the Osler Group forms the basal Keweenawan strata in the Thunder Bay, Ontario, area. The sediments are mainly sandstones that evidently were deposited in streams or in lakes within the elongate depression.

The features that developed are typical of those that form during the early stages of the break up of a continent. A good modern-day example is the major rift-valley system in eastern Africa, where the eastern edge of Africa is gradually being pulled away from the remainder of Africa. Indeed, 1,100 million years ago, the Lake Superior region was quite comparable to modern-day east Africa.

The belt of subsidence (the rift) developed in what is now the Lake Superior Basin and extended southward down the St. Croix River valley and on through southeastern Minnesota, across Iowa, at least to central Kansas. Near the eastern end of Lake Superior the belt curved southward again, extending under what is now lower Michigan. It appears to have ended somewhere near the Michigan–Ohio border (Figure 4–11).

Figure 4-13: Contact between the Bessemer Quartzite and Portage Lake Lava Series. The contact is dipping steeply to the left with basalts on the left and quartzite on the right. North of Bessemer, Michigan.

Basaltic lavas broke through to the surface and spread out in extensive layers, covering the land surface for hundreds of miles. The basal lava flows are pillowed, an indication that they were extruded into bodies of water (probably lakes). Locally, as near Bessemer, Michigan, one can find places where sand from the ancient lake bottom squeezed up between pillows, indicating that the sediments underlying the basalts had not been converted to rocks when the basal flows were extruded. The lower part of the basalt sequence consisted of very fluid lavas that spread out in broad thin flows called *flood basalts* similar to the much younger lava flows that can be seen along the Columbia River Gorge in Washington and Oregon. Continued extrusion of basaltic lava formed an immense pile of volcanic rocks perhaps 2 to 3 miles thick that covered most of the Lake Superior region. The lava flows probably extended 100 miles or more on either side of the main rift zone.

In addition to the lava flows, innumerable basaltic dikes were formed as magma cooled in the fractures leading to the surface (Figure 4–14A). These dikes may well have been feeders for overlying lava flows. Literally hundreds of dikes, many more or less parallel to one another, formed roughly parallel to the axis of the rift. In addition, a large "swarm" of basaltic dikes extends northward from Lake Superior across northern Ontario.

Subsidence along the central rift continued during volcanism and resulted in thicker accumulations of basalt along the main rift. Later stages of volcanism was evidently mainly restricted to the central rift zone, where the total thickness of basaltic lava flows reached approximately 12 miles (Figure 4–14B). This immense thickness of basalts is not an estimate; it has been verified by various geological studies in and around Lake Superior, especially recent seismic studies conducted during exploration for possible petroleum deposits associated with the rift.

While we do not know precisely when the initial doming began, or when the central subsidence (rift) began, radiometric dating indicates that volcanism began 1,109 million years ago, for that is the age of the basal lava flows. We also know that volcanism ended 1,084 million years ago, for that is the age of the uppermost lava flows. Therefore, Keweenawan volcanic activity in the Lake Superior region lasted 25 million years.

The style of eruption was probably similar to that which formed the Columbia River and Snake River basalt field in Washington, Oregon, and Idaho, and undoubtedly produced features like those that can be seen today in Craters of the Moon National Monument near Arco, Idaho, and Kingsbowl Rift some 40 miles to the southeast (Figures 4–15 and 4–16).

Gases dissolved in the magma are lost shortly after eruption because of the lack of confining pressure to hold them in. The gas tends to accumulate into bubbles that move slowly upward toward the top of the lava flow. Since the top of the flow cools most quickly, the bubbles may be "frozen-in," forming a very porous, frothy top on the flow. Fragmentation of this surface by the movement of the still-molten lava beneath forms a very rubbly surface. These frothy or vesicular zones in lava flows are very useful in recognition of flow tops. Figure 4–17 is an example of a cross section of a flow top. Note the vesicular top of the lower flow and the presence of vesicular fragments in the lower, more massive

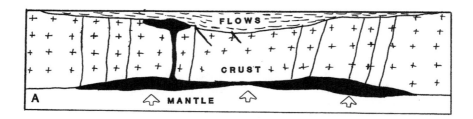

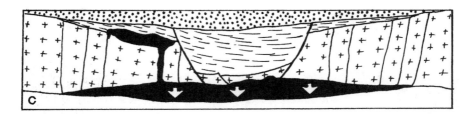

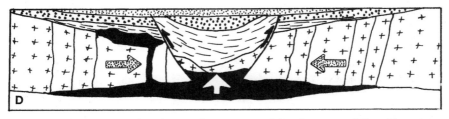

Figure 4-14: Diagram showing various stages of development of the rift system in the Lake Superior region. A. Upwelling and accumulation of basaltic magma at the base of the crust associated with formation of an extensive blanket of basalts, numerous basaltic dikes and several large gabbroic intrusions. B. Major subsidence and volcanism in central graben accompanied by thinning of the crust due to extension. C. Extension and volcanism end, basaltic magma chamber cools, and subsidence results in a broad sedimentary basin over the rift. D. Compression converts the major boundary faults into reverse faults which results in uplift of a central block (horst). Sedimentation continues.

part of the overlying flow. In some cases where bubbles were rising slowly through the lava, they produced tubes instead of the more common teardrop shaped vesicles. If the lava was flowing, the tube or "pipe" vesicles would probably be bent in the direction the flow was moving. This characteristic is, in fact, one of the few things we can use to indicate the direction of the flow.

These vesicles are generally filled after the flow is cooled and form what we call amygdules. Any other openings such as cracks or lava tunnels may also be partially or completely filled with a wide variety of secondary minerals. Probably the most common are quartz and calcite, along with a wide variety of zeolites such as stilbite, heulandite, thomsonite, and a whole host of others. In parts of northern Michigan, native copper (discussed later) fills the cavities. The famous Lake Superior agates were formed by the filling of cavities in the basalts. Silica, dissolved out of the basalts along with minor amounts of iron oxides, is

Figure 4-15: Pahoehoe surface on lava flow formed by surging of the lava beneath the still plastic crust, deforming it into a series of folds. Kingsbowl Rift, Idaho.

Figure 4-16: Pahoehoe surface on a basalt flow exposed on the Lake Superior shoreline at Temperance River, Minnesota.

transported to the cavities. The silica gradually fills them in roughly concentric layers. While this process probably takes many years, it may start while the lava flow is still warm. Variations in the amount of iron in the silica produce the attractive layering. Many larger agates contain what appears to have been a "tube" through which the quartz and hematite (iron) were added in successive layers. The tube was evidently filled after most or all of the banded interior of the agate was formed. Figure 4–18 is an example of this feature.

As the flows cooled, the top and bottom hardened first. Shrinkage due to cooling caused the lava flows to crack, and as the flow continued to cool and harden, these fractures continued completely across the flow from top to bottom. These fractures intersect on the surface of a lava flow to form a rather regular pattern consisting of five- to six-sided "columns" several feet wide extending across the flow and referred to as *columnar joints*. Figure 4–19 is an example of the cross section of some of these columns seen on the top of a lava flow, and Figure 4–20 shows the columns in profile extending across the flow. The columnar jointing is responsible for the waterfalls in some of the streams along the north shore of Lake Superior in Minnesota. The rubbly and porous flow tops

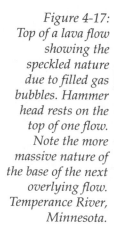

Figure 4-17: Top of a lava flow showing the speckled nature due to filled gas bubbles. Hammer head rests on the top of one flow. Note the more massive nature of the base of the next overlying flow. Temperance River, Minnesota.

are relatively easily eroded and may undercut the flow by the turbulent water at the bottom of the falls. The fractures between columns enable frost action to wedge the columns apart and eventually cause them to fall over. Collapse of the columns thus maintains the falls. Several of the waterfalls along the north shore of Lake Superior show excellent examples of columnar jointed lava flows.

Because of the immense timespan during which volcanic activity occurred, we must not presume that volcanic eruptions were daily—or even yearly—events. Indeed, there were probably long periods of time, perhaps hundreds of years, between eruptions in a given center. A considerable timespan between eruptions is indicated in many places where layers of sandstone or conglomerate are present between lava flows. The interflow sediments appear to have formed by streams and in temporary lakes on the volcanic surfaces.

Figure 4-18: Agate showing the internal layering and the "filler tube" through which the silica entered the cavity.

Curiously, the volcanic rocks are dominantly basalts, yet the sediments interbedded with them contain a substantial proportion of rhyolite fragments. In some the boulders and cobbles are dominantly rhyolitic. Clearly, therefore, there must have been rhyolites extruded intermittently during the volcanic activity. In fact, rhyolitic intrusives, flows, and tuffs are found at many places in the volcanic sequences. In northern Michigan, rhyolites, which form much of the "core" of the Porcupine Mountains, are found elsewhere at various levels in the volcanic sequences. A large quarry in a welded rhyolitic tuff (Figure 4–21) northeast of Bergland, Michigan, is worked for road aggregate and used in the White Pine mine. At the roadcut just west of Bergland, a rhyolite flow with good columnar jointing is present in an abandoned quarry. Palisade Head, a prominent landmark on the north shore of Lake Superior near Silver Bay, Minnesota, may also be a rhyolite lava flow, or a densely welded tuff.

The rhyolite magmas may have formed as the result of crystallization of large batches of basaltic magmas. The ingredients in rhyolite would have been the last material to crystallize.

*Figure 4-19:
Polygonal shape of
the cross-section of
columnar jointed
basalt. Cracks along
edges of columns are
filled with dirt.
Columns are about
two feet across.
Gooseberry Falls,
Minnesota.*

A renewal of volcanic activity following a period of quiescence may have resulted in eruption of the lighter rhyolitic magma accumulated at the top of the "magma chamber." Alternatively, the rhyolitic magma may have formed by the melting of older granitic crust as a result of heating by upwelling of basaltic magma, whatever the source of the magma.

The rhyolitic lavas, being very viscous (or stiff), probably formed very explosive eruptions. Many of the Keweenawan rhyolites appear to be welded tuffs, similar to their older counterparts in the Early Proterozoic.

Recent studies of the paleomagnetism of Keweenawan igneous rocks have proved interesting. Paleomagnetism is basically the study of the orientation of the "magnetic dipole" (or magnetic field) within the magnetite crystals in igneous rocks. When igneous rocks cool below the

"Curie point" (about 500°C), the magnetic field is "frozen" into the magnetite crystals. The magnetic field within the magnetite crystals is aligned with the earth's magnetic field at that time. By measuring the orientation of these tiny magnets, we can determine the orientation of the earth's field at the time the rocks formed.

Studies of the Keweenawan lavas reveal that the earth's magnetic field reversed itself 1,097 million years ago during the volcanic episode. This means that the magnetic north and south poles switched. (In other words, a compass that pointed north when the magnetic field was "normal" would point south when the field was reversed.) The oldest rocks (up to 1,109 million years old), the lowest flows in the South Range volcanics of northern Michigan and Wisconsin, have a normal polarity. Overlying these is a thick sequence of flows, including much of the North Shore volcanic group in Minnesota, that have reversed polarity.

Figure 4-20: Columnar jointed basalt flow at Gooseberry Falls. Vertical fractures are produced by the jointing. Gooseberry Falls, Minnesota.

Figure 4-21: Welded tuff showing typical layering, flattened volcanic fragments of older rocks.

The presence of flow sequences with normal and reversed polarity provides at least a possible way to correlate the lavas from one area to another. (In more recent time there have been more than eighty reversals during the last 70 million years.)

INTRUSIONS

In addition to the innumerable lava flows that formed during this great igneous event, there are several very large gabbroic intrusions that crystallized at some depth as well as many smaller dikes and sills. The largest of these is the Duluth Complex (Figure 4–11), which extends in a large boomerang-shaped outline from Duluth northward about 50 miles, then eastward to near the Lake Superior shoreline at the Canadian border. It is a large sill-like body intruded approximately along the unconformity between the base of the lava flows and the eroded surface of older Archean and Early Proterozoic rocks to the north and west.

The Duluth Complex (Figure 4–22) is a large, multiple intrusion composed of a wide variety of gabbroic rocks. Some of the units are well-

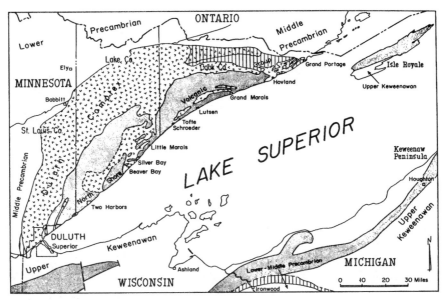

Figure 4-22: Generalized geologic map showing the Keweenawan rocks of north-eastern Minnesota and the western Lake Superior basin. Check pattern, intrusive rocks; vertical rule, Lower Keweenawan rocks (magnetically normal and reversed); stipple, Middle Keweenawan lavas (magnetically normal). Note especially the large area of intrusive rocks that make up the Duluth complex (from Green, 1972).

layered with alternating plagioclase-rich and plagioclase-poor layers (Figure 4–23) indicating oscillating conditions in the magma chamber as the mass crystallized. Intrusion of the gabbroic magma occurred before the change in magnetic polarity took place. Therefore, the gabbro intrusion is more than 1,097 million years old.

Important concentrations of copper and nickel sulfide ores have been found near the base of the complex in northeastern Minnesota. These deposits formed early in the cooling history of the immense intrusion. The magma contained small concentrations of copper and nickel and probably sulfur (although the sulfur may have been derived mainly from the intruded sediments). The sulfur combined with iron, copper, and nickel and, while still liquid, settled to the bottom of the magma and accumulated, especially in depressions on the floor of the intrusion. Here the sulfides were concentrated to constitute over 50 percent of the rock locally. These copper-nickel concentrations, major resources of these important metals, have been the object of much exploration work by mining companies.

The Mellen Gabbro in northern Wisconsin is a large sill-like mass nearly 60 miles long divided by the Mellen Granite into two segments. The western portion, called the Mineral Lake Intrusion, lies west of the town of Mellen, Wisconsin. The eastern complex, which is up to 5 miles thick, extends about 35 miles eastward from Mellen to near the Michigan–Wisconsin border. Like the Duluth Gabbro it was emplaced near the base of the Keweenawan lava flows, near the unconformity with the older Precambrian rocks. The eastern complex was formed by three separate intrusions of gabbroic magma, each one crystallized with an olivine-rich base and a plagioclase-rich top. Convection currents during cooling and crystallization produced rhythmic layering in the olivine-rich basal portion of the intrusions.

Figure 4-23: Rhythmic layering in the Duluth Complex. Lighter layers are plagioclase-rich; darker layers are olivine-rich. Skyline Drive, Duluth, Minnesota.

A plagioclase-rich phase of the intrusion has been quarried east of Mellen. Rock from these quarries has been marketed as "black granite." Local residents are proud of the fact that "black granite" from Mellen was used in the Eternal Flame memorial to John F. Kennedy.

The Mellen Granite intrudes the Mellen Gabbro as well as the basalts. Similar granitic rocks intrude Keweenawan basalts east of Superior, Wisconsin, and forms extensive units called *red rock* in the Duluth Complex in Minnesota. It is likely that these granitic magmas were formed by the differentiation of the same parent magma that produced the Mellen Gabbro and Duluth Complex.

Large gabbro intrusions evidently formed in a number of locations along the rift. For example, a huge intrusive complex is present in eastern Iowa. It extends along the Mississippi River from southeastern Minnesota to near the Illinois border. Although it is completely covered by Paleozoic sedimentary rocks, its presence is known from geophysical studies and several deep drill holes that penetrate the intrusion.

Structurally, the Keweenawan rift is rather complex, consisting of a number of fault-bounded blocks (or segments) along its length. The segments were produced by differences in subsidence along the rift as it opened. In many segments the subsidence was mainly on one side of the rift, producing a wedge-shaped block of rocks along a curved fault zone. In some segments the subsidence was mainly on the northwest side, while in neighboring segments the subsidence was mainly on the southeast side of the rift. Therefore, adjacent blocks commonly have wedge-shaped accumulations of volcanic rocks that thicken toward opposite sides of the rift zone. This results in a complex pattern along the rift with major cross fractures ("compensation zones") that separate the various blocks (Figure 4–24). As the crustal blocks on opposite sides of the rift zone were gradually pulled apart, basaltic rocks from the mantle kept the rift more or less filled. Continued spreading of the rift, however, removed some of the "support" for the tremendous thickness of basalts, causing them to sink into the earth. As discussed earlier, some of this sinking occurred during the volcanic episode, but considerable subsidence occurred after the end of volcanic activity as well.

Flow-direction studies using pipe amygdules indicate that the basalts flowed from the present Lake Superior Basin southward into Michigan and Wisconsin. Since the lava must have flowed downhill, the present Lake Superior must have been at least as high as the surrounding lands. Continued subsidence of the basalts into the earth's crust after volcanic activity ceased, however, resulted in an elongate

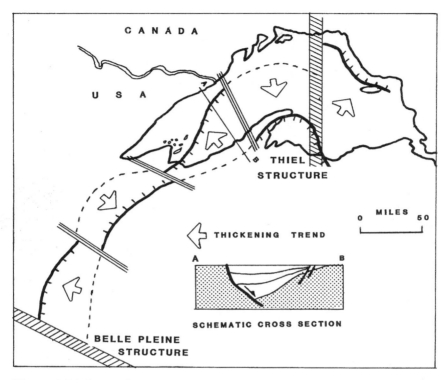

Figure 4-24: Map of a portion of the Keweenawan rift zone illustrating the alternating direction of thickening of blocks of sediments. This pattern results from subsidence on alternating sides of the rift.

trough. Erosion of basalt and rhyolite highlands (volcanoes ?) provided much of the sediment to fill the basin; however, granitic terranes outside the volcanic belt also contributed materials. The cessation of volcanic activity thus ushered in a major period of sediment deposition.

THE KEWEENAWAN SANDSTONES

The change from dominantly igneous activity to the deposition of sediments was the last major rock-forming event in the Proterozoic history of the Lake Superior region.

Overlying the volcanic sequences in northern Wisconsin and Michigan is a thick sequence of sediments (Figure 4–14C) called the Oronto Group that formed during a period of 30 to 40 million years. A substantial part of the sedimentary rocks is composed of sand-size grains and larger clasts of volcanic rocks similar to the underlying lava flows. This suggests that the volcanic rocks extended well beyond their present extent and were eroded to produce the thick pile of sedimentary rocks within the rift (Figure 4–25). The basal unit of this sequence is the Cop-

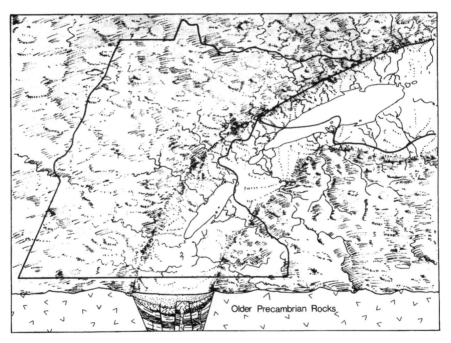

Figure 4-25: Reconstruction of how the Lake Superior region may have appeared after cessation of volcanic activity. A new basin formed largely on the depressed lava flow sequences. The faults separating the flows from adjacent rocks are hypothetical. Once the topographic low appeared, streams began filling it with sediments, locally to a thickness of 5,000 m. Note the lakes. Their presence is suggested by the more quartzose nature of rock units such as the Hickley Sandstone, which may have resulted from the cleaning up of feldspathic sands in a shallow lake with considerable wave and current action. (From Ojakangas and Matsch, 1982, with permission from the University of Minnesota Press.)

per Harbor Conglomerate, which consists of brown to red sandstone and conglomerate with boulders and pebbles of basalt and rhyolite in a sandy matrix. This conglomerate extends the length of the Keweenaw Peninsula and continues southwestward into Wisconsin. It ranges in thickness from about 200 feet to an astonishing 7,000 feet in places. Most geologists who have studied this formation have concluded that it is a fluvial deposit; that is, it was formed by streams flowing northward over the volcanic terrane. To accumulate to such a great thickness, the conglomerate must have formed in a rapidly subsiding basin or trough, probably along a major fault. The conglomerate is similar to alluvial fan deposits forming today in large fault-bounded basins in the southwestern United States. During flash floods, rapidly flowing streams carry great quantities of material into basins, where they are deposited when the streams slow down or enter a lake. The presence of lava flows in the lower portion of the conglomerate indicates that deposition began prior to cessation of volcanic activity. Cross-bedding in the sandstones and conglomerates demonstrate, however, that the streams were flowing northward into the basin, whereas the earlier lavas had flowed southward off a highland. It appears that the present site of Lake Superior changed from a volcanic highland to a lowland during a geologically short period of time. This rapid change is associated with the deposition of the Copper Harbor Conglomerate (Figure 4–26).

Following this period of conglomerate and sandstone deposition, a sequence of siltstones and shales named the Nonesuch Shale was deposited. These sediments range from 290 feet to 700 feet in thickness. The important White Pine copper deposit occurs in the lowermost 20 feet of the unit in the Iron River syncline near White Pine, Michigan. The copper deposits are discussed later.

The Nonesuch Shale is characterized by its gray to black color as distinguished from the reddish brown sedimentary rocks above and below. The principal rock type is a ripple-marked, gray, thickly to thinly laminated siltstone with reddish gray partings (Figure 4–27). In the Porcupine Mountains area, sandstone makes up a relatively small part of the formation, but the formation becomes much sandier to the east near Houghton and to the west near the Michigan–Wisconsin border.

The Nonesuch Shale is believed to have been deposited in a lake that initially lapped up onto the flood plains and alluvial fans of the Copper Harbor Conglomerate. Suszek (1991) concluded that the Nonesuch Shale was deposited in a lake within the rift zone. While the presence of mudcracks indicates intermittent exposure to the atmosphere, quiet waters were necessary to the formation of the thinly laminated dark gray silts and shales that contain organic matter and pyrite.

Figure 4-26: Copper Harbor Conglomerate dipping beneath Lake Superior. Keweenaw Peninsula, Michigan.

The Nonesuch Shale is perhaps the oldest petroleum-bearing formation in North America. Small amounts of oil seep through the cracks and drip from the rocks in the roof of the White Pine mine. While no large accumulation of petroleum is known in the area, several exploration wells have been drilled recently to test the petroleum and gas potential of the area. It is interesting and significant that the organic materials and environment necessary for the formation of petroleum existed in the Lake Superior region more than 1,000 million years ago.

Overlying the Nonesuch Shale is a thick sequence of rather impure sandstones known as the Freda Sandstone. It consists of up to 12,000 feet of reddish brown, medium- to fine-grained arkosic sandstone. Quartz content ranges from less than 50 percent to more than 60 percent. Feldspar and rock fragments make up most of the remainder of the rock, indicating rapid erosion of the source area. The reddish brown color results from hematite and goethite coating the grains.

The Keweenawan sandstones were deposited dominantly in a fluvial (stream) and lacustrine (lake) environment. Large amounts of sediment came to rest on alluvial fans at the foot of highland areas where the streams, slowing down, were unable to carry their sediment load. The great variation in thickness in some of the units suggests that the sediments may have accumulated in subsiding fault-bounded basins. The environment would be roughly comparable to the desert southwest in the Basin and Range area of Nevada, California, and Utah today. The lakes may have been intermittent, containing water only during wet periods of the year, which may account for the pervasive reddish color of the rocks, a sign of deep oxidation in an arid climate.

Figure 4-27: Nearly flat-lying Nonesuch Shale in the Presque Isle Syncline at the mouth of the Presque isle River, north of Wakefield, Michigan.

The Bayfield Group. Early workers recognized that there are two sandstone sequences in the Lake Superior area. The older sandstones (the Freda) had been tilted and deformed along with the volcanic rocks to form the Lake Superior syncline. Overlying the Freda (Oronto Group of Thwaites) is a thick sequence of flat-lying, undeformed sandstones that Thwaites named the Bayfield Group. They are well developed on the Bayfield Peninsula (from which they get their name) and extend southwestward through Superior, Wisconsin, into Minnesota, where they are called the Fond du Lac and Hinkley sandstones. Sandstones probably correlative with the Bayfield Group extend southwestward along the "Mid-Continent Gravity High" at least as far as Kansas. If the Bayfield Group is correlative with the Jacobsville Sandstone in northern Michigan, then the Bayfield Group equivalent rocks extend to the eastern end of Lake Superior and into Ontario, and probably (at depth) southeastward into lower Michigan along with the Keweenawan igneous rocks.

Outcrop data indicate that the Bayfield Group is at least 4,300 feet thick, but more recent geophysical studies indicate that it may reach a maximum of more than 7,000 feet. The Bayfield Group was subdivided into three formations: the Orienta Sandstone, the Devils Island Sandstone, and the Chequamegon Sandstone in ascending order. The Orienta is a red feldspathic sandstone about 3,000 feet thick; the Devils Island Sandstone is a well-sorted, very pure quartz sandstone about 300 feet thick; the uppermost unit, the Chequamegon Sandstone, exposed on the Bayfield Peninsula and the Apostle Islands, is again a red feldspathic sandstone with a thickness of perhaps 1,000 feet.

The Jacobsville Sandstone. A narrow belt of nearly flat-lying Jacobsville Sandstone lies along the southern shore of Lake Superior eastward from the Keweenaw Fault on the Keweenaw Peninsula of northern Michigan eastward to Munising, Michigan. The thickness ranges from less than 50 feet to more than 1,100 feet. It is a red to brown impure sandstone with moderate sorting and rounding. The Jacobsville Sandstone has abundant sedimentary features that indicate that it was formed on a land surface in a stream and lake environment. The typical cross-bedding is shown in Figure 4–28. A common feature of the Jacobsville is the presence of mottling with "bleached" greenish white spots of various size in the red to brown colored sandstone.

The reddish brown Bayfield and Jacobsville sandstones have been used locally for building stone called *brownstone*. Many of the older buildings in cities along the south shore of Lake Superior were constructed of this attractive stone.

Figure 4-28: Cross-bedded sandstone typical of the Jacobsville. Near the mouth of the Huron River east of Skanee, Michigan.

In older literature the age of the Bayfield Group and the other flat-lying nonfossiliferous sandstones, (especially the Jacobsville) in the Lake Superior region, was problematical. The sandstones were thought to be as old as 1,000 million years or perhaps as young as 600 million years. The reason for the uncertainty was that there are no minerals in them that can be dated by radiometric means, nor do they contain fossils. Some workers believed that the Bayfield Group is part of the Keween-awan succession and therefore Precambrian. They believed that the rocks are compositionally and structurally related to the other Keween-awan rocks. Alternatively, other workers concluded that the Jacobsville Sandstone and Bayfield Group are Cambrian because they have compositional and structural affinities to other Paleozoic rocks. In several areas these flat-lying sandstones have been offset by major Keweenawan faults. Therefore, the rocks must be older than the faults. Minerals along the faults have been dated at 1,040 to 1,060 million years old. This leads to the current conclusion that the sedimentary rocks are more than 1,040 million years old.

The Bayfield and Jacobsville sandstones represent the last rock-forming event in Precambrian time in the Lake Superior region. Since the sandstones are stream and lake deposits, there is no compelling reason to assume that the sandstones in northern Michigan are the same age as those in Wisconsin or Minnesota. Therefore, there may be a range in age for the deposits; however, all units appear to be older than the major faults in the Lake Superior region. The sandstones generally are rather poorly cemented, and thus would be relatively easily eroded by streams during later geologic time. As we will see, the location of these relatively easily eroded sandstones predetermined the site of Lake Superior, which formed more than a billion years after the sandstones.

THE MICHIGAN COPPER DEPOSITS

The presence of copper in the rocks on the Keweenaw Peninsula in northern Michigan has been known for centuries. Copper artifacts show that long before Europeans arrived, Native Americans throughout the upper midwest used the metal for making a variety of ornaments, tools, utensils, and weapons. While much of the copper used by the Native Americans was "drift copper" carried southward by the glaciers, primitive mining operations for copper were undertaken at several locations in northern Michigan and on Isle Royale.

The French explorers were told of the copper deposits by the Chippewa Indians in the early seventeenth century, but no mining was attempted until late in the eighteenth century by early English settlers. None of these ventures were successful. The first successful mining operations began in the 1840s following the first systematic geological survey of the area by Douglass Houghton. Copper mining has been almost continuous in the Keweenaw Peninsula area for the 150 years since then. During that time over 12 billion pounds of native copper have been mined from the area.

The ore deposits of the Michigan Copper District are of two basic types that differ in mineralogy, host rock type, and possibly in origin. Furthermore, they are separated from one another both geographically and stratigraphically. The major mining areas are shown on Figure 4–29.

1. Deposits of native copper occur in the tops of basaltic lava flows and in conglomerates interbedded with the basalts in the Portage Lake Lava Series. More than 96 percent of the native-copper production has come from an area 28 miles long, extending from just southwest of Painesdale to just east of Mohawk (Figure 4–30). Minor deposits are found in the Mass–Victoria area near Ontonagon. Over 11 billion

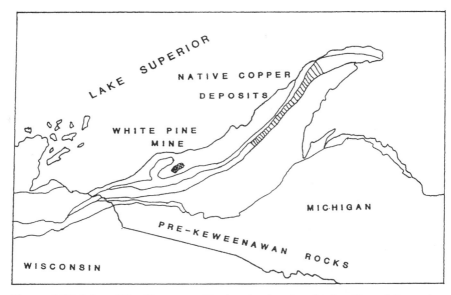

Figure 4-29: Map of the Keweenaw Peninsula showing the location of the main native copper deposits in basalt lava flows (ruled) and the White Pine deposit in the Nonesuch Shale (cross hatched).

pounds of metallic copper have been recovered from the native-copper deposits (Figure 4–31).

2. Deposits of copper sulfides (mainly chalcocite) with smaller amounts of native copper (Figure 4–32) occur in the lower 20 feet of the Nonesuch Shale just above the Copper Harbor Conglomerate. Minor amounts of copper minerals are found along this contact over a distance of 125 miles, but important deposits occur only in the Iron River syncline at White Pine and in the Presque Isle syncline on the west side of the Porcupine Mountains uplift. Over 1 billion pounds of copper have been recovered from the White Pine copper deposit.

The Native Copper Deposits. The native-copper deposits are found almost exclusively in the Portage Lake Lava Series. The lava series consists of over 200 lava flows, mostly basaltic, with twenty interbedded conglomerates and some interlayered sandstone and shale. The rocks strike parallel to the length of the Keweenaw Peninsula and dip to the

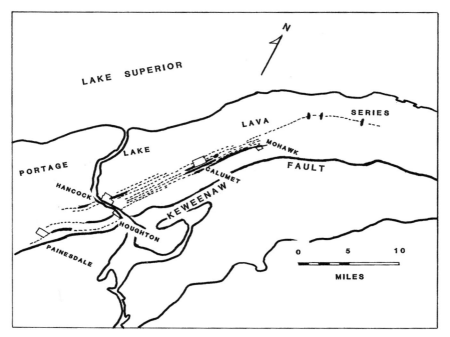

Figure 4-30: Map showing the location of the major native copper mining on the Keweenaw Peninsula. (From White, ed., 1971.)

northwest beneath Lake Superior. Some lava flows have been traced for 40 miles along the surface.

The main ore deposits are widespread, thin, blanketlike bodies found both in some of the amygdaloidal flow tops and conglomerates. The deposits are referred to locally as lodes. Commercial ore deposits, only a few of which are of major importance, are present at only about a dozen levels in the Portage Lake Lava Series. The major producers ranked in order are the Calumet and Hecla conglomerates, and the Kearsarge, Baltic, Pewabic, Osceola, Isle Royale, and Atlantic amygdaloids.

The copper is believed to have been deposited from hot water solutions rising from depth along certain permeable layers in the rocks. Because the layers are (and presumably were at the time of ore deposition) tilted down beneath Lake Superior, the solutions evidently rose along the porous tops of lava flows and up through conglomerates interbedded with the flows. The copper carried in solution in the water was deposited in cavities and pore spaces in the rocks due to changes in chemistry and/or cooling of the fluids. The reason for deposition in some places and not in others has been the subject of much study and debate.

The major factor determining the location of ore bodies is believed to be the presence of highly permeable zones as well as impermeable barriers that caused the rising copper-bearing solutions to flow through certain channels. Assuming that the solutions were widely dispersed in the rocks, barriers to circulation caused more copper-bearing fluids to pass through certain areas, which probably resulted in greater accumulation of copper at these sites.

Evidence that the copper-bearing solution was hot comes from the widespread deposition of calcite, quartz, epidote, prehnite, and a variety of zeolite minerals along with the copper. Since epidote and some zeolites form only at elevated temperatures, we conclude that the solutions must have been hot, perhaps 200°C or more. Since higher temperatures increase the solubility of all substances, copper would be more soluble at higher temperatures and less soluble as the solutions cooled. Because of this, mere cooling of the solutions could cause precipitation of the copper.

Because copper generally combines with sulfur and other elements to form sulfide minerals, the widespread occurrence of copper in its native

Figure 4-31: One and one-half inch wide crystal of native copper from the Point Prospect near Copper Harbor, Michigan.

Figure 4-32:
Cubes of native copper
from a fracture-filling
in the White Pine mine,
Michigan.

or elemental state is somewhat unusual. The absence of sulfides of copper in the Keweenawan lava flows and conglomerates in Michigan and Wisconsin indicates either that sulfur was not present or that the chemical nature of the solutions prevented it from combining with the copper.

In places native silver is found either intergrown with the copper or as independent masses or crystals. Mineral collectors avidly seek specimens of the latter two forms. While there is not sufficient silver to warrant mining, its presence in the copper increases the value of the ore mined. These copper–silver mixtures are called *half-breeds*.

The location of a source for the many billions of pounds of copper in the lava flows and conglomerates (for only a fraction of the total copper present has been mined) is another major problem. Several sources are possible: (1) the copper may originally have been contained in the lava flows and then been leached from them by the rising solutions; (2) the copper may have been added later from the slow cooling at depth of the "parent" magma that gave rise to the lava flows and gabbro intrusions described earlier; or (3) it may have risen from deep within the earth (perhaps the mantle) along deep fractures associated with the major rift that opened to permit eruption of the Keweenawan lavas. Whatever the ultimate source of the copper, it appears that it was contained in the basaltic rocks and was subsequently re-distributed by briny fluids moving through the immense pile of lava flows in the Lake Superior basin.

The White Pine Copper Deposit. The White Pine copper deposit is located near White Pine, Michigan, about 45 miles southwest of the main native-copper producing area. The mineralized area is in the Iron River syncline near the White Pine Fault lying just east of the Porcupine Mountains (Figure 4–29). The ore at White Pine in the basal part of the Nonesuch Shale consists mainly of the copper sulfide mineral chalcocite, with native copper forming about 20 percent of the ore.

Although the presence of copper mineralization in the White Pine area has been known since about 1850, successful mining operations on a large scale were not commenced until 1953. Early attempts at mining the copper in the Nonesuch Shale were small-scale, generally unsuccessful operations. Since early mining efforts recovered only the native copper present, they lost the copper that was present as chalcocite—a major constituent of the ore. It was not until technological advances made it possible to recover the chalcocite that major development of the ore body was undertaken. Since then it has been a major producer of copper in the United States, with one billion pounds of copper recovered in the first 10 years of operation. With its large reserves the White Pine District promises to continue to be a productive mining area.

Copper mineralization is present in the base of the Nonesuch Shale throughout most of its exposed length from Hancock, Michigan, to Mellen, Wisconsin. The mineralization is a blanketlike deposit parallel with the bedding and ranging in thickness from one inch to as much as 50 feet. However, only in the Iron River syncline at White Pine and in the Presque Isle syncline west of the Porcupine Mountains is the mineralization rich enough to warrant mining. The copper is not uniformly distributed throughout the mined interval; some layers contain much more copper than others. The ore zone consists of dark gray siltstones and shales interbedded with red to brown siltstones and sandstones. The copper occurs as minute grains disseminated in the gray to black organic-rich layers. The tiny grains of ore minerals, concentrated in certain layers, impart a metallic appearance to the rock (Figure 4–33).

The ore zone consists primarily of chalcocite (Cu_2S) and native copper in minute grains. Rocks overlying the copper-rich zone contain abundant pyrite (iron sulfide) but little copper, and a narrow "fringe

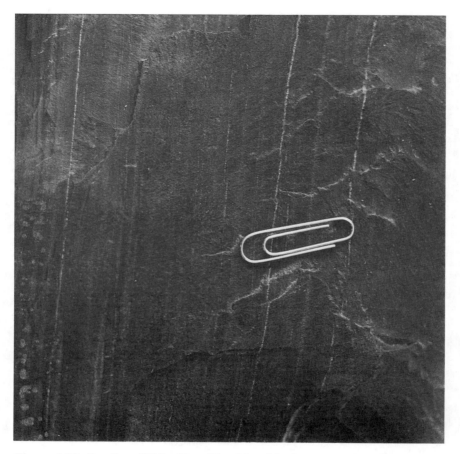

Figure 4-33: Ore from White Pine. The thin white layers are the copper sulfide (chalcocite); the dark material is the host rock for the ore, black siltstone and shale. Paperclip is 1 inch long.

zone" of copper–iron sulfides separates the copper-rich ore zone from the overlying pyritic zone.

Chalcocite, the principal ore mineral in the Nonesuch Shale, occurs as silt-size grains between the quartz and other minerals that compose the siltstone and sandstones. Native copper occurs with the chalcocite as separate, generally larger grains. In those areas that contain native copper, native silver is also found, and silver occasionally rims the copper grains or, more commonly, occurs as separate grains.

The origin of the White Pine copper deposit has been the subject of controversy for many years. Many of the earlier workers concluded that the copper deposits are epigenetic, and that the copper was introduced by hydrothermal (hot-water) solutions rising along the White Pine Fault and spreading laterally into the sediments. Some workers have proposed that the copper deposit is syngenetic, that is, the copper was deposited at the same time as the sediments by sedimentary processes. More recently it has been recognized that the deposit has a complex origin, with iron sulfide deposited as part of the sedimentary processes and the copper added later by hydrothermal fluids.

Field and laboratory data collected by numerous workers using a variety of techniques have provided a definitive answer to the question of the genesis of the deposit. For example, the sulfur in the chalcocite is largely of biological (bacterial) origin, formed by anaerobic bacteria converting the sulfate ($SO_4=$) ions in the basin waters within the sediments into sulfide ($S=$) ions. These then combined with metal ions (especially iron) to form an insoluble precipitate such as pyrite (FeS_2). Thus at least the sulfide part of the deposit is probably of sedimentary origin, for the bacteria live in the muds on the basin floor and utilize the sulfate from pore water between the particles. Later addition of copper-rich fluids converted the iron-sulfide (pyrite) to copper-sulfide (chalcocite). Thus, original iron-rich layers became copper ore bodies.

Recent studies on the age of the Michigan copper deposits indicate that they were formed between 1,060 million and 1,047 million years ago. This date shows that the mineralization occurred about 20 million years after volcanism in the area. This age also indicates that mineralization occurred after deposition of the Freda Sandstone. The long time lag (20–30 million years) between igneous activity and mineralization suggests that the mineralizing fluids were probably derived by compaction of sediments in the Lake Superior Basin rather than the result of igneous activity.

SUMMARY OF THE KEWEENAWAN STRUCTURE

The Keweenawan event began with the upwelling of basaltic magma from the mantle. The magma accumulated at the base of the crust, producing a broad domal uplift up to 100 miles wide and perhaps 1,000 miles long. Fractures and local subsidence occurred in a linear pattern along the uplift. Sandstones and other sediments accumulated along streams and in intermittent lakes within the down-dropped areas. The

Bessemer Quartzite, Nopeming, and Puckwunge formations, and the Osler Group are examples of the sediments.

Basaltic volcanism commenced about 1,109 million years ago, filled the depressions (locally forming pillow lavas in lakes) and spread out in an extensive blanket over the region. The basaltic flows, called the Portage Lake Lava Series, accumulated to a thickness of several miles, and may have extended 100 miles outward from the main rift zone. Numerous basaltic dikes and several large gabbroic intrusions were emplaced along the zone of volcanism. A gentle sag along the main axis of volcanism produced a broad syncline that was to be the future site of Lake Superior. A reversal of the earth's magnetic field that occurred 1,097 million years ago is recorded in the volcanic sequence.

Later stages of volcanic activity were concentrated mainly along the central part of the rift, where basaltic lava flows accumulated to a thickness of at least 12 miles. This great outpouring of basalt was accompanied by major subsidence and thinning of the lower part of the crust during rifting. Periodic explosive eruptions of rhyolitic lava punctuated the generally quiescent eruptions of basaltic lava. Streams and lakes developed on the surface of the flows between eruptive episodes, forming sandstone, conglomerate, and silty layers.

Volcanism ended about 1,084 million years ago and the great "pool" of basaltic magma at the base of the crust began to cool. The weight of the immense pile of lava flows and cooling at the base of the crust resulted in continued subsidence along the rift. Streams flowing into the subsiding basins eroded the volcanic landscape and deposited thousands of feet of red sandstones and conglomerates on alluvial fans, and sands, silts, and mud in lakes that occupied the central part of the rift from time to time.

Subsidence was very irregular, occurring as a number of fault-bounded blocks. Typically, one side of the rift acted as a hinge, with subsidence mainly on one side of the block. This resulted in wedge-shaped accumulations of sediments. Commonly adjacent blocks tilted in opposite directions so that the sediments on alternate blocks thickened on opposite sides of the rift. Blocks of the crust 50 to 80 miles long were involved in the tilting.

From about 1,064 million to 1,040 million years ago, the Lake Superior region was subjected to compressive forces that resulted from a continental collision in eastern North America. The compression produced large curved (listric) faults on which large blocks within the rift were uplifted (refer to Figure 4–14). In places, fault-bounded blocks were uplifted in the central part of the rift, forming large *horsts* of volcanic rocks thrust on top of sedimentary rocks that had been deposited on top of the volcanics (Figure 4–34). One of these, the St. Croix Horst, is well-developed southwest of Lake Superior, where the Douglas Fault and the Lake Owen Fault form the boundaries of the horst. In other areas, such as the Keweenaw Peninsula of northern Michigan, only one large thrust fault developed. The Keweenaw Fault is a thrust fault that brings basaltic lava flows up over the Jacobsville Sandstone. In places, movement on the curved fault surfaces rotated large blocks of rocks. An example is the Gogebic Iron Range of northern Wisconsin and Michigan (Figure 4–35) where the originally horizontal Keweenawan lava flows

Figure 4-34: Douglas Fault in Amnicon Falls State Park. The fault is dipping about 40° to the right with the older basalts on the left thrust up over the younger flat-lying Bayfield sandstone on the left.

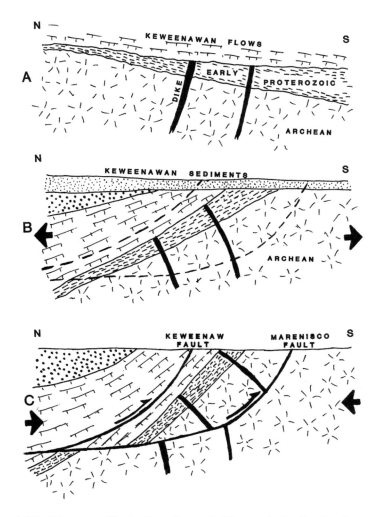

Figure 4-35: Diagrams illustrating the probable events in the development of the Gogebic Range in northern Wisconsin and Michigan. A.Early stages of vol-canism with widespread basalt flows on gently south-dipping Early Proterozoic rocks. Note the vertical dikes. B. Northward tilting of the rocks as a result of rifting with associated volcanism and sedimentation. Note that rocks in the southern part of the area were eroded during the tilting. Dashed lines show the future site of the Keweenaw and Marenisco Faults. C. Further rotation north-ward as a result of compression and thrusting on curved (listric) faults (the Keweenaw and Marenisco Faults).

are now rotated nearly 90°. Widespread deposition of copper and associated silver was also associated with the compression.

Uplift and/or rotation on the large faults resulted in additional erosion and deposition of sedimentary rocks along the major faults. Since faulting appears to have occurred over a period of 10 million years or so, there was considerable erosion and deposition of sediments. Some sediments deposited earlier were uplifted and "reworked" during the faulting episode. This resulted in the formation of "cleaner," more thoroughly weathered sandstones along the margins of the uplifted blocks.

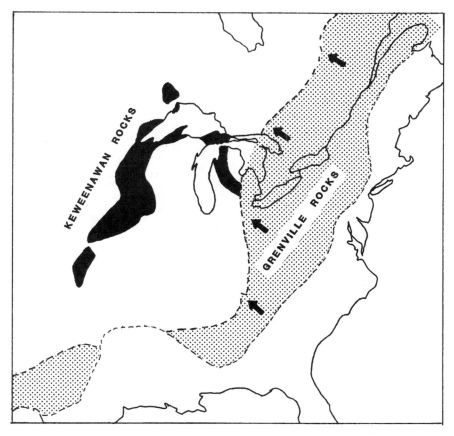

Figure 4-36: Sketch map of North America showing the relationship between the Keweenawan of the Mid continent and the "Grenville Province" to the east.

Stated very briefly, the events of the Keweenawan represent the early stages of a continental breakup. As such, they are similar to the events that occurred in the Early Proterozoic. The Keweenawan differs from the Early Proterozoic breakup in that the continent never broke up. No oceanic crust, or marine sediments, of Keweenawan age have been recognized. Continental breakup was prevented by a collision between North America (as it existed then) and another continental mass along eastern North America. The collision was a major mountain-building event called the *Grenville Orogeny*. The western edge of rocks deformed and metamorphosed during the Grenville Orogeny extends from the coast of Labrador southwestward to Lake Huron and the southern part of lower Michigan (Figure 4–36).

With the end of uplift along the faults, around 1,040 million years ago, erosion presumably slowly leveled the Lake Superior region to a gently rolling plain. This erosion evidently continued for the last 500 million years of Precambrian time. At least we have no record of any rock-forming event in the Lake Superior region during this vast span of time.

SUGGESTED ADDITIONAL READINGS

Anderson, J. L., and Cullers, R. L., 1978, Geochemistry and evolution of the Wolf River Batholith, a Late Precambrian rapakivi massif in north Wisconsin, U.S.A., Precambrian Research, vol. 7, pp. 287–324.

Cannon, W. F., and others, 1989, The North American Mid-continent rift beneath Lake Superior from GLIMPSE seismic reflection profiling, Tectonics, vol. 8.

Cannon, W. F., Peterman, Z. E., and Sims, P. K., 1990, Structural and isotopic evidence for Middle Proterozoic thrust faulting of Archean and Early Proterozoic rocks near the Gogebic Range, Michigan and Wisconsin, in Proc. 36th Annual Meeting Institute on Lake Superior Geology, Thunder Bay, Ont., pp. 11–13.

Mauk, J. L., Seasor, R. W., Kelly, W. C., and Van der Pluijm, B. A., 1989, The White Pine stratiform copper deposit, in Precambrian Geology and Metal Occurrences, Michigan's Upper Peninsula, G. B. Margeson, editor, Field Conference, Society of Economic Geologists. Fall Field Conference, October 1–5, 1989.

Myers, P. E., Sood, M. K., Berlin, L. A., and Falster, A. U., 1984, The Wausau Syenite Complex Central Wisconsin, Field Trip 3 Guidebook, 30th Annual Institute on Lake Superior Geology, Wausau.

Nicholson, S. W., Cannon, W. F., and Schulz, K. J., 1992, Metallogeny of the Midcontinent Rift System of North America, Precambrian Research, vol. 58.

Ojakangas, R. W., and Matsch, C. L., 1982, Minnesota's Geology, University of Minnesota Press, Minneapolis.

Van Schmus, W. R., Medaris, L. G., Jr., and Banks, P. O., 1975, Geology and age of The Wolf River Batholith, Wisconsin, Geological Society of America Bulletin vol. 86, pp. 907–914.

Weege, R. J., and Pollock, J. P., 1971, Recent Developments in the Native Copper District of Michigan, in Guidebook for Field Conference, Michigan Copper District, W. S White, editor, Sept. 30–Oct. 2, 1971, Society of Economic Geologists.

White, W. S., 1968, The native copper Deposits of northern Michigan, in Ore Deposits of the United States, 1933-1967, (Graton-Sales Volume), J. D. Ridge, editor, American Institute of Mining Metallurgical and Petroleum Engineers.

Wold, R. J., and Hinze, W. J., 1982, Geology and Tectonics of the Lake Superior Basin, Geological Society of America Memoir 156.

5

THE PALEOZOIC

Horizontal layers of Upper Cambrian Mt. Simon Sandstone unconformably overlying Precambrian granite with vertical foliation. Exposure is at Hay Creek Dam, Clark County, Wisconsin.

▲ THE ENCROACHING SEAS ▲

t the beginning of the Paleozoic Era about 570 million years ago the North American continent was nearly the size it is now and was mainly above sea level. In fact, it had been emergent, and thus undergoing erosion for several hundred, possibly 600 to 700 million years. This long period of erosion of the Precambrian rocks probably produced a gently rolling landscape with a few prominent hills (monadnocks) standing well above the surrounding plains, resistant to erosion. Among these hills were the ring of quartzite hills around Baraboo, Wisconsin (Figure 5–1), Rib Mountain at Wausau, the Barron Hills in northwestern Wisconsin, a series of rhyolite knobs in south central Wisconsin, an elongated highland of basaltic rocks in northern Wisconsin–Michigan, and a highland in most of northeastern Minnesota and adjacent Ontario.

At the beginning of Cambrian time the seas were restricted to eastern, western, southern, and northern coastal areas of North America, roughly

Figure 5-1: Lower Narrows of the Baraboo River near Portage, Wisconsin. The high hills are Baraboo Quartzite that stood as a ring of hills some 800 or more feet about the surrounding area when the Cambrian seas advanced.

in the present Appalachian and Rocky Mountain areas, the Arctic coast, and to the present Gulf Coastal Plain. Then, about 570 million years ago either the continents began to "sink" or sea level began to rise, because the seas slowly spread out over the land surface. It took nearly 100 million years for the seas, advancing from the east and south, to reach the Lake Superior area. The rate of advance of the shoreline was only a few miles per million years and would not have been noticeable had there been people living along the shoreline at the time.

The advance of the sea over the continents probably was not due simply to a rise in sea level with the water gradually flooding the land. The development of numerous basins and domes or arches on the continents (Figure 5–2) suggests that the continental areas were not completely

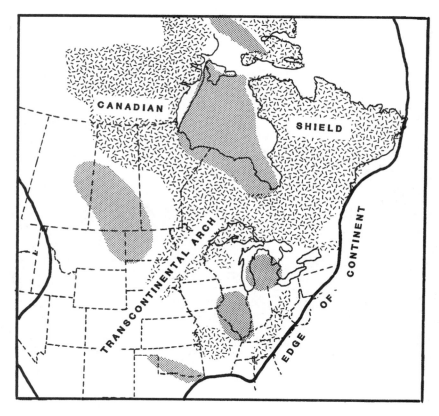

Figure 5-2: Sketch map showing the distribution of basins and domes or arches in part of North America.

passive. Forces deep within the earth caused mild downwarps in some areas and uplifts in the adjacent areas. Some downwarps (basins) were active for several hundred million years. As these areas became stable, basins developed elsewhere. Many of these basins and domes may have developed as a result of movements on older (Precambrian) structures, especially faults.

A thick mantle of weathered material developed on the continent during the long period of weathering prior to the advance of the Cambrian sea. Some of this material was undoubtedly saprolite (chemically weathered rocks) similar to that shown in Figure 5–3. Where the rocks were less chemically weathered, they had a consistency like that of the "rotten" granite (Figure 5–4).

The surf of the advancing sea stripped off the weathered materials. The quartz from the granites and quartzites was carried along the shoreline to produce vast sandy beaches while the clay (mud) formed from the weathering of the feldspars and other minerals was carried out into

Figure 5-3: Deeply weathered rocks called saprolite. Saprolite has the consistency of soil, and the geologist is hoeing the exposure to show the folding. Photo taken in western South Carolina.

the deeper waters of the basins. Figure 5–5 is an example of a granite that was stripped clean of weathered material and then buried by sands as the seas continued their relentless advance over the land surface. Thus the sandstones and shales deposited in the Lake Superior region by the Paleozoic seas were derived mainly from the rocks over which the seas advanced.

When the sea finally reached the Lake Superior region, it advanced farther north into Minnesota and Michigan than it did into Wisconsin because Wisconsin remained a relatively high area or "arch" extending across northern Michigan into Ontario. In contrast, deeper basins developed around the arch. An elongate basin extending northeast from Missouri to Ontario (the "Michigan–Illinois" Basin) flanked the arch on the east and south, and the north-trending Forest City Basin lay to the west in Iowa and eastern Minnesota. The Forest City Basin is bounded on the west by the Transcontinental Arch, and the Michigan–Illinois Basin is bounded on the east by the Cincinnati Arch. These basins and arches are

Figure 5-4: Disintegrated or "rotten" granite, a rock widely developed in Central Wisconsin today, and present when the Cambrian seas advanced over the area. Photo taken south of Marathon.

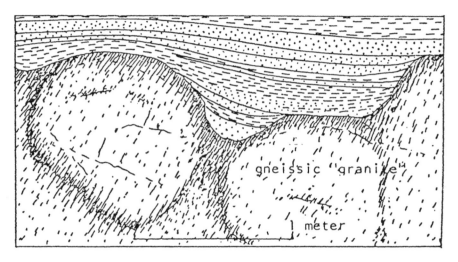

Figure 5-5: Drawing of an exposure in a quarry west of Neillsville, Wisconsin. The gneissic granite was spheroidally weathered, eroded, and then overlain by the Cambrian Mt. Simon Sandstone. (From P. E. Myers, 1978.)

shown on the map in Figure 5–6. The Forest City and Michigan Basins are almost centered over the high-density Keweenawan age basalts and gabbros of the "Midcontinent Gravity High" and may have formed as a result of the subsidence of these rocks. The Wisconsin Arch is more or less centered on a major gravity low in which the exposed rocks are dominantly granites. Since they would not tend to "sink" into the crust, these lower density rocks may have contributed to Wisconsin's remaining as a positive or topographically high area during the lower Paleozoic. Whatever the cause for the development of the Wisconsin Arch and surrounding basins, they had a great influence on the type, thickness, and pattern of sedimentary rocks produced in the Lake Superior region.

An east–west cross section through Wisconsin today (Figure 5–7) shows the arch shape with the younger sedimentary rocks dipping off the Precambrian core to the east and west. Because the rock layers thin and become more sandy as they approach the arch, we believe that Wisconsin stood above the surrounding areas during Cambrian and Ordovician time. For example, the basal sandstone unit ranges in thickness from less than 300 feet in west-central Wisconsin to about 2,000 feet in northeastern Illinois and 3,500 feet in southern Illinois. Obviously subsidence was much greater to the south than it was in Wisconsin.

The Cambrian sea did not advance at a uniform rate over the land; instead there were numerous advances separated by minor withdrawals, causing the shoreline to migrate back and forth several hundred miles. Ostrom (1967) has recognized a series of five advances and withdrawals of the sea that affected Wisconsin and the surrounding states. The result was a distinctive cyclic pattern of sedimentary rocks. The cycles are best represented in the rocks of southwestern Wisconsin and adjacent parts of Minnesota, Iowa, and Illinois.

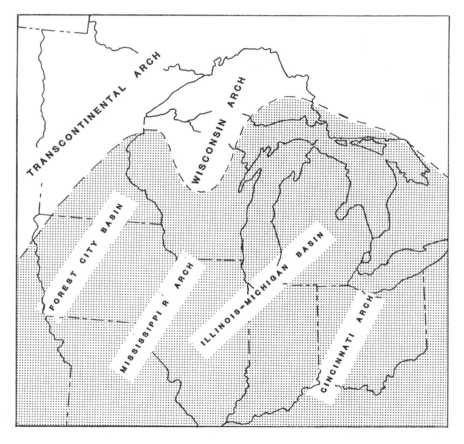

Figure 5-6: Sketch map of the Great Lakes area showing the location of the embayments around the Wisconsin Arch and the probable position of land to the north.

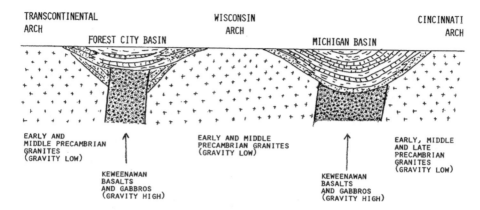

Figure 5-7: Diagrammatic east-west cross section across the Great Lakes region showing the relationship between gravity highs and basins and between gravity lows and arches.

According to Ostrom (1970) a cycle is a recurring sequence of rocks arranged in the same order, and these lithologic cycles record the physical conditions produced by geological events. In the Cambrian and Ordovician of the upper Mississippi Valley, the cycles were produced by transgressions and regressions of the sea over the area. The rock types deposited at a given place and time are controlled mainly by the position of the shoreline at that time, the source areas of sediment, and the patterns of longshore currents.

The beach (littoral) zone is a relatively high-energy environment in which clean, well-sorted, thick-bedded sand with well-developed cross-bedding accumulates (Figure 5–8). Offshore is a *nondepositional zone* in which little or no sediment is deposited. Currents carry the finer silt and clay across the zone, reworking some of the sand deposited in the littoral zone. A thin-bedded deposit is produced (Figure 5–9), incorporating some clay into the sand, making it less pure than that in the beach zone. Farther offshore on the *depositional shelf* shaley sandstone or shale is deposited. These sediments are typically silty or shaley thin-bedded deposits that are gradational with those of the reworked quartz sandstone. The *biogenic zone* is offshore from the shaley zone. Here abundant lime-secreting organisms produced calcium carbonate deposits, some with small reeflike mounds called *bioherms*. These sediments are converted to limestones, some of which may later be converted to dolomite (Figure 5–10).

Figure 5-8 (above): Cross-bedding in the Mt. Simon Sandstone. Major layering is horizontal and the cross beds are inclined down to the right. They form from current carrying the sand from left to right. Chippewa River Valley, Eau Claire, Wisconsin. Photo by Paul E. Myers.

Figure 5-9 (below): Shaly Eau Claire Sandstone, typical of the non-depositional shelf. The shale is added to the sandstone as the sediment is carried across the already deposited sand.

*Figure 5-10: Dolomite (carbonate) unit deposited mainly by biological activity.
Lone Rock member of the Franconia Formation. Near Arcadia, Wisconsin.*

This sequence of rocks is laterally gradational between each adjacent
unit. All form at the same time and are called *sedimentary facies*. As the
sea transgresses, however, the units are deposited one on top of the
other, and this sequence is used to determine the location of the shoreline at any given time. For example, when a thick-bedded, well-sorted,
cross-bedded quartz sandstone was deposited in an area, the shoreline
was close by, but when a limestone was deposited in that area, the shoreline must have been some distance away. Mapping of the distribution of
these various rock types permits us to determine the oscillations of the
shoreline and the fluctuations in sea level. By studying the fossils contained in the rocks from place to place, we can correlate these changes
over large areas. Ostrom (1970) (Figure 5–11) shows that the abundant
sandstones in the vicinity of the Wisconsin Arch become thicker and
grade into dominantly carbonate rocks (limestones) to the southeast as
one approaches the Appalachian region.

The sequence of Paleozoic rock units in Wisconsin is different from
the sequences in Minnesota and in Michigan because Wisconsin is
located on an arch and Minnesota and Michigan are in basins. As shown
in Figure 5–11, Ostrom places a sandstone unit at the base of each cycle

representing a new advance of the sea onto the Wisconsin Arch. Each of these basal sandstone units overlies an erosion surface formed when the seas withdrew from the Wisconsin Arch. We can determine how far the sea withdrew during each of these regressions by tracing the limits of the erosion surface formed at that time. The sandstones were formed when the sea advanced over the erosion surface. As the advance continued, the shoreline got farther and farther away from a given site, and deeper water (offshore) sediments were deposited on the sandstones. The limestone and dolomite units were deposited during the maximum advance of the seas. Because the seas did not advance an equal distance

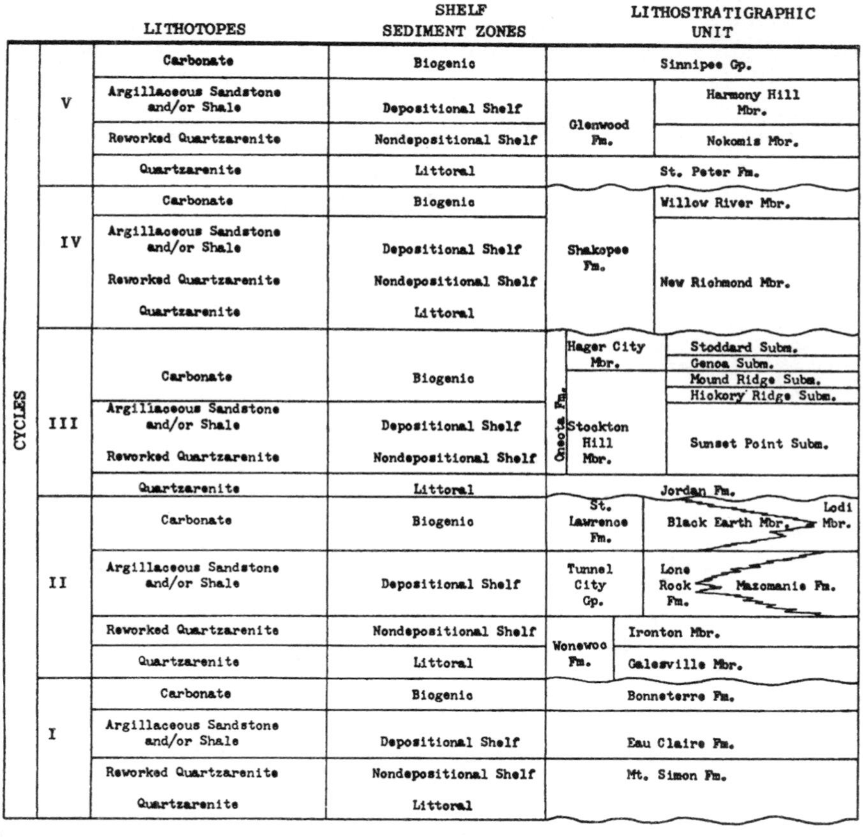

CYCLES		LITHOTOPES	SHELF SEDIMENT ZONES	LITHOSTRATIGRAPHIC UNIT		
	V	Carbonate	Biogenic	Sinnipee Gp.		
		Argillaceous Sandstone and/or Shale	Depositional Shelf	Glenwood Fm.	Harmony Hill Mbr.	
		Reworked Quartzarenite	Nondepositional Shelf		Nokomis Mbr.	
		Quartzarenite	Littoral	St. Peter Fm.		
	IV	Carbonate	Biogenic	Willow River Mbr.		
		Argillaceous Sandstone and/or Shale	Depositional Shelf	Shakopee Fm.		
		Reworked Quartzarenite	Nondepositional Shelf	New Richmond Mbr.		
		Quartzarenite	Littoral			
	III	Carbonate	Biogenic	Hager City Mbr. (Oneota Fm.)	Stoddard Subm.	
					Genoa Subm.	
					Mound Ridge Subm.	
					Hickory Ridge Subm.	
		Argillaceous Sandstone and/or Shale	Depositional Shelf	Stockton Hill Mbr.	Sunset Point Subm.	
		Reworked Quartzarenite	Nondepositional Shelf			
		Quartzarenite	Littoral	Jordan Fm.		
	II	Carbonate	Biogenic	St. Lawrence Fm.	Black Earth Mbr.	Lodi Mbr.
		Argillaceous Sandstone and/or Shale	Depositional Shelf	Tunnel City Gp.	Lone Rock Fm.	Mazomanie Fm.
		Reworked Quartzarenite	Nondepositional Shelf	Wonewoc Fm.	Ironton Mbr.	
		Quartzarenite	Littoral		Galesville Mbr.	
	I	Carbonate	Biogenic	Bonneterre Fm.		
		Argillaceous Sandstone and/or Shale	Depositional Shelf	Eau Claire Fm.		
		Reworked Quartzarenite	Nondepositional Shelf	Mt. Simon Fm.		
		Quartzarenite	Littoral			

Figure 5-11: Correlation of lithologic cycles with lithotopes, shelf sediment zones, and lithostratigraphic units.

during each transgression, the limestones are not all the same or equally developed. The maximum regression of the sea occurred during middle Ordovician time. The sandstone and carbonate rocks deposited on this erosion surface was during perhaps the greatest transgression of the Paleozoic seas over the continent.

The pattern of rock types, however, is not the only evidence for repeated transgression and regression during the Cambrian and Ordovician periods. The presence of fossils in the sedimentary rocks provides additional evidence, since evolution brings slow but constant change in the type and kind of organisms living in a particular environment. Some organisms present during one advance of the sea had changed or may have become extinct prior to the next advance. Thus, there are "breaks" or "gaps" in the fossil record in areas from which the sea withdrew, while a more or less complete record of the evolutionary changes is present in those deeper parts of the basins from which the seas did not withdraw.

▲ PALEOZOIC LIFE ▲

When the seas advanced over the continents during Cambrian times, they were different from all the previous seas. For the first time in the geologic record the seas contained abundant animal and plant life (Figure 5–12). Skeletons and other remains (impressions, burrows, tracks, etc.) of these organisms attest to their presence. Fossil remains of these organisms are helpful in reconstructing environments and are invaluable for correlating rock sequences from one area to another. These animals and plants did more than leave their imprint on rocks, for many limestones are <u>composed</u> almost entirely of skeletal remains of some of these organisms.

The presence of fossils is the most definitive basis for establishing that the sedimentary rocks in the Lake Superior region are, in fact, Paleozoic in age. Furthermore, the presence of fossils in Paleozoic rocks marks such a major change from all the Precambrian rocks that a brief discussion of some of the major forms of life is presented here as a background for the section on the history of physical events in the area.

Over the long period of crustal stability and erosion during the last 400–500 million years of Precambrian time, the earth's atmosphere became sufficiently oxygen-bearing for animal life to evolve. The fossil record for practically all of Precambrian time indicates that the forms of

Figure 5-12: Restoration of plant and animal life of the Middle Cambrian. Life forms include colonies of branching sponges, trilobites, sea cucumbers, jelly- fishes, and an arthropod somewhat like modern crustaceans. (Photo courtesy of The Field Museum, Neg #GE080872, Chicago.)

life on earth were almost entirely plants (algae) and bacteria. Then, in an almost startlingly short period of time at the beginning of the Paleozoic, we find an evolutionary burst of life unlike anything before or since.

The lower Cambrian strata contain a wide diversity of life with every phylum except the vertebrates represented. While one might expect this record of early animal life to be made up mainly of very primitive types of organisms, there are, in fact, numerous highly evolved, complex organisms. The trilobites, for example, are the most abundant type of animal. The presence of these rather complex creatures suggests a long period of evolution prior to their appearance in the fossil record. Several factors may have contributed to this apparent paradox. Remember that marine organisms live mainly in the shallow waters of the continental shelf; few organisms can live in the abyssal depths of the oceans. Remember also that during the last few <u>hundred million</u> years of the Precambrian, the continents were emergent, and thus the area of shallow seas was greatly restricted to the continental margins. Since rocks that formed along the continental margins at that time are only sparsely pre- served and exposed, we do not have a good picture of the depositional environment. Where rocks of late Precambrian age are exposed, how- ever, they contain abundant coarse clastic rocks (sandstones and arkoses) that are poor environments for the preservation of fossils. It is unfortunate that perhaps the major evolutionary event of all time occurred during a period of such crustal stability that few rocks from that period survived unchanged and exposed at the earth's surface today. We may never find answers to the riddle of the origin and early evolution of animals, but perhaps this mystery makes us search all the harder.

Whatever the origin of animals, they were abundant and diversified by the beginning of Cambrian time some 570 million years ago. As the seas slowly advanced over the continents, the area of shallow seas available for marine life increased perhaps a thousand times. With all the new environmental niches to fill, an amazing diversity of organisms developed.

CAMBRIAN LIFE

The lands over which the seas advanced were very bleak, forbidding places, for there is no evidence of any forms of plants or animals that may have inhabited them. Perhaps the lone exception to this is the likelihood that lichens probably grew in moist places on some of the rocks. Clearly, however, the scene would have been one of utter desolation by modern standards. The continents were to remain naked for nearly 200 million years longer.

In marked contrast, however, the seas teemed with a great abundance and diversity of plants and animals. The plants consisted of a wide variety of seaweeds and algae that provided food for many of the animals. In some shallow areas where little or no sand or mud were deposited, the algae left distinctive deposits of calcium carbonate called *stromatolites* or *algal structures*. Some of these algae were very similar to their present-day descendants (blue-green algae) and to their Precambrian ancestors that had lived some 1500 million years before.

The most abundant animals in the Cambrian seas were the trilobites, a type of Crustacean and a biologically complex organism. The trilobites were so numerous and diverse that they constituted nearly 60 percent of the varieties of Cambrian life. Some were excellent swimmers and may have been among the first predators; others were scavengers, eating organic debris from the shallow sea floor. They ranged from diminutive creatures less than an inch long to giants nearly 20 inches long weighing possibly 10 pounds. They were able to move freely about the oceans and dominated the animal world for over 100 million years. So abundant were they that the Cambrian period is often referred to as the "age of trilobites." Diminishing in diversity and proportion of the total population during the Ordovician period, they never regained the prominence they held in the Cambrian.

A wide variety of upper Cambrian trilobite fossils are present in rocks in the Great Lakes area, each with its own distinctive form. Most species existed only for a geologically short period of time (perhaps several million years). Therefore, since fossils of these species occur only in rocks formed during a specific span of time, they serve as a reliable basis for correlating rocks throughout the area. *Crepicephalus*, *Cedaria*, *Norwoodia*, *Coosia*, and *Dikelocephalus* (Figure 5–13) are varieties of trilobites found in

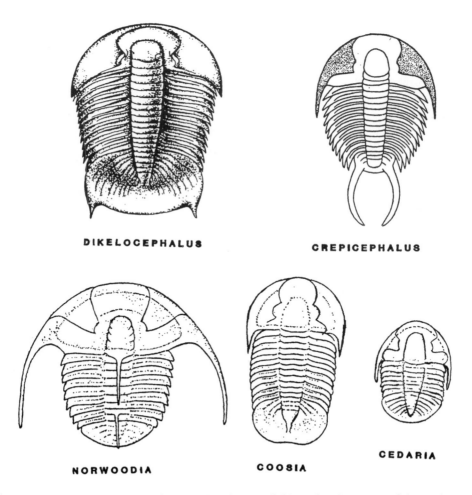

DIKELOCEPHALUS

CREPICEPHALUS

NORWOODIA

COOSIA

CEDARIA

Figure 5-13: Drawings of Upper Cambrian trilobites showing some of the variations found in the region. All are natural size.

Cambrian rocks in the area. Most trilobite fossils are fragments of their skeleton, since complete skeletons are rare.

Second to the trilobites in importance were a wide variety of brachiopods. They made up nearly 30 percent of the Cambrian fauna and experienced a spectacular development during the Cambrian. Unlike the mobile trilobites, brachiopods were covered with protective shells and attached to the bottom. Most of the early Cambrian forms had a phosphatic shell, while the later ones had a calcium carbonate shell. They must have been extremely abundant in relatively clear limy bottoms, as evidenced by the fact that some limestones are composed in large part of brachiopod shells. Brachiopod fossils are present in most of the carbonate rocks in the Lake Superior region and are abundant in some. Brachiopods reached their peak development and diversity during the Middle Paleozoic periods (Ordovician–Devonian), but remained major marine invertebrates throughout the Paleozoic era. Very few brachiopods exist today, but one, *Lingula*, has remained virtually unchanged since early Cambrian time, and represents one of the longest ranged animals on earth.

Worms and other soft-bodied creatures must have been present in considerable numbers and variety. Because of the lack of any hard skeleton, however, these organisms do not often occur as fossils. Only in extremely foul, stagnant waters would these soft-bodied animals be preserved as fossils, for in more hospitable waters the scavengers would clean up the remains long before they could become buried and fossilized. Burrowing worms, however, can and do leave a record of their existence. The sand and mud on the ocean floors were gently stirred up by these organisms much as is done by present day worms.

The burrowing may obliterate the normal layering in sediments and burrows themselves may be preserved as fossils. While we cannot tell with certainly what particular type of organism made the burrow, it is evident that burrowing worms must have been abundant—again a marked change from Precambrian times.

Gastropods (snails), cephalopods, and most other animal phyla made their appearance during the Cambrian. In fact, the vertebrates are the only major group of animals not represented in the Cambrian seas. They were to make their appearance during the Ordovician Period.

ORDOVICIAN LIFE

The vast shallow seas of the Ordovician Period swarmed with invertebrate animals, many of which were very similar to their Cambrian ancestors (Figure 5–14). Trilobites and brachiopods were still abundant,

a. **Hudsonaster**

b. **Edrioaster**

c. **Ischadites**

d. **Sowerbyella**

e. **Batostoma**

f. **Fusispira**

Figure 5-14: Typical Ordovician fossils found in the Mackville quarry, near Appleton, Wisconsin. (a) Hudsonaster, perhaps the oldest starfish; (b) Edrioaster, a primitive echinoderm; (c) Ischadites, a small sponge; (d) Sowerbyella, a brachiopod; (e) Batostoma, a branching bryozoa; (f) Fusispira, a high-spired gastropod.

but a number of new groups also became prominent. Among them are the graptolites, true corals, crinoids, bryozoans, and clams. The widespread limy middle Ordovician rocks in North America contain fossils of nearly 3,000 different species, a considerable number of which are present in the Lake Superior region. The limy skeletons of bryozoans, brachiopods, and crinoids form a substantial part of many Ordovician limestones and dolomites, and locally appear to have formed small reefs. Trilobites probably reached their peak development in early and middle Ordovician, but they were greatly diminished in number and variety by the end of Ordovician time.

Graptolites were free-floating animals that were very abundant and widespread during the Ordovician. Because they were floating animals, the graptolites are exceedingly widespread—an almost universal fossil. They drifted wherever the winds blew them, probably often to their death in cold or highly saline waters. They are present in deepwater shales and shallower limestones as films of carbon on bedding planes. They apparently were not often preserved in sandy areas since they had no hard skeletons, and because they may have been eaten by scavengers. Most genera existed only a relatively short time before becoming extinct. Thus, graptolites are excellent fossils for correlating rock sequences from one area to another, even from one continent to another.

Although not found in the Lake Superior region, one of the most significant Ordovician fossils is the remains of a primitive fish that had a bony armored skin. These represent the first record of vertebrates in the fossil record and led to a large family of *Ostracoderm* fishes in the Silurian and Devonian Periods to follow.

A new predator appeared on the scene in the form of the rapidly developing cephalopod (Figure 5–15). Besides being perhaps the fastest swimmers of their time, they possessed numerous tentacles that probably permitted them to catch and eat any animal that did not have a hard shell. Some of these squidlike animals had long cone-shaped, chambered shells up to 15 feet long and 10 inches in diameter. Most, however, were much smaller. The development of these predators may have resulted in a decline in other types of animals that previously had been without superior enemies. Cephalopod fossils are present in limestones throughout the Great Lakes area.

Meanwhile on the land, the first vascular plants capable of drawing water from the soil appear to have developed. Such plant spores, indicative of higher orders of plants, have recently been discovered in the rocks in Poland. The nature and extent of these land plants, however, is not known.

It is therefore evident that there is a significant difference between the kinds of fossils in Ordovician rocks and those in the Cambrian. Even

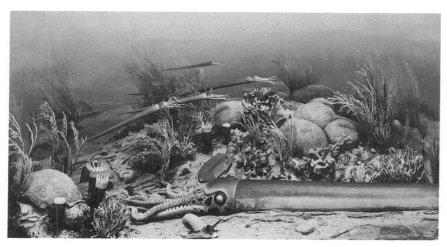

Figure 5-15: Restoration of an Ordovician sea floor in the vicinity of Chicago. The fauna and flora depicted here include trilobites, seaweed, straight shelled cephalopods, "honeycomb" corals, gastropods, and nautiloids (swimming). (Courtesy of The Field Museum, Neg #GE080820, Chicago.)

though most of the same phyla are represented, the genera and species are usually quite different. An example would be the difference between Ordovician trilobites and their Cambrian ancestors. These differences are invaluable in distinguishing the rocks of one age from those of the other.

SILURIAN LIFE

Like the Cambrian and Ordovician, the Silurian is characterized by its own distinctive group of fossils. Also like the Cambrian and Ordovician, nearly all the fossils found in central North America are of animals that flourish in warm tropical seas. We must therefore conclude that at that time North America was in a much more tropical environment than it is now. Indeed, it is generally accepted that North America straddled the equator during the early Paleozoic era.

In the Silurian seas, the invertebrates still were the dominant animals. Trilobites, molluscs (cephalopods), and graptolites were much less common, but brachiopods, corals, and echinoderms (crinoids and cystoids) emerged as major groups of animals. Bryozoa continued to be an important

Figure 5-16: Restored Silurian sea floor showing the fauna and flora typical of Silurian reefs. Tall crinoids stood up from the sea floor inhabited by trilobites, brachiopods, coiled cephalopods, and a variety of corals (honeycomb coral, Favosites, chain coral, Halysites, tube coral, Syringopera, and a solitary coral). (Courtesy of the Milwaukee County Museum.)

Figure 5-17: The Silurian trilobite, Sthenarocalymene calebra, designated as the Wisconsin State fossil, from the Hartung quarry in Wauwatosa, Wisconsin. (Photo by Steve LoDuca)

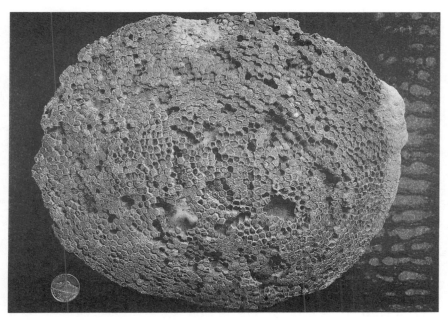

Figures 5-18A(above) and 5-18B (below): The Silurian corals, Favosites ("hon-eycomb coral") (upper) and Halysites ("chain coral") (lower) were important reef-builders in the Great Lakes region. (Photos from the University of Wisconsin Museum, courtesy of Klaus Westphal.)

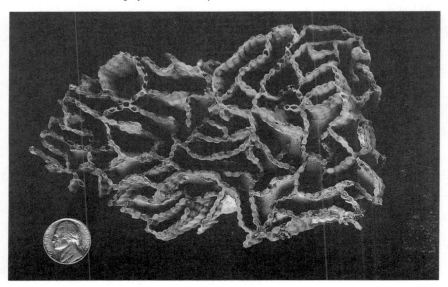

group. Included among the Silurian fossils is the trilobite *Sthenarocalymene calebra* (Figure 5–17), which has been designated the Wisconsin State fossil.

The prominent development of corals in the clear waters of the shallow limy seas resulted in the first major development of coral reefs. Two of the more common corals are the colonial "honeycomb" coral, Favosites, and the "chain" coral, *Halysites* (Figure 5–18). These corals are so distinctive that the Silurian has been called the *Age of Corals*. A large number of these reefs formed around the Michigan Basin and are discussed later.

Associated with the coral reefs were a variety of other animals and plants that lived in the warm shallow waters. Lime-secreting algae formed algal mats and dome-shaped "algal structures." Crinoids grew on long slender stems from their "foot" in the bottom sediments, the "head" waving to and fro in the currents. These graceful animals looked somewhat like plants and are often referred to as "lilies of the sea." They were common in the Silurian and were even more abundant throughout the Devonian and Mississippian periods.

In places, brachiopods became so abundant that their shells accumulated to form mounds or shoals on the sea floor. In particular, shells of the brachiopod *Pentamerus* form layers up to 10 feet thick that extend for over half a mile in features called *biostromes* in Silurian dolomite near Fond du Lac, Wisconsin.

Primitive fishes, although not reported from the Great Lakes area, became much more common in the Silurian, but were even more common and diversified in the Devonian. The appearance of fish signals the beginning of vertebrate fossils, and although they were very primitive creatures, they mark a major evolutionary step. They probably represent the common ancestor of all higher forms of vertebrates.

DEVONIAN LIFE

The Devonian marks the beginning of the last half of the Paleozoic era. The warm tropical seas that had alternately advanced over and withdrawn from the main upper Midwest were making their last stand except in some of the major basins.

In the seas, corals were even more abundant than in the Silurian, forming numerous coral reefs (Figure 5–19). The corals were more varied in form than those of their Silurian ancestors, and both colonial and solitary corals were common. Brachiopods were at their climax with more than 700 different varieties recognized in North America. Many of these brachiopods lived on the reefs along with bryozoa, crinoids, blastoids,

Figure 5-19: Restoration of a Devonian sea floor showing the assemblage of animals found in the mid-continent region. Most of the animals shown are corals. Also shown are a nautiloid cephalopod, several trilobites, a gastropod, a crinoid, a straight shelled cephalopod, and brachiopods. (Neg./trans. no. 333958. Courtesy Department of Library Sciences, American Museum of Natural History.)

and pelecypods (clams). Sponges with siliceous spicules or skeletons were also common in places.

The tremendous development of fish has caused some geologists to refer to the Devonian as the "Age of Fishes." Fish became common, and many different types are represented in the fossil record. Fish with well-developed vertebra and bones, as well as sharks with only a cartilaginous backbone were common. The fish left a number of well-preserved fossils, but from sharks only the teeth and tiny scales were preserved. Most of the fishes and sharks were less than a few feet long, but some sharks evidently grew to nearly 20 feet in length.

Since freshwater fish also were common during the Devonian, other forms of freshwater life must also have existed. Among the freshwater fish were several groups of "lungfish" in which the swim-bladder was connected with the throat so that air could be inhaled and exhaled at will. The walls of the bladder were lined with blood vessels to absorb oxygen, forming primitive lungs. Several genera of lungfishes are still living in Africa and Australia, and we know their habits well. During dry seasons they are able to breathe air as well as extract oxygen from the water. They have peculiarly developed fins that enable them to crawl on land. An early adaptation of this evolutionary trend led to the development of amphibians, the first land animals, during the Devonian. Fossil insects of Devonian age have also been found in some parts of the world.

Another major change in the continents occurred in the Devonian period. The first evidence of land plants is found in early Devonian rocks. By 360 million years ago, lowland forests with trees up to 30 feet tall were present (Figure 5–20). While the trees and other plants were very different from those of today, they made a profound change in a landscape that had stood naked for over 4 billion years except for probable lichens and algae coatings on the rocks. As hardier varieties of plants evolved, the entire land surface was covered, and in the following Mississippian and Pennsylvanian periods vast swamplands covering much of eastern North America stood for millions of years. The decaying wood that fell into the water was slowly converted to coal.

The spreading of plants over the land was followed closely by air-breathing amphibians during the Devonian. With the development of lungs, animals had a vast new array of environments to inhabit. During the next 100 million years, a great variety of land animals evolved, including amphibians, reptiles, and innumerable insects.

Figure 5-20: Restoration of early land plants of the Devonian period. Plants shown include early tree ferns that grew 30 to 40 feet high, horsetail rushes, a primitive plant that had no leaves (Psilophyton), and a lycopod, the tall tree without leaves which is covered with short spike-like projections that served as leaves. (Courtesy The Field Museum, Neg #73898, Chicago.)

The amphibians almost certainly evolved from the fish, which made their appearance in the Silurian. The evolution of vertebrates initiated a major new line of evolution among animals.

With the evolution of land plants and animals the surface of the land changed forever. Plants helped to hold the soil on slopes, retarding erosion, yet decay of plant materials provided various "humic acids" that promoted chemical weathering of soils. Indeed, the addition of organic matter to the soils by more primitive plants and worms was probably important to the development of more advanced, specialized kinds of plants.

With this brief sketch of Paleozoic life to indicate some of the major biological events during the first half of the Paleozoic era, let us return to the sequence of rocks formed in the Great Lakes region during this time.

THE PALEOZOIC HISTORY
▲ OF THE ▲
LAKE SUPERIOR REGION

EARLY TRANSGRESSIONS
AND REGRESSIONS

The basal Paleozoic unit formed by the advance of the upper Cambrian sea (about 500 million years ago) is the Mt. Simon Sandstone. It is a blanketlike deposit of sand formed by the coalescing of innumerable beaches, offshore bars, spits, etc., along the coastline. Much of the sand was carried into the sea by rivers flowing off the land areas to the north, but some was derived directly by the surf attacking the higher lands of that ancient landscape. In places where the surf was eroding the shoreline, basal conglomerates were formed with locally derived boulders and cobbles. The waves stirred up the sand on the floor and rounded the grains. The ocean currents then sorted the finer silt and clay from the sand and carried it out into deeper waters. The currents also produced cross-bedding with the inclined layers formed on the downstream side of underwater "deltas" (Figure 5-8). The currents flowed mainly south and southwest, roughly parallel to the shoreline. Since ocean currents are produced mainly by the wind, this suggests that the dominant wind direction in Wisconsin at that time was from the north and northeast. This, and paleomagnetic data, have led Dott and Batten (1970) to postulate that Wisconsin was located south of the equator at that time, in the Southeast Trade Wind Belt.

The Mt. Simon Sandstone forms a continuous blanket that covers much of the Midwest, including Illinois, Iowa, Missouri, and lower Michigan. It evidently did not cover northwestern Minnesota along the Transcontinental Arch or northern and northeastern Wisconsin and northern Michigan, which were exposed as a ridge from north of Sault Ste. Marie westward to near the Minneapolis area.

Farther offshore where less sand was available and where the water was somewhat deeper, the Mt. Simon Sandstone was reworked by the waves and currents, and some silt and clay were incorporated, producing a rather poorly sorted, more thinly bedded sandstone. This represents the nondepositional shelf deposit. As the sea advanced, this type of material, formed farther offshore, was deposited on top of the more typical nearshore phase of the Mt. Simon Sandstone that had been deposited earlier.

In the basins flanking the Wisconsin Arch, more silt and clay were deposited and mixed with the sand. This is referred to as the depositional shelf environment. Glauconite (a mineral similar to biotite) was chemically (or biochemically) precipitated in this zone, locally producing extensive beds of "green sand." The Eau Claire Formation was formed in this way. Fossils such as trilobite fragments and brachiopods are relatively common in this unit.

Still farther offshore in deeper water a carbonate unit, the Bonneterre Formation, was deposited mainly in the Illinois Basin. Since it is not exposed in the Lake Superior region, it is not discussed further. In the older geologic literature, the Mt. Simon and Eau Claire sandstones are referred to as *Dresbach*.

The first transgressive cycle ended with an uplift of the Wisconsin Arch that caused a regression of the sea and erosion of the newly formed sediments. The seas evidently withdrew approximately to the latitude of central Illinois and then began the slow advance of the second cycle of deposition.

The Wonewoc Formation is the basal sandstone of the second advance of the sea. It is similar to the Mt. Simon Sandstone, and is spectacularly exposed in the Dells of the Wisconsin River and in numerous buttes and other erosional remnants in western Wisconsin (Figure 5–21). Overlying the Wonewoc is the Tunnel City Group which formed offshore on the depositional shelf. It is almost identical to the Eau Claire

Figure 5-21: Erosional remnants of the Galesville member of the Wonewoc Sandstone. Camp Douglas, Wisconsin.

Formation formed during the first cycle, but contains a different suite of fossils. The St. Lawrence Dolomite represents the carbonate zone of the maximum transgression of this cycle. Like most of the carbonates it is quite fossiliferous, with well-preserved trilobites and brachiopods present in places. Following the deposition of the St. Lawrence Formation, the seas again withdrew and exposed the sediments on the Wisconsin Arch to erosion. In older literature the Wonewoc was called the Galesville and Ironton formations, and the Tunnel City Group was called the Franconia Formation.

Although the rock units defining these cycles are distinct in western Wisconsin and adjacent parts of Minnesota, Iowa, and Illinois, no recognizable subdivisions of the cycles are apparent in northern Michigan. These first two cycles are represented in northern Michigan by the Chapel Rock and Miners Castle sandstones of the Munising Formation. Both of these units apparently represent nearshore (littoral) environments and suggest that the seas barely covered the Upper Peninsula during these advances.

The Jordan Sandstone represents the nearshore sand deposited by the third advance of the sea about 475 million years ago (about 25 million years after the first advance). The Jordan is the youngest deposit of Cambrian age in the Midwest and is similar to the Mt. Simon and Wonewoc

Figure 5-22: Cross-bedded Jordan Sandstone, typical of the basal transgressive sandstone units. Berlin, Wisconsin.

Figure 5-23: Typical exposure of the Prairie du Chien Dolomite forming resistant hill tops overlying the weaker sandstone. Near Galesville, Wisconsin.

sandstones (Figure 5-22). The Oneota Formation containing dolomite formed during the maximum advance of the seas onto the Wisconsin Arch and represents the first sedimentary deposit of the Ordovician period. Its deposition was followed by another southward retreat of the sea.

The fourth advance of the sea is represented by the New Richmond Sandstone of the Shakopee Formation, which rests on an erosion surface developed on the Oneota Dolomite and older formations. The Shakopee (Prairie du Chien) Dolomite (Figure 5–23) was deposited during the maximum advance of the seas during this cycle. A common feature of the Prairie du Chien Dolomite is the widespread development of stro-matolites and oolites (Figure 5–24), both of which indicate a very shal-

Figure 5-24: Stromatolites common in the Prairie du Chien Dolomite. View looking down on the dome-shaped tops of the algal structures. South of Prairie du Chien, Wisconsin.

low, perhaps intertidal environment, in which few marine invertebrates lived. As a result there are relatively few fossils in the Prairie du Chien Dolomite. Thus the sea appears to have been very shallow even though the shoreline was many miles away.

After deposition of the Shakopee (Prairie du Chien) Dolomite, a major uplift occurred in the Great Lakes region, with the shoreline retreating south to central Kentucky. Paleozoic sediments in much of the northern midcontinent region were subjected to erosion by streams flowing over the "new" land. Since no land plants or animals had yet evolved, the landscape must have been very bleak and erosion excessive. An unknown amount of material was carried south and east into the surrounding seas, for the streams cut valleys hundreds of feet deep into the sedimentary rocks. When the middle Ordovician sea advanced over the continent for the fifth time, it did so over a very irregular surface.

The St. Peter Sandstone is the basal unit formed during this advance of the sea. It is an extremely pure, well-sorted sandstone with well-rounded grains, and it exhibits large variations in thickness due to the fact that it fills in valleys and covers hills (Figure 5–25). The high purity and rounding of the sand may have resulted from its having been subjected to the wave and current action of five advances of the sea, for parts of each of the older sandstone units were weathered and eroded to form the St. Peter Sandstone. Much of the sand in the St. Peter is "frosted," similar to that in most sand dunes. Indeed, it is likely that extensive sand dunes were present along the shoreline of the advancing sea, much like modern-day beaches. Without vegetation on the land,

Figure 5-25: Quarry in a channel filling of St. Peter Sandstone. The sand is used for molding sand in nearby foundries. Utley, Wisconsin.

Figure 5-26: Platteville Dolomite overyling the St. Peter Sandstone. Because the sandstone is poorly cemented, it weathers much more readily than the overlying dolomite. New Glarus, Wisconsin.

there may have been sizable areas of sand dunes extending far inland. It is estimated that it took 5 million years for the sea to advance during St. Peter time. If this is so, the St. Peter (Simpson) Sandstone in Oklahoma is 5 million years older than it is in Wisconsin, and by the time the St. Peter was deposited in Wisconsin, a thick sequence of shale and limestone had already accumulated in Oklahoma.

A sequence of carbonate rocks up to 350 feet thick was deposited during the maximum transgression. In places, the Glenwood Shale overlies the St. Peter Sandstone with the carbonate rocks overlying the shale. In other places, the carbonates rest directly on the St. Peter Sandstone (Figure 5–26). The Platteville–Decorah–Galena formations formed during a long period of carbonate deposition in the upper Midwest and represent the thickest accumulation of carbonate rocks to occur in the Lake Superior region during the cyclic transgressions and regressions of the upper Cambrian and Ordovician periods. Major zinc and lead deposits present in the Galena limestone are discussed later.

In Wisconsin this sequence of carbonates is referred to as the Sinnipee Group. In northern Michigan rocks of this age are called the Trenton and

Black River dolomites. These dolomites are quite fossiliferous, commonly containing well-preserved brachiopods.

With the deposition of the Galena Dolomite of the Sinnipee Group in the Great Lakes region, the cyclic pattern of transgressions and regressions characteristic of the upper Cambrian and Ordovician ceased. While the cause or causes for this cessation is not clear, it resulted in a change in the pattern and type of sediments deposited.

The pattern of rocks, however, is not due strictly to simple transgression and regression of the seas to form a series of blanketlike layers. In Minnesota, for example, Morey (cited by Austin, 1972) shows that movements on Keweenawan faults during the Paleozoic have resulted in local unconformities and locally thicker deposition of some units. Although the evidence is less clear in the Michigan Basin, Dorr and Eschman (1970) cite local abrupt changes in thickness of some Paleozoic formations. Paull and Paull (1977) show that faults also developed in the Illinois basin during deposition of Paleozoic sediments. These faults, and gentle folds elsewhere, suggest movements in the Precambrian "basement" on which Paleozoic formations were deposited.

MIDDLE PALEOZOIC ROCKS: INFLUENCE FROM THE EAST

A subtle erosion surface separates the Galena Dolomite from the overlying Maquoketa Shale in most of the upper Midwest. Evidently a minor regression of the sea and associated minor erosion of the Galena Dolomite occurred before deposition of the Maquoketa.

In Michigan and Wisconsin the Maquoketa is primarily a gray to greenish gray shale with silty and dolomitic layers and lenses (Figure 5–27. In Iowa it contains much more limestone and dolomite, while in Minnesota it is composed predominantly of dolomite. Unlike all the underlying rock units, the Maquoketa was not derived from the erosion of the rocks in the Great Lakes area. During the late Ordovician, the Taconic Mountains (ancestors of the Appalachian Mountains) were formed in the northeastern United States. Folding and faulting and volcanic activity produced relatively high lands in New England, which were vigorously eroded by streams flowing westward into a sea that covered most of North America at that time. Near the eroding mountains graywackes and sandstones accumulated to great thickness, and the finer muds and volcanic ash were carried westward to the Great Lakes area, accumulating to form the Maquoketa Shale (Richmond Shale

Figure 5-27: Maquoketa Shale exposed in a quarry at the Oakfield Brick Plant. The main quarry face is shale. The lighter layers in the upper portion are dolomite. Glacial till forms the gentle hill on top.

in Michigan). The layer of muds gradually thinned to the west and changed to a carbonate sequence in western Iowa. Organisms evidently flourished on the muddy bottom during deposition of the Maquoketa since it is relatively fossiliferous wherever it is exposed.

Volcanic ash layers in the Midwest became thicker and more common to the east, suggesting that the source was in the Taconic Mountains. No volcanic activity at that time is known in the western United States. This implies, therefore, that the prevailing winds in the United States were from the east.

Because the shale is much more easily eroded than the dolomites that underlie and overlie it, the Maquoketa does not crop out in many places. Some of the more accessible places are at a quarry for brick making at Oakfield, Wisconsin, in Calumet County Park on the eastern edge of Lake Winnebago north of Stockbridge, and at Kittell Falls east of Green Bay, Wisconsin. However, because of the ease with which it is eroded, the Maquoketa has had a marked influence on the landforms in eastern Wisconsin. Green Bay, the Lake Winnebago lowland, Horicon Marsh, and the Rock River valley all occur in the lowlands formed by erosion of this soft shale.

Overlying the Maquoketa in eastern Wisconsin is the Neda Formation of probably late Ordovician age. There appears to be a gradational contact with the top of the Maquoketa. The Neda consists of sand-sized pellets of hematite (Fe_2O_3) and geothite ($FeO(OH)$) called oolites that are concentrically layered like an onion. The iron-rich Neda occurs as a series of discontinuous lenses along the top of the Maquoketa throughout eastern Wisconsin (Figure 5–28). Some of the lenses are as much as 50 feet thick and were mined for iron ore at Neda near Mayville, Wisconsin, during the late 1800s and early 1900s.

At Neda the lower part of the formation is iron-rich shale at the top of the Maquoketa overlain by oolitic goethite; the upper one foot is a harder, more massive structureless hematite. The top layer (the hard one) appears to be reworked with fragments of hematite up to two inches across set in a hematite matrix.

Like the Precambrian iron ores, the origin of the Neda is a problem. It is similar to other Paleozoic sedimentary iron deposits in the eastern United States. The Clinton iron ores of Silurian age extend from Alabama to New York, and the Wabana iron deposits of Newfoundland

Figure 5-28: Lens-shaped mass of Neda iron ore (dark layer sloping down to the right) overlain by massive Mayville Dolomite of Silurian age. North of Neda, Wisconsin.

are also of Silurian age. The Neda is overlain unconformably by the Silurian Mayville Dolomite, and some geologists have suggested that the Neda also is Silurian.

In eastern and northern Iowa there is a well-developed erosion surface at the top of the Maquoketa. In Northern Michigan the Maquoketa is believed to be gradational into the overlying Silurian rocks without a break. At Neda the Mayville Dolomite lies unconformably on the Neda.

The Neda is composed dominantly of chemically precipitated iron and contains virtually no detrital materials. Furthermore, it is directly overlain by a carbonate, also devoid of clastic material, that presumably formed in deeper water, or at least offshore from any sediment source.

I suggest that the erosional surface at the top of the Maquoketa on which the Neda iron deposits occur was developed by submarine erosion where the Maquoketa Shale was elevated to near sea level. Perhaps small islands developed during the erosion. Reworking of the top of the Maquoketa and chemical addition of iron may have produced iron-silicate (chamosite) oolites similar to those of most other oolitic iron deposits. The iron presumably came from the sea water. The oolites formed in the shallow, agitated waters and subsequently were converted to iron oxides. The reworked upper part of the Neda suggests that deposition of the iron ended while the deposit was still in shallow water. Some parts of the area may have been elevated above sea level and may have been oxidized to iron oxides relatively shortly after deposition. When these islands were again submerged, the Mayville Dolomite was deposited on top of the Neda.

THE MICHIGAN BASIN

During the early and middle Silurian an extensive blanket of limestones was deposited from New York State west at least as far as Wisconsin. Within this area of carbonate deposition, however, some localities subsided much more rapidly than others. One of the areas of subsidence was located under what is now lower Michigan. Indeed, the development of the Michigan Basin is the dominant feature developed in the Great Lakes region during the Silurian.

During the Cambrian and Ordovician periods one rather elongate basin extended from Missouri northeastward through Illinois and lower Michigan. This basin was bounded on the northwest by the Wisconsin Arch and on the southeast by the Cincinnati Arch. During the middle Silurian the Kankakee Arch developed across northeastern Illinois, forming two separate basins (Figure 5–29). Although it did not form a land

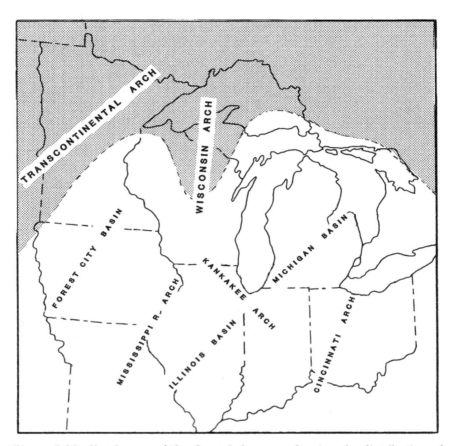

Figure 5-29: Sketch map of the Great Lakes area showing the distribution of basins and arches during Silurian time. Note that the Kankakee Arch restricted circulation to form the Michigan Basin.

barrier, it greatly restricted circulation within the Michigan Basin. The rate of subsidence within the Michigan Basin increased markedly, and a series of coral reefs developed along the Kankakee Arch and in the shallow waters along the western and southern margins of the basin. Some of these reefs can be seen today in the large limestone quarry at Thornton, Illinois, on the south side of Chicago, and at Racine, Wisconsin. Smaller reef mounds (bioherms) and extensive shoals can be seen in some of the quarries in Fond du Lac, Wisconsin, area. The fossil corals are especially well preserved in Door County, Wisconsin.

These reefs are among the first examples of <u>coral</u> reefs in the geologic record. Organic reefs are formed from lime-secreting organisms such as algae, coral, and other organisms. Earlier reefs were constructed mainly by lime-secreting algae. Assuming that the Silurian reefs formed in an environment similar to modern reefs, we can infer something about the Great Lakes area during this time. All modern reefs grow on a shallow bottom, no deeper than the depth of light penetration (generally about 200 feet). Most modern reefs extend up almost to the surface and may be partly exposed at low tide (Figures 5–30 and 5–31). Furthermore, coral reefs are restricted to tropical regions where water temperatures are consistently above 77°F. Thus, the presence of extensive reefs around the Michigan Basin during the Silurian suggests a shallow tropical or subtropical environment. Well-preserved fossils are present in most of these ancient reefs. Outward from the reefs the limy muds accumulated on the floor of the vast shallow seas, generally producing thinly bedded dolomite that contains few fossils.

Figure 5-30: Coral reef largely exposed at low tide. Green Island, Great Barrier Reef, Australia.

Figure 5-31: A modern coral reef showing some of the varieties of coral, sponges, starfish, etc. that make up the reef. Green Island, Great Barrier, Australia.

New discoveries of significant aspects of the past history of the earth come to light at unexpected times and places. In the late 1980s, a major discovery of fossils of soft-bodied animals that lived in the Lake Superior region during the Silurian was made in a dolomite quarry in Waukesha, Wisconsin. Organisms without hard parts are rarely preserved in rocks, and, therefore, little is known about the past history of these types of organisms. A special set of conditions must have occurred on the sea floor from which the dolomite in the quarry in Waukesha formed. The fossils and enclosing rocks unearthed in the quarry have been carefully studied to learn as much as possible from this rare discovery. Figure 5–32 shows several of the rare fossils from the site.

It appears, then, that a subsiding circular basin was present in lower Michigan surrounded by shallow waters. At that time the Great Lakes area was near the equator, and as a result, there was extensive evaporation of sea water. Normal salt water was constantly added to the Michi-

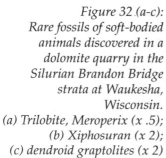

Figure 32 (a-c):
Rare fossils of soft-bodied
animals discovered in a
dolomite quarry in the
Silurian Brandon Bridge
strata at Waukesha,
Wisconsin.
(a) Trilobite, Meroperix (x .5);
(b) Xiphosuran (x 2);
(c) dendroid graptolites (x 2)

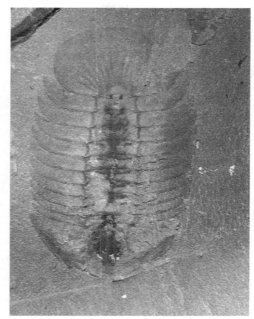

A

B

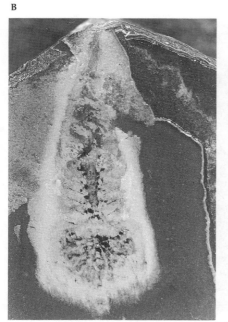

C

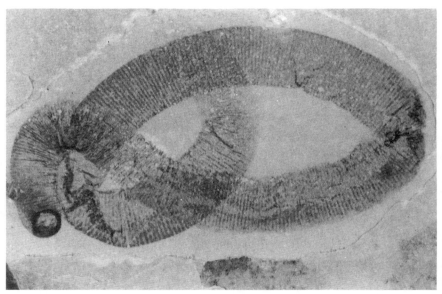

D

E

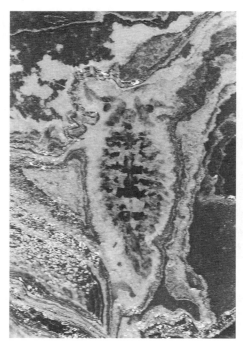

Figure 5-32 (d and e):
Rare fossils of soft-bodied animals
discovered in a dolomite quarry in
the Silurian Brandon Bridge strata
at Waukesha, Wisconsin.
(d) leech (x 1.5);
(e) remipede crustacean (x 2).
(All photos courtesy of Donald
Mikulic.)

gan Basin through shallow passages in the reefs (Figure 5–33). Waters in the basin became progressively saltier as surface evaporation continued year after year. Since the higher salt concentration caused the water to become heavier, the highly saline water settled to the bottom of the basin rather than mixing with the inflowing fresher waters from the surrounding seas. The conditions were roughly analogous to the present-day Mediterranean Sea where water from the Atlantic flows in over the rather shallow restriction at the Straits of Gibraltar. The arid climate in

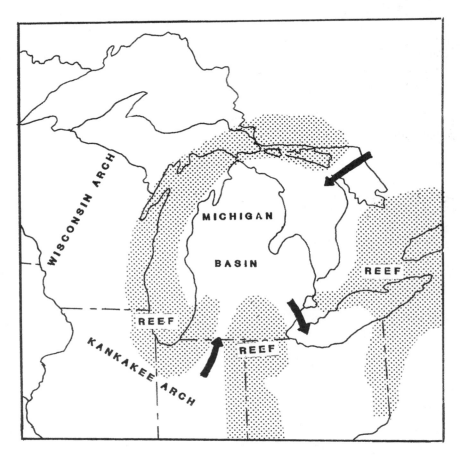

Figure 5-33: Paleogeography of the Great Lakes regions during the Silurian when extensive evaporites were deposited. Reefs or shallow water carbonate banks isolate the Michigan Evaporite Basin from the open sea, restricting inflow of normal sea water.

the region evaporates the sea water and concentrates the salt. The heavier, highly saline water sinks to the bottom and cannot escape through the Straits of Gibraltar and therefore tends to accumulate. In this way the salt concentration in the Michigan Basin was built up until gypsum ($CaSO_4 \cdot 2H_2O$), anhydrite ($CaSO_4$), and finally rock salt (NaCl) were chemically precipitated on the underlying carbonates. An aggregate thickness of 2,000 feet of gypsum and salt accumulated in the basin, with one bed of salt nearly 500 feet thick. It would take a column of sea water nearly 600 miles deep to form a layer of salt 2,000 feet thick. Great thicknesses of anhydrite and gypsum are also present. The deposition of this immense volume of salt took perhaps 15–20 million years and ended about 390 million years ago. The Michigan Basin is one of the greatest areas of rock salt accumulation in the world, and these sediments have been the basis of major chemical and plasterboard industries in Michigan. (For more information on the evaporites of the Michigan Basin, refer to Dorr and Eschman for an excellent summary). (See Figure 5–33.)

The thick sequence of Silurian dolomite that surrounds, and dips gently under, the Michigan Basin is very resistant to erosion. Therefore, it tends to form a prominent topographic feature and many outcrops. The eroded edge of these rocks forms an escarpment that can be traced almost continuously along the eastern part of Wisconsin, the Upper Peninsula of Michigan, and on east to New York State where Niagara Falls is formed by waters flowing off the "Niagaran" Dolomite onto the softer underlying shales. This escarpment is generally referred to as the Niagara Escarpment.

The extensive development of offshore carbonate rocks and an absence of sandstones and shales suggests that no landmass was present in the Great Lakes area, and therefore the Silurian seas must have completely covered the Wisconsin Arch.

With the deposition of the late Silurian evaporites in the Michigan Basin, the midcontinent was uplifted, and once again the seas withdrew from the Great Lakes area. The Michigan Basin remained as a small landlocked sea. Erosion during this major regression resulted in practically all of the Silurian and some of the Ordovician sediments being removed in Iowa, southern Minnesota, and probably much of Wisconsin.

When the seas returned again during middle Devonian time about 350 million years ago, they deposited sediments on lower Devonian rocks in the Michigan Basin, on Silurian rocks in eastern Wisconsin, and on Ordovician rocks in western Wisconsin and Iowa. A wide variety of Devonian sediments were deposited in Michigan, including sandstones, shales, limestones, and evaporites. In Illinois, Wisconsin, Minnesota, and Iowa, the Devonian rocks are dominantly limestones and dolomites, suggesting that virtually the entire region was covered by the Devonian seas.

The middle Devonian sediments are largely offshore limestones with excellent development of coral reefs in a number of places such as at Alpena in the northern Lower Peninsula of Michigan and in Iowa. The upper Devonian in Michigan and Wisconsin is characterized by deposition of black shales (the Antrim shale in Michigan and "Kenwood Formation" in Wisconsin) that thicken to the east. These muddy sediments were derived from erosion of an uplift in the northern Appalachian region in the New England states known as the Acadian Mountains, precursors of the present Appalachian Mountain range.

Black muds deposited in the Great Lakes region during early Mississippian time had their source in the eroding Acadian Mountains in the Appalachian region. This shale and some sandstone accumulated to thicknesses totaling nearly 3,000 feet in the Michigan Basin. Farther west, in Iowa, Mississippian sedimentary rocks are mainly limestone. Again, the lack of sandstones or other nearshore sediments suggests that the early Mississippian seas covered virtually all of the Great Lakes region and that the present lack of the rocks on the Wisconsin Arch is due to subsequent erosion.

During middle and late Mississippian time, there was another upwarping of the midcontinent region with the withdrawal of the sea, first from the higher lands of the major arches and domes, including the Wisconsin Arch. This was followed by a final retreat of the Paleozoic seas from the entire midcontinent during the Pennsylvanian, approximately 260 million years ago.

The thick accumulation of late Devonian and Mississippian shales on the resistant Silurian dolomites around the western, northern, and eastern margins of the Michigan Basin was very important in determining future topographic features in the area. As was mentioned earlier, the resistant dolomites form a bedrock high, almost completely encircling the basin. Erosion of the softer shales by streams and later by glaciers resulted in the formation of Lake Michigan and Lake Huron. Thus the sites of these two lakes were predestined by events that occurred more than 300 million years ago. (Remember that the location and shape of Lake Superior was determined by events in Keweenawan time, some 1,000-1,200 million years ago.)

This concludes the long and restless chapter of the Paleozoic history of the Great Lakes region. The era, lasting nearly 250 million years, saw the seas advance over the area and withdraw at least ten times over a period of some 200 million years. The cause for these repeated oscillations of sea level and the development of a series of basins and domes on the continent has remained largely a mystery. While we have been able to decipher what has happened and where, we do not yet fully understand why it happened. Nor do we understand why these fluctuations in sea level largely ended in the Great Lakes area at the close of the Paleozoic era.

▲ ECONOMIC IMPORTANCE OF PALEOZOIC ROCKS ▲

The wide variety of Paleozoic sedimentary rocks has provided the raw materials for a number of industries, both large and small, in the Great Lakes area. This brief discussion mentions a few of these rock types and is presented to show how events that occurred hundreds of millions of years ago influence our lives today.

SANDSTONES

Recall that there were five layers of sandstone deposited during the Cambrian and Ordovician transgressions of the sea. The sandstones are generally very porous rocks with pores large enough to permit water to flow through readily. These various sandstone layers are rocks from which water can readily be extracted in relatively large quantities. They provide the source of water for many municipal water supplies and innumerable private wells, including irrigation wells in some places.

The sandstones are also used extensively as a source of sand for making molds for metal casting, for glass making, and for fill and ice control on roads, as well as for the all-important sandboxes. Because the sandstones were reworked during several advances of the sea, they are very clean, well-sorted deposits. Many of them are only poorly cemented so that they can be quarried and used without crushing.

In some areas the sandstones are thoroughly cemented, very hard rocks. The layering might be emphasized by yellow-brown iron oxide cement producing an attractive pattern in the rocks. Some of these rocks are quarried and used for building stones.

SHALE

Shale does not form bold outcrops in the Great Lakes region. Because of the extremely fine-grain size of shale, the pores between grains are also tiny. As a result water does not flow readily through shale, and shales, therefore, act as barriers to movement of underground water.

Shale is quarried at several places in the Great Lakes area and used in the manufacture of bricks and tiles. Baking (firing) of the clay converts it into the extremely resistant bricks and tile. Brickworks can be seen at Rockford, Iowa (Devonian shale), Oakfield, Wisconsin (Ordovician shale), and Grand Ledge, Michigan (Pennsylvanian shale).

LIMESTONE

As mentioned earlier, limestone and dolomite are put to a wide variety of uses and locally provide the basis for industries. The use for which a particular deposit is suitable depends largely upon the nature of the rock. For example, practically all of the carbonate rocks were originally deposited as limestones by the accumulation of skeletons of lime-secreting organisms. Most of these limestones in the Great Lakes area were converted to dolomites by the circulation of magnesium-rich brines through the limestone. This may have occurred shortly after deposition or many tens of millions of years later, or some of it may have resulted from downward percolation of waters during chemical weathering and erosion.

Limestone is used in the manufacture of Portland cement, which is produced by burning and grinding a mixture of clay (or shale) and limestone. Dolomite cannot be used. The chemical reaction that occurs when cement hardens involves the formation of calcium-aluminum minerals, and the magnesium in dolomite results in an inferior product. Limestones may also be used for building stone or crushed to form aggregate for concrete, road metal, or agricultural "lime."

Dolomite is put to the same uses as limestone, except that it cannot be used to make Portland cement or mortar. Many local industries have developed around limestone and dolomite quarry operations (Figure 5–34).

Since limestone and dolomite are rather brittle, they tend to be very fractured near the surface. Generally the rocks are rather impervious to the downward movement of water and groundwater tends to be channeled into the cracks and crevices. Because the rocks are relatively soluble in groundwater (dissolved carbonates are what make water "hard"), the

Figure 5-34: Dolomite quarry south of Fond du Lac, Wisconsin. The thinly bedded units are quarried and cut into blocks for building stone while the more massive units are crushed for aggregate for making concrete and for agricultural lime.

flowing of water along the channelways dissolves caverns and caves in rocks. In carbonate rocks, groundwater may actually flow in underground rivers through the dissolved caverns. In places these caves and caverns may be the basis of tourist business (Figure 5–34). In many areas with carbonate rocks near the surface, serious problems of groundwater pollution occur because of the underground streams. Instead of the waters percolating slowly downward through a porous rock (e.g., sandstone) and being purified, the rapid downward movement along cracks prevents natural purification of the water before it joins the groundwaters of the underground streams. Several areas in the Lake Superior region have encountered groundwater problems because of the carbonate bedrock in the area.

LEAD AND ZINC

The upper Mississippi valley lead-zinc district covers an area of about 4,000 square miles in southwestern Wisconsin and adjacent parts of Illinois and Iowa (Figure 5–35). The district has been a major producer of lead and zinc since its discovery by the early French explorer Nicholas Perrot in the late seventeenth century. Early mining for lead was carried on by Indians using primitive mining methods taught them by the French. Julien Dubuque established a smelter for lead in 1788 at what is now Dubuque, Iowa. His operations ceased in 1810, and the area reverted to "Indian Territory." With the influx of American settlers in the 1820s, lead production from the area greatly increased, and by 1840 the district was the major lead producer in the United States, a position it maintained until about 1860.

Prior to 1860, zinc was not recovered in the mining operations, but technological advances by 1860 made the recovery of zinc feasible, and the district has been primarily a zinc producer since. Minor amounts of copper and barite have also been recovered.

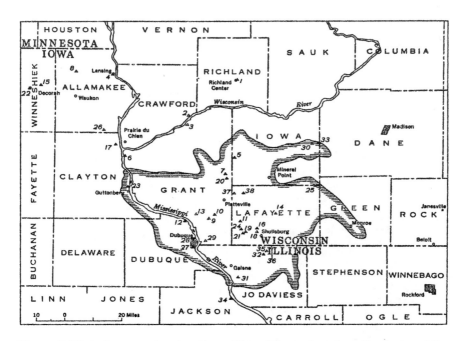

Figure 5-35: Index map showing the outline of the main mineralized area of the lead-zinc district in southwestern Wisconsin and adjacent Iowa and Illinois. (From Heyl and others, 1959.)

Figure 5-36: Three-inch calcite crystal surrounded by sphalerite crystals with a coating of fine grained marcasite. Shullsburg mine, Shullsburg, Wisconsin. Photo by David DeBruin.

Figure 5-37: Five-inch tall "thumb" of iridescent marcasite blades from the Blackstone Mine, Shullsburg, Wisconsin. Photo by David DeBruin.

Lead-zinc ore consists of two basic types of minerals: *primary* minerals formed by the rising ore-bearing solutions, and *secondary* minerals formed by chemical alteration of the primary minerals when they were subjected to nearsurface weathering. The primary minerals are sphalerite (ZnS) called *blackjack* by the miners, galena (PbS), chalcopyrite ($CuFeS_2$), pyrite (FeS_2), marcasite (FeS_2), and barite ($BaSO_4$). Secondary minerals include smithsonite ($ZnCO_3$) called *dry-bone* by the miners, ochre (iron oxides), some cerussite ($PbCO_3$) and anglesite ($PbSO_4$). Minor amounts of azurite and malachite (hydrous copper carbonates) and several other minerals are present. The change from primary to secondary minerals is due to the breakdown of the sulfide minerals through oxidation of the sulfur in the weathering zone above the groundwater table.

The mineral deposits occur as cavity fillings in faults, joints and solution openings (Figures 5–36 and 5–37), and as bedding replacements. All deposits are structurally controlled and genetically related to an intricate system of folds, faults, and joints. The ore bodies are primarily in the lower part of the Galena Dolomite, the Decorah Formation, and the upper part of the Platteville Limestone of middle Ordovician age (Figure 5–38). Thus, over the district as a whole the deposits have a very restricted stratigraphic range of less than 200 feet. However, individual

Figure 5-38: Entrance to a zinc-lead mine near Shullsburg, Wisconsin. Because the rocks are nearly flat-lying, the vehicles can be driven into the mines.

ore bodies have crosscutting relations with the enclosing rocks. In map view the deposits are linear features, much longer than they are wide. In cross section the ore bodies have a distinctive shape, as shown in Figure 5–39 with different minerals in different parts of the structure. The "crevice" ore bodies are predominantly galena, whereas the "pitches," "flats," and "core ground" contain some galena, but are much richer in sphalerite. Copper (chalcopyrite) is found with the sphalerite in the "pitch and flat" type deposits.

Many theories have been proposed for the origin of the primary minerals in the deposits, including hydrothermal solutions rising from some unknown granitic intrusion at depth, downward percolating groundwaters, laterally moving groundwaters, and combinations of these. The deposits lie on the eastern flank of Forest City Basin near the crest of the Wisconsin Arch (Figure 5–7). While minor lead and zinc mineralization are present in rocks below the St. Peter Sandstone, commercial mineralization is restricted to the Platteville and Galena formations along fractured and folded zones immediately above the St. Peter. It should be noted that minor sphalerite and galena mineralization are present in the lower Paleozoic carbonate rocks throughout much of the Great Lakes area, suggesting a widespread source of lead and zinc in the rocks of that age.

Recent studies of the highly saline pore waters (brines) that are forced out of sedimentary basins by compaction and the flow of underground waters provide tantalizing ideas on the origins of the zinc and lead ores in the upper Mississippi valley. These brines can be relatively warm and contain considerable dissolved metal ions. Studies of fluid inclusions in the minerals in the ore bodies show that they formed at temperatures between 75 and 121 degrees centigrade.

The St. Peter Sandstone is very permeable and would provide an excellent channelway for solutions moving upward and out of the Forest City Basin, which lies just west of the district. The flow would be confined by the more impervious shaly base of the Platteville Dolomite (the Glenwood Formation). When these solutions encountered fractures in the overlying rocks, they would rise upward toward the surface, depositing their dissolved minerals as they cooled and chemically reacted with the surrounding carbonate rocks. These relationships are shown diagrammatically in Figure 5–40. Whether the zinc, lead, and copper were contained in the muds originally deposited in the basin or whether they were derived in part by the leaching from underlying Keweenawan basalts of the Midcontinent Gravity High by deeply circulating basin waters is not known. The presence of this and other lead-zinc districts on the flanks of sedimentary basins suggests that there may

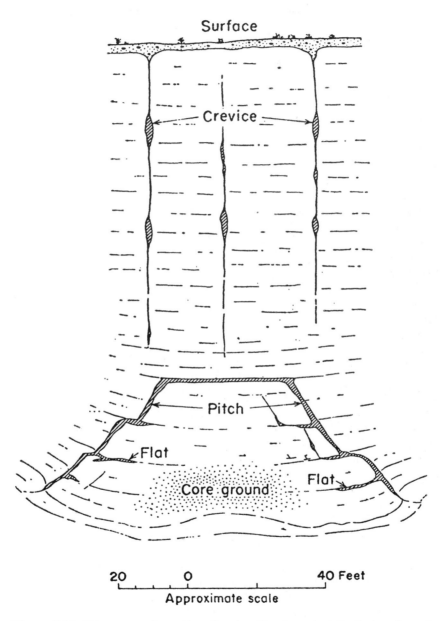

Figure 5-39: Diagrammatic section showing the characteristic forms of crevice and "pitch and flat" ore deposits. (From Flint and Brown, 1956.)

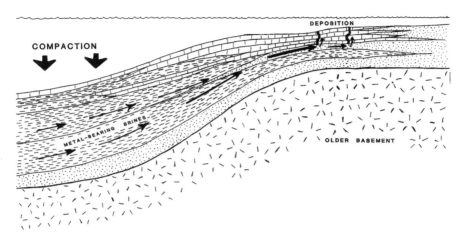

Figure 5-40: Diagram showing possible origin of the lead-zinc deposits. Compaction of shales within the basin expel heated briny fluids that dissolve lead, zinc, iron, and copper from the shale. The metal-bearing fluids move laterally out of the basin. Deposition occurs at relatively shallow depths where solutions encounter fractures in overlying carbonate rocks.

be a genetic relationship between them. For an excellent comprehensive review of the zinc-lead district, refer to United States Geological Survey Professional Paper 309, "The Geology of the Upper Mississippi Valley Zinc-Lead District," by Allen V. Heyl, Jr., et al., 1959, and Economic Geology Monograph 3, "Genesis of Lead-Zinc-Barite-Fluorite Deposits," edited by J. S. Brown, 1967.

IRON ORE

Several occurrences of iron ore in Paleozoic rocks have been the basis for local mining operations. The oolitic iron ores in the late Ordovician Neda Formation in Dodge County in eastern Wisconsin have already been mentioned. The iron ore at Neda, Wisconsin, was discovered in 1845, and mining operations commenced shortly thereafter, including construction of a smelter at Mayville, Wisconsin, in 1849. Mining operations continued more or less continuously until 1928. Mining ceased because the ore was not as high a quality as that from the Precambrian iron formations; it contained significantly higher amounts of phosphorous and sulfur, causing the finished iron to be more brittle. Furthermore, the ore bodies were not of large size, and therefore could not compete with the larger, open-pit ore bodies of the iron ranges farther north, which could be more highly mechanized.

Iron ores in Paleozoic rocks also occur in Filmore, Olmsted, and Mower counties in southeastern Minnesota. Mining in this area continued from 1942 to 1968 and produced over 8 million tons of iron ore. These ores were developed from the weathering of siderite-rich layers in the middle Devonian Cedar Valley Formation. They are believed to have formed during Tertiary weathering. Thus, these ores are quite different in nature and origin from the Neda deposits.

SUGGESTED ADDITIONAL READINGS

Austin, G. S., 1972, Paleozoic lithostratigraphy of southeastern Minnesota, in Geology of Minnesota: A Centennial Volume, P. K. Sims and G. B. Morey, editors., Minnesota Geological Survey.

Brown, J. S., editor, 1967, Genesis of Lead-Zinc-Barite-Fluorite Deposits, Economic Geology Monograph 3.

Dorr, J. A., Jr., and Eschman, D. F., 1970, Geology of Michigan, University of Michigan Press, Ann Arbor.

Heyl, A. V., Jr., et al., 1959, The geology of the Upper Mississippi Valley zinc-lead district, U.S. Geological Survey Professional Paper 309.

Ojakangas, R. W., and Matsch, C. L., 1982, Minnesota's Geology, University of Minnesota Press, Minneapolis.

Ostrom, M. E., 1967, Paleozoic stratigraphic nomenclature for Wisconsin, Wisconsin Geological and Natural History Survey Information Circular 8.

Paull, R. K., and Paull, R. A., 1977, Geology of Wisconsin and Upper Michigan, Including Parts of Adjacent States, Kendall/Hunt Publishing Company, Dubuque, Iowa.

Paull, R. K., and Paull, R. A., 1980, <u>Field Guide, Wisconsin and Upper Michigan</u> (Kendall/Hunt Geology Field Guide Series), Kendall/Hunt Publishing Company, Dubuque, Iowa.

Webers, G. F., 1972, Paleoecology of the Cambrian and Ordovician Strata of Minnesota, in <u>Geology of Minnesota: A Centennial Volume</u>, P. K. Sims and G. B. Morey, editors, Minnesota Geological Survey.

6

THE
PLEISTOCENE

Continental ice sheet showing the gently sloping front of the ice and meltwater streams flowing out of the terminus. The southwest margin of the Barnes Ice Cap, Baffin Island, N.W.T., Canada. This is a remnant of the Pleistocene Ice Sheet. (Photo by Robert Baker)

he final chapter of the geologic history of the Lake Superior region was different from all the preceding events, and it too left a major imprint on the area. Several times during the Pleistocene "ice age," huge masses of glacial ice several thousand feet thick (some geologists estimate up to 10,000 feet) covered most of the northern half of North America. The glaciers removed most of the weathered rock that had been accumulating north of the Great Lakes since the withdrawal of the Paleozoic seas some 270 million years earlier. Much of this debris was carried southward, and when the ice melted, was deposited in lower Michigan, Illinois, Wisconsin, Iowa, and southern Minnesota. The combination of glacial erosion and deposition greatly altered the landscape, filling some valleys, deepening others and in general modifying the previous drainage patterns. The Great Lakes were formed by glacial erosion, as were many other lakes. Thousands of smaller lakes were formed largely by deposition of glacial materials. Many distinctive landforms and deposits were produced by glacial action. Studies of these landforms and deposits enable us to interpret the direction of ice movement, its thickness, where it came from, where it melted, and where all the water from the melting ice went. The following brief picture of the ice age, though not intended as a comprehensive review of Pleistocene geology, should nonetheless give a general understanding of this interesting part of our geological heritage.

▲ BEFORE THE ICE ▲

Much of the Lake Superior region was subjected to erosion for at least 250 million years after the final withdrawal of the Paleozoic seas. In Minnesota, however, the presence of Cretaceous sediments some 70–100 million years old indicates that much of that state was covered by the sea at least one more time. During this immense span of time a number of well-developed river systems were established and drained the area. Available evidence suggests that removal of the relatively soft Paleozoic sediments had reduced the area to a gently rolling plain. The surface of the plain was probably the resistant dolomite layers of lower Paleozoic age. Since these dolomites dip gently off the Wisconsin Arch to the east, south, and west, the plain probably did the same. After the streams cut through the dolomite into the underlying sandstone layer, continued erosion broadened the valleys with a "floor" on the next lower resistant layer or on the Precambrian basement. Thus, the erosion surface was a series of gently sloping surfaces on each successive dolomite layer, similar to the shingles on a roof. The eroded edge of each dolomite layer produced a steplike rise (called a *cuesta*) above the underlying unit (Figure 6–1). A number of sandstone buttes and mesas capped with dolomite undoubtedly were present in front of each cuesta. Remnants of this topography are still present in southwestern Wisconsin.

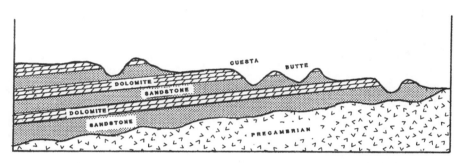

Figure 6-1: Sketch of the cross section of the eroded Paleozoic rocks showing the resistant dolomites and soft sandstone layers that produce the distinctive topography in southern Wisconsin.

The edges of the dolomite units formed escarpments that extended for hundreds of miles. For example, the Niagara Escarpment extends along most of eastern Wisconsin, and similar escarpments are present in southern and western Wisconsin. Some of these escarpments and associated lowlands were to be important in controlling the movement of ice during glaciation.

The exposed Precambrian Shield in the northern part of the region presented a different landscape. Two broad high areas, one in northern Wisconsin–Michigan and one in northern Minnesota, were separated by a lowland in which is now Lake Superior. Much of the highland was probably quite flat except for prominent hills such as Rib Mountain, the Barron Hills, ridges of Keweenawan basalts along the south edge of the Superior lowland, and the highland formed by the Duluth Gabbro complex in northeastern Minnesota. The flat topography in central Wisconsin is probably typical of much of the area.

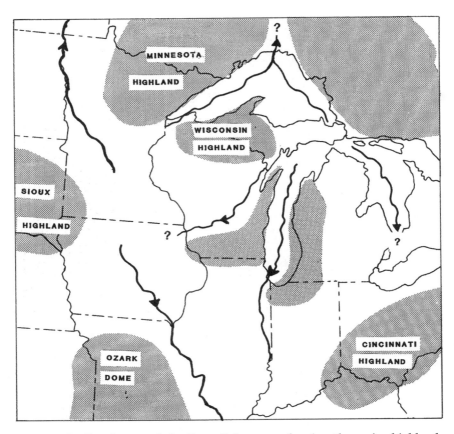

Figure 6-2: Sketch map of the Great Lakes area showing the major highlands and the probable pre-glacial stream valleys.

Surrounding these broad uplands were several prominent river valleys (Figure 6–2). On the west a major bedrock valley that deepens to the north extends along the Minnesota–Dakota border. This ancestral Red River valley was evidently a major north-flowing river along the west side of the "Minnesota Upland."

Another major stream valley was developed in the soft Keweenawan sediments in the Lake Superior basin. This stream also appears to have flowed to the north. On the south the Minnesota ancestral Mississippi River had its headwaters in north central Iowa. A bedrock high (or divide) separates this ancient valley from the ancestral Red River valley. The ancestral Wisconsin River (named the Marquette River by Stewart,

Figure 6-3: Smooth, grooved bedrock ridge formed by glacial erosion removing the weathered material. Near Sudbury, Ontario.

1977) originated in northeastern Wisconsin and flowed southwest to join the preglacial Mississippi. It flowed through a long-established gorge in the Baraboo Quartzite just west of Portage and left the Baraboo range via the gorge now occupied by Devil's Lake. The preglacial Wisconsin River may have flowed from Sauk City to Prairie du Chien in its present course. Since the Missouri and Ohio Rivers were probably not tributary to the Mississippi in preglacial times, the Mississippi may have been considerably smaller than it is today.

A south-flowing stream valley also appears to have existed in the Lake Michigan basin in preglacial times. Therefore, the drainage pattern in the Lake Superior region appears to have been very different than it is today. The highlands and stream valleys were to play an important role in the movement of ice over the region during the Pleistocene Ice Age. Other river valleys probably also existed and may have influenced ice movement. Their recognition is uncertain, however, and difficult to establish due to the tremendous amount of erosion and deposition by the glaciers.

The long exposure to weathering had also produced a thick mantle of weathered rock (saprolite) similar to that shown in Figures 5–3 and 5–4. The thickness of this saprolite varied greatly from place to place and was controlled, in part, by the nature of the underlying rock. Most of the weathered rock was removed by glacial erosion in north-central North America. South of the glaciated parts of North America, however, much of this mantle of weathered material still remains.

The fossil record indicates that North America had a mild, moist climate for many millions of years prior to the Pleistocene. Throughout most of the Tertiary Period the climate was milder than at present. During this period a wide variety of plants and animals (especially mammals) evolved in central North America. The evolution of grasses during the Tertiary undoubtedly produced vast open prairies. Trees similar to modern species evolved and provided both deciduous and hardwood

Figure 6-4: Bedrock surface with grooves and sets of curved fractures formed by boulders frozen in the ice gouging the underlying rock. Redgranite, Wisconsin.

forests. There existed an abundance of animal life, with many of the animals markedly different from those now present. Horses, which evolved in North America during the Tertiary, were common. (Horses were <u>not</u> present in North America when Europeans first arrived. Thus, although they originated here, horses had emigrated to Eurasia before recorded history.) Mammoths, giant ground sloths, camels, ancestors of rhinoceros, and others roamed over much of the country. Carnivorous ancestors of dogs and cats, including the famed "saber-toothed tigers" were also common. Thus, the American heartland must have resembled the grassy regions of Africa, teeming with mammals. In fact, many of the animals were similar to those now native to Africa. Curiously, nearly all of these animals, so common before and during the ice age, became extinct or migrated out of North America before the end of the Pleistocene. Never before in geologic history had so many groups of animals become extinct in such a short period of time!

▲ DEVELOPMENT OF ▲ CONTINENTAL GLACIERS

Somewhat more than 3 million years ago the climate in North America became much cooler; the summers cooled sufficiently that all the snow that fell the previous winter did not melt. With a cooling of the climate a greater percentage of the annual precipitation probably also fell as snow. These changes were felt first in the more northerly latitudes of northern and central Canada, particularly in areas with considerable surface irregularities. Initially the snow probably remained only on the north slopes of hills, but each year the area covered by snow during the summer increased. This old snow developed a porous granular texture typical of late-winter snowbanks today. Geologists call this granular snow *firn*. After many years of accumulation the lower layers were compacted by the weight of the overlying snow and gradually recrystallized to form ice. With continued accumulation of snow the thickness of ice gradually increased. At some critical point the lower part of the pile was no longer able to support the weight of the overlying ice and it began to flow gradually down the slope due to recrystallization of the ice crystals. This ice that flows under its own weight marks the development of a glacier. The ice flowed off the higher lands into valleys, where it met and coalesced with the ice from neighboring high lands. This union formed more extensive areas of ice that gradually deepened, eventually burying the hills on which the ice originally accumulated. Continued accumulation of ice caused it to spread out from the original centers of accumulation.

Mapping of glacial geology in North America has shown that there were several main centers of accumulation of ice that affected the Lake Superior region: the Keewatin Center just west of Hudson Bay, the Labrador Center east of Hudson Bay, and possibly the Patrician Center south of Hudson Bay. As the ice accumulated in these centers it spread out in all directions. Eventually the ice from the centers merged and continued to spread southward over eastern North America. It should not be assumed, however, that the ice spread out equally from all three centers, or that all three were major centers of ice accumulation at the same time. During the Pleistocene as much as 30 percent of the land surface of the earth was covered by glaciers, compared with about 10 percent today.

Near the margins of a glacier more snow and ice melt each year than accumulate. Farther up on the glacier the reverse is true. There, accumulation of snow exceeds melting. Thus, there is a balance between accumulation of ice upstream and melting downstream. If total accumulation is greater than total melting, the front of the ice advances.

If melting and accumulation are the same, the ice front remains stationary. Because ice moves slowly, it is doubtful that short-term variations in accumulation and melting would be noticeable. However, prolonged changes in the rate of accumulation or melting would produce changes in the position of the ice front. Thus, the formation of the glaciers that advanced over much of North America was the result of a colder, and perhaps wetter climate during the Pleistocene. Similarly, the retreat of the glaciers by melting was the result of a warmer and perhaps drier climate. Within this general trend, however, there were numerous major advances and retreats of continental glaciers. Older geological literature refers to four advances (stages) of glaciation. From oldest to youngest they are the Nebraskan, Kansan, Illinoian, and Wisconsinan. Recent studies indicate that this picture is too simple, and that there were more than four advances, possibly ten or more, however, the number of major advances is not yet known. The glaciers advanced approximately in the same areas with each successive glaciation, and therefore tended to obliterate and erode the evidence for earlier advances. Although it is likely that glaciers advanced into the Lake Superior region a number of times, evidence of the last glaciation is best preserved, and we are left largely to speculate on earlier advances. The sequence of glacial events is covered later in this section.

The ice reached thicknesses as great as 10,000 feet in the main centers of accumulation, although large areas were probably much thinner, on the order of 1,000–2,000 feet. It is estimated that up to 8 percent of all the earth's water was tied up in glacial ice during the Pleistocene, compared with about 3 percent today. This had two major consequences:

1. It lowered sea level several hundred feet, exposing large areas of the sea floor along the present coastlines.
2. The weight of this water (ice) on the land surface depressed the crust locally as much as 2,000 feet from its normal position.

Removal of the ice by melting caused the sea level to rise and allowed the land surface to rise back to its normal level. The depression and *rebound* of the earth's surface occurred during each advance and retreat of the continental glaciers. The adjustment (or rebound) of the earth's surface is a relatively slow process and is still in progress from the last melting of glaciers from the Lake Superior region. The effects of depression and rebound strongly influenced the drainage of the Great Lakes and are discussed later.

The southward-flowing ice moved inexorably over the land surface, destroying everything in its path. The cooling of the climate associated with glaciation caused a gradual southward migration of vegetation zones and animals as glaciers advanced. For example, tundra vegetation probably extended several hundred miles in front of the ice, with a spruce forest beyond that, and a mixed deciduous forest still farther from the ice front. Animals inhabiting these various environments therefore also lived at varying distances from the ice front. The front of the glacier may have advanced only a few tens or hundreds of feet a year. Considerable ice probably melted near the margins of the glacier each summer, however, the entire area was snow covered during the winter. When warm, moisture-laden south winds blew up onto the several-thousand-foot-high ice sheet, cooling resulted in precipitation of the moisture, adding snow to a large area of the glacier. In this way, the ice sheet may have grown significantly by additions of snow near its margins.

▲ GLACIAL EROSION ▲
▲ AND TRANSPORT ▲

The movement of the immense ice sheets modified the landscape in several ways. In the general region of ice accumulation, glacial erosion removed practically all the weathered material as well as most of the

Figure 6-5: Cross section of a glacier showing folded and thrust faulted layers carrying debris to the top of the glacier. Wrangell Mountains, Alaska. Note the man in the upper right hand part of the photo.

fractured bedrock. The thickness of material removed probably ranged from a few feet to several hundred feet, depending on how fractured the rock was and how susceptible it was to erosion. This material became frozen into the ice and was transported by the advancing glacier. To a limited extent the ice also abraded solid bedrock, but it is unlikely that any great thickness of solid rock was removed. The rasping section of material frozen into the bottom of the glacier smoothed the rough edges and polished and scratched the underlying bedrock as shown in Figures 6–3 and 6–4. The scratches and marks produced by rocks frozen into the bottom of glaciers is extremely useful for determining the direction of ice movement.

Easily eroded rocks such as shales and deeply weathered zones along faults tended to be excavated by the advancing ice producing elongate bedrock valleys or basins. Many of the lakes in Ontario, and the northern parts of Minnesota, Wisconsin, and Michigan owe their existence to this type of glacial erosion. Where the trend of the weak zones paralleled the direction of ice movement, the excavation was especially pronounced. In many instances in the Great Lakes area, major bedrock trends controlled the direction of ice movement. The abundance of relatively fresh bedrock at the surface in much of northern Michigan, Wisconsin, Minnesota, and Ontario attests to the ability of the ice to remove the weathered rock.

The materials picked up by the ice range in size from boulders more than 20 feet across to fine silt and clay. Much of the material was frozen into the ice at the bottom of the glacier, and was transported and deposited farther downstream. Figure 6–5 illustrates how rock debris can be carried to the top of the glacier along thrust faults and by folding. Once on top of the ice, or even well up into the glacier, the material might be carried long distances before being deposited. Boulders and smaller debris protect the ice from melting; boulders perch on ice pedestals where surrounding ice has melted, and dirty (debris laden) ice forms prominent ridges on the glacier. In this way the large boulders or

Figure 6-6:
Aerial photo of a
portion of the western
margin of the
Greenland Ice Cap,
showing a lobe of ice
flowing out from the
main body of ice.
Photo was taken
between Nuuk and
Sonderstrom.

"erratics" may have been transported for tens or hundreds of miles by the ice. For example, boulders of Keweenawan copper have been carried from Lake Superior to central Illinois, and large boulders of Precambrian igneous and metamorphic rock were carried hundreds of miles from their source.

When the advancing glaciers reached the Lake Superior region, the ice was diverted into the major stream valleys, where it advanced as great tongues or lobes similar to, but much larger than the lobe shown in Figure 6–6. One major lobe moved southward in the stream valley that is now Lake Michigan. Another moved in a more westerly direction in the valley that is now Lake Superior. A third major lobe moved southward

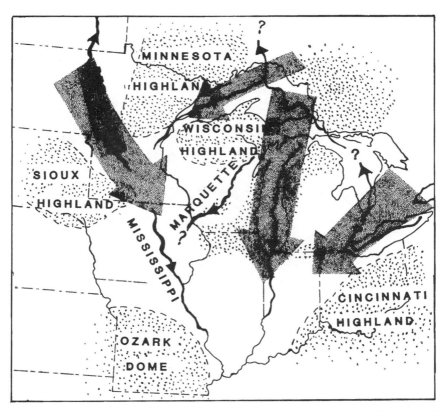

Figure 6-7: Sketch map of the Great Lakes area showing the general movement of ice lobes along pre-glacial valleys.

over western Minnesota and Iowa in what is now the Red River valley (Figure 6–7). Similar lobes carved the eastern Great Lakes. The ice did not advance in all of these valleys at the same time. Moreover, the timing of the various advances is still not well understood.

The channeling of ice coupled with the soft underlying bedrock resulted in much erosion in these valleys, deepening them hundreds of feet. Thus, Lake Superior is over 1,300 feet deep and Lake Michigan more than 900 feet deep. The eroded material was carried uphill out of the basins and deposited when the ice melted. These valleys controlled the major directions of ice movement in the upper Midwest.

Highlands bordering these major valleys also influenced the movement of ice. For example, the ice tended to move around the highlands of northern Minnesota and northern Wisconsin–Michigan. While the ice advanced to central and southern Illinois from the Lake Michigan Lobe and into southern Iowa in the Des Moines Lobe, it moved only to central Wisconsin between these large lobes. Thus, although the ice eventually covered northern Wisconsin, the highland clearly acted as a barrier to ice movement.

▲ GLACIAL DEPOSITION ▲

Deposition of the debris carried by glaciers is at least as important as erosion in modifying the landscape. When glaciers melt they deposit the debris carried by the ice, producing a variety of distinctive materials and landforms. Debris deposited directly by the melting ice consists of an unsorted, unlayered mixture of boulders, sand, silt, and clay called *till* (Figure 6–8). Till deposited from the bottom of the ice forms an extensive blanket of material ranging up to several hundred feet thick. It is characterized by a surface of gently rolling hills and is called *ground moraine*. Most of the upper Midwest north of the Missouri and Ohio Rivers is covered with ground moraine. Streams flowing over the ground moraine gradually erode the material and modify the topography. Thus, ground moraine from early glacial advances is typically thinner and has a more subdued topography than younger deposits.

Since till is deposited mainly near the front of the glacier, continued advance of the ice results in partial to complete erosion of earlier formed till. Distinctive elongated hills called *drumlins* are produced by partial erosion near the margin of the ice. A more detailed discussion of drumlins is presented later in this chapter.

Figure 6-8: Exposure of glacial till showing the unsorted nature of materials deposited directly by the ice.

When the climate warms to the point that the glacier melts at the same rate that it is flowing forward, the front of the glacier remains in the same position. This results in continued deposition of till along the front of the ice. In time a considerable thickness of till accumulates to form a prominent ridge of debris. These ridges are called *end moraines* and mark the farthest advance of the ice. End moraines extend in an almost unbroken line from the Atlantic Coast on Long Island to the Rocky Mountains (Figure 6–9). They form prominent ridges through much of Indiana, Michigan, Illinois, Wisconsin, Iowa, and Minnesota. The end moraine marking the farthest advance of the ice is called the *terminal moraine*. End moraines may also form by minor advances during a general retreat of glaciers. These are referred to as *recessional moraines*. End moraines are very useful in interpreting the glacial history of a region, and several are referred to later.

Literally thousands of cubic miles of water flowed off the front of melting glaciers, carrying immense quantities of glacial debris. These debris-laden streams deposited most of this material in front of the ice. Coarser cobbles, pebbles, and sand were deposited near the glaciers, but the silt and clay were carried hundreds of miles downstream. Thus, unlike the glaciers, meltwater streams were able to sort out the debris according to size. Furthermore, running water always deposits material in layers, so these deposits are both sorted and layered. Since they are carried out in front of the ice, they are referred to as *outwash.*

Commonly large, gently sloping "aprons" of outwash sand and gravel formed in front of the ice. The stream valleys were probably very broad, for during warm spells in the summer huge quantities of water would cover the valley bottom, preventing growth of much vegetation. During more temperate weather the valleys were an interconnected network of sediment-laden streams like that shown in Figure 6–10. Channels

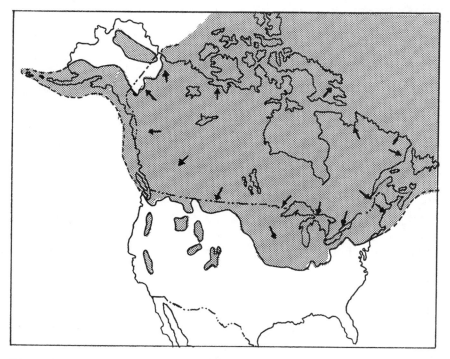

Figure 6-9: General locations of the boundaries of the Pleistocene ice sheet in North America and the terminal moraine that marks the maximum advance of the ice.

Figure 6-10: Typical "braided" glacial meltwater stream with innumerable shifting sand bars. During warm spells the entire mile-wide channel was awash with sediment-laden water. Nizina River, Alaska.

Figure 6-11: Cross-section of typical sand and gravel deposits formed by melt-waters in front of a glacier. Near Michigamme, Michigan.

constantly change due to deposition of gravel and sand bars along on part of a stream and erosion along another. A cross-section of outwash deposits reveals a complex pattern of channels of sand and gravel as shown in Figure 6–11.

The meltwater streams carried hundreds or thousands of cubic miles of silt and clay (and some sand) down the major meltwater channels, such as the Mississippi River and its tributaries. Much of this material was transported to the Gulf of Mexico where it was deposited as a major addition to the delta of the Mississippi River. However, significant amounts of the silt and clay were deposited during periods of flooding along the river channels. During lower water levels, these deposits were exposed and left to dry. Winds blowing over the broad Mississippi and Missouri Rivers' meltwater channels periodically picked up great clouds of silt and clay particles, carrying them downwind. The dust gradually settled, in part being held by grasses and other vegetation along the streams. The scene probably looked similar to that shown in Figure 6–12. The long-term result was the accumulation of a blanket of silt and clay (called *loess*) many feet thick extending almost the entire length of the Mississippi River. The blanket of loess thins in the northern tier of states,

Figure 6-12: Wind-blown silt in a glacial meltwater stream forming dense dust clouds covering many miles. Copper River at Chitina, Alaska.

Figure 6-13: Stream in an ice tunnel behind the author flowing out of the front of a glacier. Recent collapse of the roof produced the abundant ice. Nizina Glacier, Wrangell Mountains, Alaska. It is in such intraglacial streams that eskers form.

Figure 6-14: An esker exposed by melting of the ice at the front of the Barnes Ice Cap, Baffin Island, Canada. The gravel ridge is largely frozen, and parts of the ridge have been eroded by meltwater flowing off the glacier at the left. (Photo from Robert Baker.)

but it covers a large area. Loess forms an excellent soil, since many of the fragments are relatively unweathered and contain abundant plant nutrients. The soils of the famed "corn belt" are formed mainly on loess. Thus, the effects of glaciation are felt far from the ice itself.

Numerous streams flow on the surface of melting glaciers, and when they encounter a crevasse, they drop down to flow within or at the bottom of the ice. Ultimately, they emerge from a tunnel at the front of the ice (Figure 6–13). Sand and gravel is deposited by these streams, just as it is along surface streams. Thus, the bed of the stream could contain 10 to 50 feet of gravel, with walls of ice holding it in the channel. When the glacier melts, these stream deposits formed under the ice form winding gravel ridges called *eskers* (Figure 6–14) that often extend for miles across the land surface (Figures 6–15 and 6–16).

Where sediment-laden streams on top of the ice fall into a crevasse, much of the sand and gravel is deposited if the velocity of the water decreases. The water sometimes carves a more or less circular basin in the ice which, in time, will be filled with sediment. When the ice melts, these local accumulations of sand and gravel are "let down" on the underlying till and form hills we call *kames* (Figure 6–17). Kames and

Figure 6-15: Aerial photograph of an esker near Whitewater, Wisconsin, showing the serpentine course of the gravel ridge. (Photo by Jack Travis.)

Figure 6-16: Cross section of an esker in a gravel pit near Jump River, Wisconsin. Layering of the gravel is scarcely visible. Many eskers have been almost completely consumed as gravel resources.

Figure 6-17: Dome-shaped hill typical of many kames. Near Eden, Wisconsin.

eskers as well as outwash are excellent sources of sand and gravel, and have been widely used as such.

In places, large areas of stagnant ice were present near the retreating margin of the glacier. Much of the ice was covered with debris carried to the top of the glacier. Widening of crevasses by melting produced a very irregular surface on the ice. Meltwater streams flowing into crevasses formed numerous tunnels in and under the ice. Local collapse of the roof of these tunnels produced depressions, adding to the irregularity of the surface of the ice like that shown in Figure 6–18. Some depressions were

Figure 6-18: Irregular topography and lakes formed from stagnant ice at the end of a glacier. The glacier movement is from the left to the center of the photo. Barnard Glacier, Wrangell Mountains, Alaska.

filled with several hundred feet of debris while large blocks of ice remained nearby. When the ice finally melted, the areas occupied by ice blocks became depressions because little glacial debris had accumulated there. Because most of the debris has been transported by water, it is a form of outwash. Later melting of the buried ice forms depressions, so these deposits are called *pitted outwash*. They form by outwash being deposited on stagnant ice. Many of these depressions later become lakes or swamps. Figure 6–19 shows the hummocky, lake-dotted, pitted outwash

Figure 6-19: Hilly landscape with numerous lakes probably formed by melting of stagnant ice. Near Hayward, Wisconsin.

country of northern Wisconsin. Similar areas are present in northern Michigan and central Minnesota.

Many hypotheses have been advanced to explain the development of continental glaciers, and particularly of the ice sheets that covered north-central North America. Flint (1943) argued for a continuous mass of ice extending from the Rocky Mountains eastward into the Atlantic Ocean with a single main center of accumulation in the present site of Hudson Bay. He believed that all the glacial features were essentially contemporaneous. With the advent of ^{14}C dating of glacial deposits we now know that glacial events occurred at different times in different areas. For example, during the last glacial maximum, glacial advances in the eastern Great Lakes occurred earlier than those in the western Great Lakes and Great Plains regions. The recognition that the advances and retreats of the ice were different from one area to another argues against a single large center of accumulation. Early workers proposed a number of smaller, independent centers of ice accumulation east and west of Hudson Bay, and that ice moved out radially from these various centers and may, at times, have coalesced with ice from other centers. However, greater accumulation of ice in one center would have produced much greater flow of ice from that center during a particular period of time. This may, in fact, be one of the causes of the great ice lobes that advanced and retreated more or less independently over the Great Lakes area during the Pleistocene.

Recent evidence (Shilts, et al., 1979) strongly supports the concept of multiple centers advocated around the turn of the century, but largely abandoned following Flint's (1943) report.

The various lobes of the Pleistocene ice sheet, such as the Des Moines Lobe, the Superior Lobe, the Lake Michigan Lobe, can be thought of as large valley glaciers. They advanced along preglacial valleys, eroding them much deeper than the earlier streams had done. They differed from valley glaciers in mountains in that these valleys were very broad and had gently sloping sides, allowing the ice to spread out laterally from the valleys. Thus the ice in the Lake Superior Basin moved mainly to the west, but spread southward across the high land in northern Wisconsin. Similarly the ice from the Lake Michigan and Green Bay lobes moved mainly southward, but spread westward across eastern Wisconsin and Illinois.

▲ PLEISTOCENE ▲ STRATIGRAPHY

Stratigraphy is a basic principle used by geologists in deciphering the geologic history of a region. It involves the recognition of depositional units and their relationship to other units in the sequence. It also involves correlation of units and sequences from one area to another. Finally, stratigraphy involves the dating (or chronology) of events that produced the deposits. We must recognize and separate two different kinds of stratigraphic units. *Rock stratigraphic units* are deposits that have recognizable characteristics and boundaries, such as a particular till sheet or outwash deposit. Generally, they are deposits formed by a particular process or in a relatively uniform environment. However, since geological processes continue through time, these deposits have a different age from one place to another. *Time stratigraphic units* are those deposits formed during a given interval of time. Since a number of different processes occur simultaneously, the deposits formed during a given interval of time may differ markedly. For example, till may form beneath a glacier at the same time that outwash and loess are deposited by streams and wind in front of the ice, yet all represent a time stratigraphic sequence. Considerable confusion exists in the geologic literature because rock stratigraphic units and time stratigraphic units have been used interchangeably by some geologists.

The extreme local variability in environment during the Pleistocene makes it difficult to correlate events throughout the Lake Superior region. Lake deposits in one area formed at the same time as till or outwash in another area. Older deposits are often eroded or buried by later glacial events. Furthermore, deposits formed by the same process (for example, a till) can be virtually identical in widely separated areas, yet one might be thousands of years older. The best way to establish the time sequence is by dating the deposits using one or more of the radioactive elements, such as Carbon-14. These techniques are expensive and are not applicable to all deposits, however, so a great deal of judgment remains.

While we have a general understanding of the major events of the Pleistocene, the timing of events and correlation of units is still subject to much revision. Therefore, the following brief summary of Pleistocene stratigraphy is subject to change as new data become available. Indeed, recent studies throughout the Midwest indicate that the sequence of events is more complex than older literature suggests. However, since no new chronology of events has yet been proposed, the accepted sequence is presented as a frame of reference. The general sequence of events is based upon the recognition of major drift sheets separated by outwash and loess deposits and soil horizons.

The *Nebraskan* glacial stage is the oldest named glacial advance. It is named for deposits in Nebraska, but is also well preserved in northern Missouri and northeastern Kansas. Nebraskan deposits are best preserved west of the Mississippi River, showing that the maximum advance was in that area. The current best guess is that the Nebraskan advance occurred about 1,800,000 years ago.

The *Aftonian* interglacial stage was a major warm spell that resulted in the almost complete melting of the Nebraskan ice sheet. It is represented by loess deposits and an extensive soil horizon developed in Nebraskan drift. It may have lasted for many thousands of years.

The *Kansan* glacial stage represents another cold period that produced a major advance of the ice west of the Mississippi River. Kansan glacial deposits overlie Nebraskan drift and Aftonian soils in Kansas and Nebraska. The Kansan stage was the maximum advance of ice down the Great Plains. Both the Nebraskan and Kansan ice probably came from the Keewatin center. The Kansan advance probably occurred between about 900,000 and 600,000 years ago.

The *Yarmouthian* interglacial stage followed the Kansan glacial stage. The warm climate melted the Kansan glaciers and allowed the development of soils on the Kansan drift. The Yarmouthian lasted for thousands of years.

The *Illinoian* glacial stage was yet another major cooling of the climate, and resulted in ice sheets again covering large areas of the Midwest. Illinoian drift is best preserved in Illinois, with the maximum movement of ice from an eastern (Labrador) center. It represents the most southerly advance of ice east of the Mississippi River. The Illinoian stage lasted from about 400,000 to 300,000 years ago.

The *Sangamon* interglacial stage represents the major warming of the climate that largely melted the Illinoian glaciers. Extensive soil development on Illinoian drift in Illinois and Iowa resulted from weathering and plant growth. A distinctive mineralogy of soils produced during the Sangamon interglacial aids in correlating this soil horizon.

The *Wisconsinan* glacial stage was the last major advance of continental glaciers in North America. Its deposits are widely exposed and therefore the best understood of the various glacial advances. The Wisconsinan glaciation consisted of several advances and retreats of the ice, each with several small pulsational advances. Correlation of these various advances and retreats is still unresolved. It is likely that similar pulsational advances occurred during earlier glacial episodes, but poor pre-servation of older deposits makes resolving (or even recognizing) these events almost impossible. The Wisconsinan stage began about 100,000 years ago and ended about 8,000 years ago.

The *Altonian* (or mid-Wisconsinan) advance lasted from 70,000 to 30,000 years ago. Ice moved down Lake Michigan and Green Bay and spread west into Wisconsin and Illinois. Ice from the Lake Superior Lobe spread southward over the northern Wisconsin highland into central Wisconsin. The Des Moines Lobe moved southeast through western Minnesota into central and eastern Iowa. The ice retreated during *Farmdalian* time from about 30,000 to 22,000 years ago. A cool, moist climate persisted with possible permafrost (permanently frozen ground) in the Lake Superior region (Figure 6–20). *Woodfordian* time was a cold period that saw the maximum advance of glaciers during the Wisconsinan stage. Ice from the Lake Michigan and Green Bay lobes extended into central Illinois and central Wisconsin. The Lake Superior Lobe again topped the northern Wisconsin highland, but did not extend as far south as Altonian ice. The Des Moines Lobe had its maximum advance later than the Lake Michigan Lobe and extended into southern Iowa. The final retreat of Woodfordian ice was marked by a number of minor advances. During at least one of these minor advances the ice overrode forests established on deposits in front of the receding ice sheet. Remnants of one of these buried forests can be seen along the Lake Michigan shoreline at Two Creeks, Wisconsin.

With the final retreat of ice, the major geological events that produced the Lake Superior region came to a close. The rocks, lakes, streams, and soils had been established. Subsequent erosion has modified the deposits slightly and soils have gradually improved with time. The present erosion is part of the on-going geological history of the region. We can only speculate on what the future holds in store. Clearly, however, the area has already experienced a wide variety of events, each of which has left its imprint on the area.

Older geologic literature discusses four major advances of glacial ice separated by prominent interglacial periods. Recent studies in glaciated parts of North America indicate clearly that there were more than four advances of glacial ice during the Pleistocene ice age. Because much of the record of glaciations on land has been eroded by later glacial advance or stream erosion, it is difficult to establish the number and sequence of events. However, the glacial record in the ocean basins is not so subject to erosion, and therefore, is much more complete. The marine record of glaciation, established from studies of numerous core samples of ocean floor sediments, indicates that there were a minimum of <u>eleven</u> major advances of glacial ice. The four events that have been named probably do not represent four successive events. Therefore, current geological literature de-emphasizes the importance of the four <u>named</u> advances in the Pleistocene.

Figure 6-20: An ice-wedge cast in pre-Woodfordian outwash formed by infill of surface material during alternate freezing and thawing of surface layer of permanently frozen ground. Near Fairchild, Wisconsin.

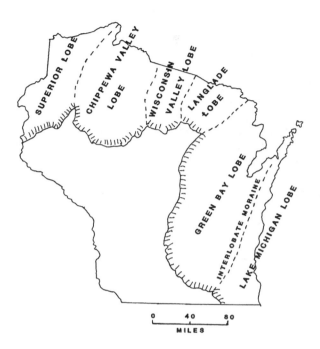

Figure 6-21: Map showing the main Woodfordian sub-lobes of the Michigan and Superior Glaciers that produced the prominent end moraines in Wisconsin.

▲ GLIMPSES OF OUR ▲ GLACIAL HERITAGE

THE ICE LOBES

As mentioned earlier the southward-flowing glaciers were channeled into preexisting valleys or lowlands along the southern margin of the ice sheet. The ice flowed much farther in the lowlands than it did over the highlands between the valleys. These long tongues of ice are called lobes, and their movement and interaction produced many of the present landforms in the region. While the maximum extent of the various lobes has been known for many years, our understanding of the timing of the advances and retreats of the lobes is still far from complete. Radio-

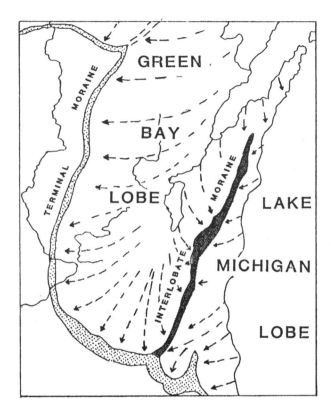

*Figure 6-22:
Location of
interlobate moraine,
northeastern
Wisconsin, formed
where ice from the
Green Bay Lobe
encountered ice
from the
Lake Michigan
Lobe.*

carbon dates reveal that each of the lobes advanced and retreated more
or less independently during the general advance and retreat of the ice
sheet as a whole. Therefore, the map in Figure 6–21 shows the distribution and extent of the major lobes, but it does not indicate the time
sequence of maximum development of the various lobes.

Figure 6–22 is a map of the Lake Michigan basin showing the end
moraine produced by the Lake Michigan Lobe and the smaller Green
Bay Lobe to the west. Perhaps due to the close proximity of the two
lobes, their major advances and retreats were roughly synchronous. This
produced an unusual feature called an *interlobate moraine* along the contact between the two lobes. The following scenario may illustrate at least
one stage in the development of this feature.

The Lake Michigan Lobe advanced down the Lake Michigan lowland, with the major ice movement down the axis of the basin. However, the ice also spread laterally to the east and west onto the surrounding uplands. At the same time the Green Bay Lobe advanced southward up the Fox River and Winnebago lowland and spread out both east and west. To the west the ice, spreading out over the gently sloping Paleozoic sediments, encountered progressively higher elevations as it moved westward. Since the ice flow was largely unhindered, it spread westward some 50 miles into central Wisconsin. To the east, however, the ice encountered the 300 foot high Niagara escarpment. Although the ice overtopped the escarpment, it soon encountered the ice moving westward out of the Lake Michigan basin. In Door County, ice from the two lobes merged and probably continued moving slowly southward. Farther south, however, debris accumulated along the contact between the two lobes. Meltwater streams flowed along the ice valley between the two lobes, burying blocks of ice, and filling depressions with till and outwash. When the ice finally melted back, it left an especially hummocky topography with numerous depressions and gravelly hills. The depressions formed where blocks of ice had been buried in outwash deposited by streams flowing off the ice. These depressions are called *kettles*, and those with lakes in them are called kettle lakes. This has given rise to the name *Kettle Moraine* for this feature, which extends across eastern Wisconsin from near Valders south to Whitewater.

THE DRIFTLESS AREA

Glaciers covered most of North America north of the Missouri and Ohio Rivers at one time or another during the Pleistocene. Although there were a number of major advances of the ice, an area of some 10,000 square miles in southwestern Wisconsin and adjoining parts of Illinois, Iowa, and Minnesota (Figure 6–23) appears to have escaped glaciation. The driftless area, so named because it lacks the glacial deposits so typical of the surrounding lands, provides an area of topography unique in the upper Midwest. Although the driftless area is completely surrounded by glacial deposits, it never was completely surrounded by glaciers. The reason is that the glacial deposits around the driftless area are not all the same age. The western border of the driftless area in northeastern Iowa and southeastern Minnesota consists of Nebraskan drift perhaps 2 million years old. In central Wisconsin the drift may be Illinoian in age, perhaps 200,000 years old. The eastern margin contains Wisconsinan drift about 20,000 years old. Thus, the glacial deposits sur-

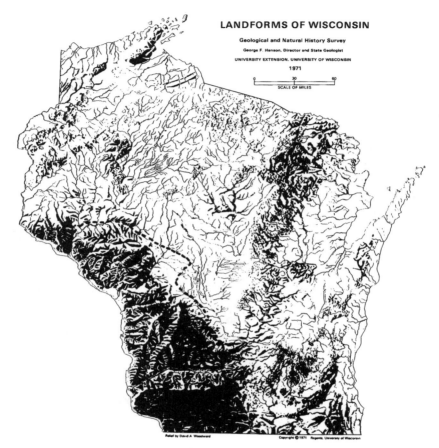

Figure 6-23: Map showing the location of the driftless area in southwestern Wisconsin. Note the distinctive landforms within the driftless area compared with the glaciated landforms elsewhere in the state.

rounding the driftless area are of very different ages. Mapping of glacial deposits suggests that the driftless area was a large "embayment" into the ice margin and had an opening to the south. During both the Kansan (second) and Illinoian (third) advances, this opening appears to have been nearly closed.

Since the driftless area was not glaciated, it is tempting to conclude that the topography in the area shows what the area looked like before glaciation. The alternating layers of sandstone and dolomite in the driftless area are not exposed far outside the area, however, and studies of the topography indicate that erosion continued during the Pleistocene. Thus, much of the topography in the driftless area appears to be Pleistocene in age, and therefore the appearance of the area may be rather different than the preglacial landscape.

The driftless area is characterized by extensive flat to gently sloping surfaces incised by narrow steep-walled stream valleys. Mesas, buttes, and small pinnacles (see Figures 5–21 and 6–29) are present along the eroding escarpments. Most of these features are characteristic of a youthful stage of erosion, consistent with a Pleistocene age for the features.

Erratic boulders transported many miles are characteristic of glaciated regions. These boulders are conspicuously absent in the driftless area. Indeed, it was this absence of erratic boulders that led early workers to the conclusion that the area had not been glaciated. The boundary of the driftless area is marked by prominent end moraines and outwash of young Wisconsinan drift along its eastern border from Madison to Stevens Point. However, the older drift borders on the north and west have no topographic expression. Instead, the drift gradually thins to a feather edge toward the driftless area. Erosion along streams and burial of this thin drift with loess makes locating the true boundary of the driftless area very difficult. As a result, different workers have placed the boundary in different places over the years. Our present understanding of the boundary is shown in Figure 6–21.

Soils in the driftless area are also different from those in most of the rest of the Lake Superior region. These soils are formed largely on residual materials from the weathering of Paleozoic rocks in addition to the wind-blown loess along the major rivers. Elsewhere, the soils are developed on glacially transported materials. Thus, in terms of landscape, geologic history, and soils, the driftless area is different from the surrounding area.

THE MISSISSIPPI RIVER

The Mississippi River as we know it did not exist prior to the Pleistocene glaciations. Glaciation alters the drainage of a region in several ways: (1) during glacial advances, ice fills the stream valleys, forcing the streams to establish new channels and valleys, (2) the huge volumes of water carried by the streams from the melting glacier may cause the streams to be incised in their new valleys, and (3) deposits left by the melting ice may completely fill former stream valleys that the glacier overrode. Many of the major rivers in the upper Midwest have had their course determined by glacial activity.

*Figure 6-24:
Map showing the
approximate location
of the lobe of
Nebraskan ice that
resulted in the
Mississippi River
Channel. Erosion
along the eastern
margin of the lobe
produced a deep
valley which the
river has occupied
most of the time
since it formed.*

On a broad scale the course of the Missouri and Ohio Rivers is a result of glaciation because they flow along the margins of the maximum advance of the continental ice sheet. Buried valleys indicate that preglacial drainage was quite different than the present system, and that fewer streams were tributary to the Mississippi. For more detailed information on the history of these rivers, consult Wright and Frye (1965).

In the upper Midwest the course of the ancestral Mississippi River is difficult to establish precisely. However, deep bedrock valleys completely filled with drift indicate an earlier drainage quite different from the present. Figure 6–2 shows the ancestral Mississippi valley across

Figure 6-25: Bluffs along the Mississippi River, now standing only half as high above the river as they did during pre-glacial times. South of LaCrosse, Wisconsin.

Iowa. This bedrock valley appears to join with a northwesterly trending bedrock low across western Minnesota approximately along the present course of the Red River (Figure 6–2). The bedrock valley in the Red River valley slopes northward, however, "suggesting" that there may have been a divide between the ancestral Mississippi and ancestral Red Rivers. Perhaps 2 million years ago ice of the Nebraskan stage moved down this valley, blocking the older drainage. Meltwaters flowing off the eastern edge of this lobe resulted in a new channel essentially in its present course between Minnesota-Wisconsin and Iowa-Illinois. Thus, the present course of the Mississippi in that area marks the eastern limit of the advance of a lobe of Nebraskan age ice (Figure 6-24). The river was so entrenched in its new channel that it did not revert to its earlier channel when the ice retreated. Thus, the present course of the Mississippi was established some 2 million years ago, and the prominent bluffs along the river (Figure 6–25) are, therefore, very young features. Continued erosion during Kansas, Illinoian, and Wisconsinan glaciations resulted in deepening the channel to nearly 1,000 feet. During later stages of the Wisconsin glaciation, at least 500 feet of gravel, sand, and silt were deposited on the bedrock floor in parts of the valley. Thus, during the maximum erosion the bluffs along the Mississippi were at least twice as high as they are now.

The ancestral Wisconsin River (called the Marquette River by Stewart, 1977) appears to have had its headwaters in northeastern Wisconsin in the present valley of the Wolf River. Prior to Pleistocene glaciation it flowed southwestward across the state through the Baraboo Range near Portage and on to Sauk City. In the Baraboo Range it carved major gorges through the resistant Baraboo Quartzite, one of which was blocked on both ends by glacial debris to produce Devils Lake. Below Sauk City the preglacial course of the Wisconsin River appears to be largely unchanged. However, ice from the Green Bay Lobe filled the preglacial valley north of Portage. A new channel for the northern part of the Wisconsin River was established, in part, along the western margin of the ice in the Green Bay Lobe. Entrenchment of the new valley and filling of the earlier channel resulted in a permanent westward shift of up to 50 miles westward for the northern part of the river.

MULTIPLE GLACIATIONS IN NORTH CENTRAL WISCONSIN

Throughout the world the sequence of glacial advances is determined by studying the deposits left by the ice. The concept of multiple glacial advances has been developed by observing one drift overlying another, in some places with a soil horizon developed on the older drift. An excellent example of multiple glaciations is present in north–central Wisconsin. It has been established in many areas that till from a particular glacier has a uniform character over large areas. Evidently the finer materials in the till are thoroughly "blended" by glacial action. This uniformity permits recognition of a till sheet over large areas. More recently, studies of prolonged weathering of drift sheets have been used as an indicator of age. Prolonged weathering (associated with the formation of soil) dissolves out the soluble carbonate minerals in the drift. Therefore, assuming a comparable source, the older the soil the less carbonate minerals it would contain. The nature of the clay minerals also changes with age. For example, older drift commonly has a higher content of the clay mineral smectite (formed by the weathering of micas in the clay size fraction of soils). Multiple glaciations can also be recognized by the boulder content in the drift. Since glaciers pick up rocks from areas they override, the rock types differ from place to place, ice moving into an area from one direction may have a quite different boulder content than ice arriving from another direction. Thus, exposures in stream cuts, roadcuts, or auger samples may reveal layers having boulders from different source areas. This would indicate more than one glacial advance into an area. In some cases distinctive rocks are carried by the ice from a small area. Mapping the distribution of boulders (the boulder train) from such distinctive localities enable us to determine the direction the ice was moving. Striations on bedrock surfaces and the orientation of elongate boulders in till also enable us to determine the direction of ice movement.

The complex glacial history of north-central Wisconsin has long been recognized. This has led to a number of different interpretations of the glacial history of the area. The margin of the last (Woodfordian) advance of ice left prominent end moraines throughout most of Wisconsin (Figure 6–21). Therefore, there has been little dispute among geologists about the margins of the various lobes.

However, older glacial deposits that thin almost imperceptibly into the driftless area occur south and west of these prominent moraines. The age and origin of these glacial deposits has been the subject of debate by geologists for nearly 100 years. New data and new techniques of studying the deposits have resolved much of the problem.

The area covered by these glacial deposits is characterized by a well-developed drainage system (few, if any, lakes), a gently rolling surface, and thin cover of glacial debris. This is in marked contrast to the features of the more recently glaciated areas to the north and east. The older landscape is typical of one produced by prolonged stream erosion. Early workers believed that this flat topography indicated a much greater age for these glacial deposits. Weidman (1907) distinguished three separate drifts (tills) in north central Wisconsin based on: 1) grouping of moraines in relation to possible ice lobes, 2) correlation of buried moraines (from water well records), 3) average thickness of ground moraine, 4) average thickness of drift sheet borders, 5) degree of weathering of drift shown by color, clay content, weathering of included boulders, and depth of weathering, 6) degree of compaction and cementation of the drift, 7) presence or absence of swamps and sag and swell topography, and 8) areal extent. Later workers disagreed with Weidman on the number and age of these "older" drifts.

Recent mapping has revealed that several recognizably different tills are present in central Wisconsin. Excavations in gravel pits and during road construction have revealed one till overlying another, and auger drilling has shown that several till sheets overlie one another. Studies of the clay mineralogy of the different tills by x-ray methods indicate that the lower till contains a greater amount of the mineral smectite produced by prolonged weathering of the micas. Comparison of these results in central Wisconsin with tills of known age elsewhere in the

Midwest supports the interpretation that the tills are indeed old, and that tills of several different ages are present. Dating of organic remains by Carbon-14 methods establishes the minimum age in years of several of the tills. For example, the Merrill drift is a minimum of 40,800 years old, or early Wisconsinan in age, because organic materials in bogs developed on it. Figure 6–26 is a map of central Wisconsin showing our present understanding of the distribution of tills produced by different advances of ice into the area.

The oldest glacial deposit presently recognized is the Wausau Drift exposed in central Marathon County and in Portage and Wood Counties. It appears to thin gradually southward and form the northern border of the driftless area. Boulder trains indicate that the drift was deposited by ice moving from the west-northwest. Cretaceous fossils in the drift are most likely carried from northwestern Minnesota. Clay mineralogy and stratigraphic position indicate that the Wausau drift is pre-Wisconsinan in age. Paleomagnetic studies indicate that the Wausau drift was deposited at a time of reversal of the earth's magnetic field, or more than 800,000 years ago.

The Edgar Drift overlies the Wausau till in western Marathon County and in Wood and Clark Counties to the southwest. Till fabric measurements indicate that the Edgar till was deposited by ice moving south-southeast. The age of the Edgar Drift is believed to be similar to that of the Wausau Drift.

The Merrill Drift extends across northern Marathon County where it overlies the Wausau and Edgar drifts. The Merrill Drift was deposited by ice moving from the northwest. Carbon-14 dates of 40,800 years on organic matter in bogs developed on top of the Merrill till indicate an Early Wisconsin (Altonian) age. The Merrill till appears to be the youngest of these drifts. If it is Altonian, all the others must also be at least that old.

The "Bakersville" Drift overlies the Edgar till in western Marathon County and adjacent parts of Clark County to the west. The "Marshfield moraine" marks the approximate boundary of the Bakersville till. This prominent ridge of till extends from near Stratford, in Marathon County, to west of Neillsville, in Clark County. It is unique in this area of older drift. Till fabric measurements indicate that the Bakersville till was deposited by ice moving from the northwest. Stratigraphic position and direction of ice movement suggest that it may be correlative with the Merrill Drift.

The advance of late Wisconsin (Woodfordian) ice into the area about 18,000–20,000 years ago produced prominent topographic moraines. Ice from the Green Bay lobe entered the area from the east-southeast, over-

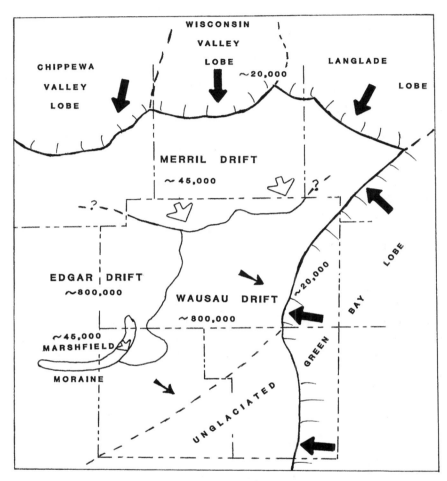

Figure 6-26: Map of central Wisconsin showing the distribution of glacial deposits of different ages. Arrows indicate the directon of ice movement of the various glacial events represented.

riding deposits of the Wausau and Merrill tills. These tills were also overridden from the north and northeast and north by ice of the Langlade, Wisconsin River, and Chippewa lobes. In eastern Wisconsin an interlobate moraine developed where ice of the Green Bay lobe met ice of the Lake Michigan lobe.

GLACIAL LAKES

During glaciation a number of large lakes formed in the Midwest when ice or glacial deposits dammed major drainageways. Melting of the glaciers resulted in greatly increased discharge in some rivers that aided in filling some of the lakes. Most of these large lakes were drained by the end of the glacial period. Since they provide an interesting part of the glacial heritage of the region, a brief summary of the history of several of the lakes is presented here.

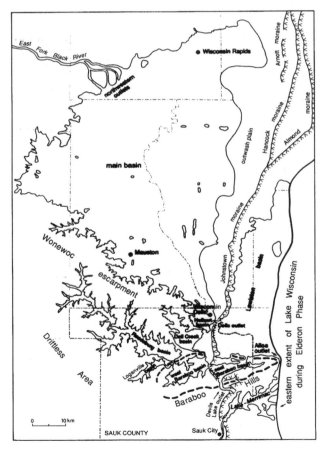

Figure 6-27: Map of central Wisconsin showing the main features of glacial Lake Wisconsin. The map shows the maximum extent of the lake during the last part of the Wisconsin Glaciation, but it never occupied this entire area at one time. The heavy dashed line is the crest of the Baraboo Hills. (From Clayton, L., and Attig, J. W., 1990, Geology of Sauk County, Wisconsin. Wis. Geol. and Nat. Hist. Survey, Information Circular 67, 68 p.)

Glacial Lake Wisconsin. A large lake existed in central Wisconsin during at least part of the "ice age." Chamberlain (1883) first pointed out the former existence of a major glacial lake in the area. Alden (1918) named it Glacial Lake Wisconsin, and provided a more complete history of the lake. Martin (1932) identified the outlet as the east fork of the Black River.

Glacial Lake Wisconsin was formed when the westward moving ice from the Green Bay Lobe encountered the ridge of Baraboo Quartzite near Portage and dammed the Wisconsin River. Water melting from the ice to the north was ponded in a lake that covered at least 1,825 square miles in central Wisconsin (Figure 6–27). The lake level is believed to have been between 960 and 1000 feet above sea level, with maximum water depths of 70 to 150 feet. The eastern margin of the lake was the outwash apron along the western margin of the Green Bay Lobe. On its western margin the lake flooded numerous stream valleys along the eastern edge of the driftless area producing a very irregular shoreline. Many sandstone buttes and pinnacles (Figure 6–28), such as those at Roche a Cri and Mill Bluff State Parks, stood as islands in the lake. The water continued to rise until it entered a stream valley leading out of the area. That valley was the east fork of the Black River, in which erosion during the existence of Glacial Lake Wisconsin removed most of the weathered material, exposing Precambrian bedrock.

Sediments carried into the lake filled depressions in the bottom of the lake to produce an extremely flat surface as shown in Figure 6–29. Streams entering the lake from the north produced a sandy bottom in

Figure 6-28: Pinnacle of Cambrian sandstone that was a small steep-sided island in Glacial Lake Wisconsin. East of Friendship, Wisconsin.

Figure 6-29: Extremely flat lands in Central Wisconsin, formed by sediment accumulating on the floor of Glacial Lake Wisconsin. South of Wisconsin Rapids.

Figure 6-30: Laminated or "varved" lake clay, with the ice-rafted cobble, dropped into the mud when the ice cake melted. Near Little Chute, Wisconsin.

the northern part of the lake. In the eastern part of the lake, however, the bottom was covered with laminated red silt and clay similar to that shown in Figure 6–30. The source of the red mud is probably from material carried by the Green Bay Lobe.

We know the probable extent, depth and duration of Glacial Lake Wisconsin during the last major advance of the Green Bay Lobe about 18,000–20,000 years ago. However, it is quite possible that a glacial lake formed more than once in central Wisconsin.

The ice dam at Portage persisted for centuries, and thus the lake must have used the Black River outlet for several hundred years. When the ice melted back to the east, the ice dam was finally removed, and the waters from Glacial Lake Wisconsin overtopped the moraine and began eroding the glacial debris. Downcutting of the outlet of such a vast lake resulted in a tremendous volume of water flowing through the new outlet. This produced rapid erosion of the glacial materials and of the soft Cambrian sandstones that underlie much of the region. The torrential flow of the waters cut a steep-walled gorge in the sandstones in a few weeks time. We now call this gorge the Dells of the Wisconsin River (Figure 6–31). Thus, one of the scenic attractions in Wisconsin was produced in a very

Figure 6-31: The Dells of the Wisconsin River, a variety of water-carved exposures of Upper Cambrian Wonewoc Sandstone.

short period of time. Once Glacial Lake Wisconsin was drained, the more normal flow of the Wisconsin River in its newly formed channel caused much less erosion.

Glacial Lake Oshkosh. In eastern Wisconsin a glacial lake with a complex history developed during the Wisconsin stage of the Pleistocene. It is now generally referred to as Glacial Lake Oshkosh (Thwaites, 1943), although some earlier reports referred to this former lake as Glacial Lake Jean Nicolet. Like Glacial Lake Wisconsin the history of this lake is recorded by limits set on its size by outlets for the lake deposits formed in it and the shorelines that developed around it.

Glacial Lake Oshkosh was drained by a number of outlets and appears to have formed and drained several times during late Wisconsin time. It occurred within the present Fox–Wolf River drainage system. The preglacial (pre-Wisconsin?) drainage of the area is believed to have been into the Wisconsin River through the Marquette (ancestral Wisconsin) River (Stewart, 1976). Stewart suggests that the river was dammed by glacial deposits during the maximum advance of late Wisconsin ice. Thus, meltwaters flowing off the Green Bay Lobe as it advanced up the Fox–Winnebago lowland were carried out the Marquette River. Glacial deposits filled the valley during continued advance of the lobe, however, and a prominent end moraine was built along the western margin of the lobe. Deposition of this end moraine and the filling of the Marquette River valley changed the drainage in the area. In particular, the dam formed by the end moraines near Portage halted the westward flow of water.

Thus, when the ice melted back from the moraine near Portage a lake formed in front of the glacier. The lake level rose until an outlet was reached over the end moraine into the Wisconsin River. The elevation of this outlet was probably about 800 feet above sea level. As the outlet was eroded, the level of the lake lowered to about 780 feet. The lake continued to grow in size as the ice from the Green Bay Lobe melted back to the east. The lake had a very irregular shoreline and numerous islands. Figure 6–32 shows its approximate maximum extent when it utilized the Portage outlet.

With continued melting of the ice in the Green Bay Lobe, a series of successively lower outlets developed into Lake Michigan. When some of these outlets were freed of ice, the level of Glacial Lake Oshkosh suddenly dropped—sometimes as much as 80 to 90 feet. These changes in lake level also produced major changes in the size and shape of the Lake. Each lower outlet resulted in a significant reduction in the size of the lake. When the channel at Sturgeon Bay was freed of ice, the lake

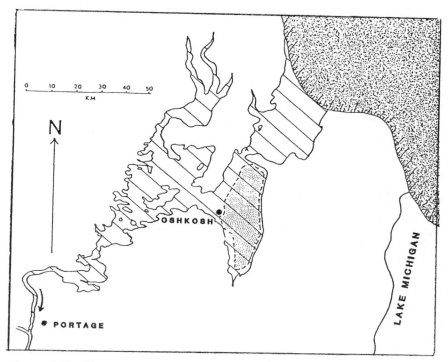

Figure 6-32: Sketch map showing the approximate size and shape of Glacial Lake Oshkosh at its maximum extent when it drained into the Wisconsin River through the Portage Outlet. (From Weilert, J. S.)

was largely confined to the present margins of Green Bay. This constituted the "draining" of Glacial Lake Oshkosh.

The history of the Glacial Lake Oshkosh is more complex than this, however, for there were several minor advances of the Green Bay Lobe during the general retreat of the glacier. Thus, as the ice advanced up Green Bay, a lake was produced in front of the glacier. As the ice advanced it successively closed the lower outlets, causing a rise in lake level and increasing the size of Glacial Lake Oshkosh again. As the ice overrode the deposits on the glacial lake floor, they were eroded, deformed, and buried by glacial till (Figure 6–33). Sufficient time elapsed between draining of the lake and the readvance of the ice that spruce forests developed in places (Figure 6–34), only to be destroyed by the advancing ice.

Figure 6-33: Deformed lake sediments (about two-thirds of the way up the quarry face) overlain by till deposited by ice moving over an earlier stage of Glacial Lake Oshkosh. Near Little Chute, Wisconsin.

The lake utilized the lower outlets again as the ice melted back. Thus, Glacial Lake Oshkosh existed a minimum of three times and had a highly variable lake level (depth), area, and outline.

Glacial Lake Agassiz. Glacial Lake Agassiz was named after Louis Agassiz, one of the early proponents of the glacial theory. Like other glacial lakes, its size and shape changed markedly from time to time. At its maximum size it covered some 200,000 square miles in southern Manitoba and adjacent parts of Minnesota, North Dakota, Saskatchewan, and Ontario (Figure 6–35). While this may seem somewhat removed from the Lake Superior region, it is covered here because its history and the preglacial history of the area had a significant influence on the glacial history of the Lake Superior region.

First, recall that Glacial Lake Agassiz developed in a bedrock low on the west side of the Minnesota upland. This lowland served as a major

Figure 6-34: Lake sediments in the lower half of the picture on which a forest had developed. Till overlying the wood and other debris shows that the ice moved over a wooded former lake bed. Near Little Chute, Wisconsin.

valley for ice movement from the Keewatin Center. The valley channeled the ice southward around the Minnesota upland, which served as a barricade to ice movement. Thus, instead of moving southward as a massive front, the Des Moines Lobe developed to carry the ice up this old stream valley into southern Minnesota and Iowa. The eastern margin of ice that moved up this valley formed the western border of the "driftless area" in southwestern Wisconsin. Therefore, the existence of the valley destined to become Glacial Lake Agassiz (and later the Red River valley) played an important role in the history of glaciation elsewhere in the Lake Superior region.

The bedrock valley was probably deepened by the repeated advances of ice during the various stages of glaciation during the Pleistocene. It is conceivable that glacial lakes existed in the valley during the advance and retreat of earlier glacial episodes. However, no deposits confirming the existence of such lakes are known. Glacial Lake Agassiz itself first

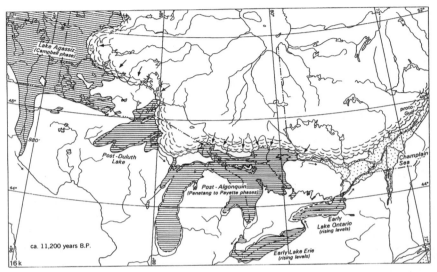

Figure 6-35: Map showing glacial Lake Agassiz and other glacial lakes. Lake Agassiz spread out over vast areas of the prairies in Canada. Lake Winnipeg is a relatively small remnant of this large lake. (From Prest, 1970)

appeared about 13,000 years ago when ice of the Des Moines Lobe melted back from a recessional moraine roughly along the bedrock high of the transcontinental arch. The lake increased in size as the ice melted back and may have been over 600 feet deep at times. Debris from melt-water streams flowing into the lake covered the lake floor with up to 600 feet of sand, silt, and clay. These deposits form the flat, in part poorly drained area now occupied by the northward flowing Red River. Lake Winnipeg is a remnant of Glacial Lake Agassiz.

For nearly 3,500 years the only outlet of the lake was Glacial River Warren, which carved a broad valley southeastward across Minnesota. The Minnesota River, which joins the Mississippi River at St. Paul, flows in this broad valley, which was eroded to bedrock in many places. About 9,500 years ago a lower outlet for Lake Agassiz opened eastward across Ontario into the Lake Superior basin. This greatly reduced the volume of water flowing down the Glacial River Warren (the Minnesota River) valley. The Lake Superior outlet was abandoned about 8,000 years ago when lower, more northerly outlets were freed of ice. The entire area formerly occupied by Glacial Lake Agassiz is now drained northward through Lake Winnipeg and the Churchill River into Hudson Bay.

THE DRUMLIN FIELDS

Drumlins are one of the more intriguing landforms produced by glaciers. Drumlins are elongated hills shaped somewhat like the inverted bowl of a spoon (Figure 6–36). The elongation of drumlins is usually parallel with striations on bedrock and boulder trains, and thus can be used to indicate the direction of ice movement. Typically drumlins have a steeper slope in the direction from which the ice came and a more gentle slope "downstream." Drumlins vary widely in size and shape. Commonly they are one-half to 2 miles long, about one-quarter mile wide, and 30 to 100 feet high. Most drumlins are composed of unconsolidated glacial debris (till and/or outwash), but some have a core of bedrock. Another interesting characteristic of drumlins is that they occur in groups. For example, Alden (1905) mapped about 1,400 drumlins in a major "field" in southeastern Wisconsin (Figure 6–37). About 80 percent of the drumlins were formed by the Green Bay Lobe, the remaining 20 percent by the Lake Michigan Lobe. Several large drumlin fields are present in central and northeastern Minnesota as well (Figure 6–38). In large areas of glaciated terrane elsewhere in North America no drumlins occur. Therefore, the formation of drumlins must require special conditions that

Figure 6-36: Profile of a typical drumlin. Ice moved from left to right producing the streamlined shape. Near Whitewater, Wisconsin.

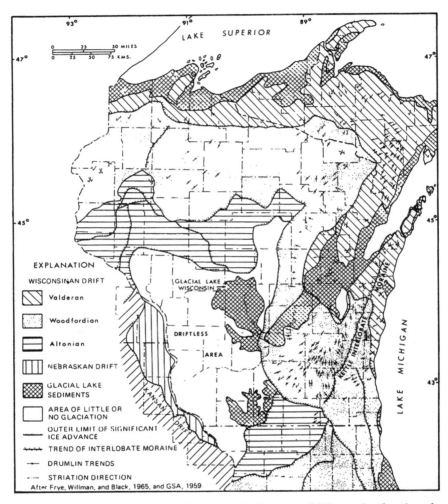

Figure 6-37: Generalized map of the glacial deposits of Wisconsin showing the drumlin field in southeastern Wisconsin. (From Paull and Paull, 1977)

develop only in certain areas. When the conditions are favorable, hundreds of drumlins form.

The origin of drumlins has been debated since they were first recognized over 100 years ago. Two basic ideas have been proposed for their origin. One idea maintains that they were formed by the deposition of material beneath glacial ice.

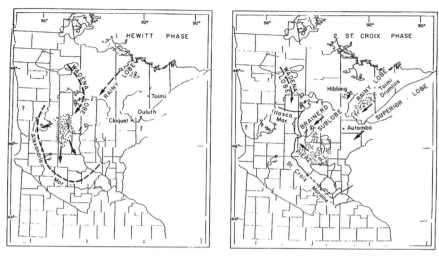

Figure 6-38: Maps showing some of the drumlin fields in Minnesota. (From Wright, 1972)

The other possible origin proposed for drumlins is that they are erosional features produced when the ice overrides deposits formed closer to the margin, or in front of the ice. Recent field and theoretical studies provide a basis for testing these two models for drumlin formation. Most drumlin fields, including those in southeastern Wisconsin, formed in a zone from about 3 to 25 miles behind the terminal moraine of a glacier. This suggests that they were produced during the main advance of the particular lobe in which they develop. The composition of drumlins is also significant. Drumlins in Waukesha County in southeastern Wisconsin and in Forest County in northeastern Wisconsin are composed largely of outwash and gravel, with a veneer of till over the outwash.

In many drumlins the outwash has been deformed. The field relationships have been interpreted to indicate the following sequence of events to produce drumlin fields. Meltwater streams deposit sand and gravel in front of an advancing glacier. The advancing ice overrides the outwash and deposits a layer of till on top of the outwash. Continued advance of the glacier results in thicker ice covering the area (Figure 6–39). At this stage erosion becomes the dominant process, and both the "advance till" and older outwash are eroded.

The drumlins actually represent uneroded areas over which the ice moves. Movement and weight of the ice may deform (fold and fault) the

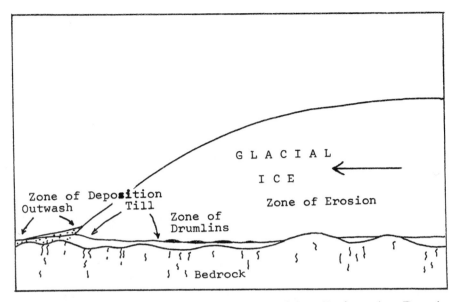

Figure 6-39: Diagram illustrating the location of drumlin formation. Deposition of outwash and till near the front of the glacier is overridden by the advancing ice. Drumlins form by erosion of till and outwash. Continued erosion destroys the drumlin form as the ice advances.

material in the drumlin, "squeezing" it into the drumlin form. Continued advance of the ice produces continued erosion and thus will eventually remove the drumlins. This may explain the occurrence of drumlins only within a limited distance of the terminal moraine. Retreat of the ice by melting produces a second layer of till over the entire area, including the drumlins. Many drumlins are composed entirely of till, and therefore this sequence of events is difficult to demonstrate. Although we cannot prove that all drumlins are erosional features, in drumlins where the necessary materials (outwash) are present, however, the preceding sequence of events seems to explain their origin satisfactorily.

THE GREAT LAKES

The Great Lakes are perhaps the most prominent feature formed by glaciation in North America. They are the result of a long and complex sequence of events, some of which have already been mentioned. All of the lakes owe their origin and location in part to events that preceded the Pleistocene epoch, particularly the occurrence of relatively easily eroded rocks. It is highly unlikely, however, that any of the lakes existed before the Pleistocene. Instead a series of stream valleys occupied the present lake basins. A brief account of the history of Lakes Michigan and Superior is presented to illustrate the complex sequence of events that produced the lakes as we know them today.

Lake Michigan. The present site of Lake Michigan is believed to have been occupied by a south-flowing river in preglacial times. The river valley was developed in the Devonian shales and was bounded on the west by the resistant Silurian dolomite. This valley served as a channel for the ice, and was responsible for the development of a large lobe of ice that moved southward hundreds of miles down the valley. It is likely that the first advance of ice deepened the valley. Drift deposited as the ice melted may also have dammed the valley, possibly forming a small lake basin. Thus, there may have been a small ancestral version of "Lake Michigan" after the retreat of the Nebraskan glaciers more than 1.5 million years ago. Glaciers advanced down the valley repeatedly during the Kansan, Illinoian, and Wisconsin stages. With each advance the lake basin was deepened to its present depth of 923 feet (or 343 feet below sea level) and widened by erosion. The material was carried uphill to the south and deposited in Indiana, Illinois, and southeastern Wisconsin. Thus, it is reasonable to assume that an ancestral lake existed during much of the Pleistocene, and that it increased in size with each major advance of the ice. Unfortunately, the last advance of the ice has obliterated nearly all evidence for the ancestral lake. Assuming that an earlier lake existed and that its outlet was (like today) through the Mackinac Straits, the Woodfordian ice probably produced effects somewhat as follows.

The advancing glacier blocked the outlet at the Straits of Mackinac, and the weight of the ice depressed the area, "tilting" the basin to the north. Meltwater was impounded in front of the ice and the lake level rose until a new outlet was reached. The area probably looked similar to the view in Figure 6–40. Ancestors of present rivers flowing through the Chicago and Des Plaines Rivers served as the outlet. This outlet to the Mississippi was used until the ice completely filled the lake basin. The ice moved far beyond the margins of the lake, and for thousands of years no lake existed. The weight of the thousands of cubic miles of ice in the basin was so great that it depressed the earth's crust in that area perhaps several hundred feet. This was to have a significant effect on the history of the lake when the ice melted.

When the ice melted back so that its border was again within the lake basin, the lake level was again controlled by the outlet to the Mississippi.

Figure 6-40: The edge of the Ross Ice Shelf in Antarctica where glaciers move into the sea. The scene is probably similar to that in the Great Lakes as the ice moved down the lake basins several times during the Pleistocene. (Photo by T. S. Laudon)

The outlet stream cut down through the drift until it reached the bedrock surface. This lake level is called the Glenwood stage of Glacial Lake Chicago (Figure 6–41) and had an elevation of 640 feet above sea level (60 feet above the present lake level). The Chicago outlet was utilized until a lower outlet through the Mackinac Straits was freed of ice. A lower lake level (620 feet) of the Des Plaines River outlet is called the Calumet stage. A series of minor advances and retreats of the Michigan Lobe alternately closed and opened the Straits of Mackinac and produced several rises and falls in the lake level. An especially low lake level called Lake Chippewa (Figure 6–42) occurred during the Two Creekan interglacial phase. It occurred because crustal depression had greatly lowered the outlet of the Great Lakes to the east through the St. Lawrence River valley. Isostatic rebound of the crust produced a gradual rise in the level of the outlet at the Straits of Mackinac, and therefore a rise in the level of the lake.

Some of the earlier shorelines persisted for centuries and cut prominent beaches into the drift and bedrock surrounding the lake. Figure 6–43 shows the terrace of Lake Nipissing stage at 605 feet.

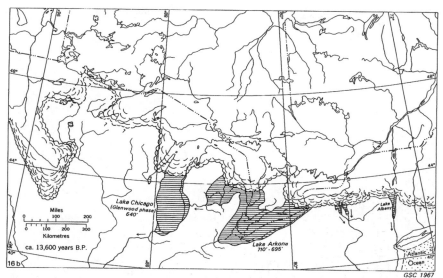

Figure 6-41: Map (top) showing the drainage pattern of the Great Lakes area with the main outlet through the Chicago River.

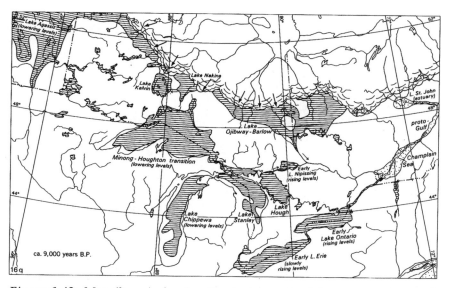

Figure 6-42: Map (lower) showing the drainage at a later stage and a much smaller size of Lake Michigan. (From Prest, 1970)

Figure 6-43: Shoreline of Green Bay showing a "notch" from the elevated beach level of Lake Nipissing. View from Peninsula State Park.

Lake Superior. The origin and history of Lake Superior is similar to that of Lake Michigan. In preglacial times a major east-flowing (?) river had developed a valley in the poorly cemented Keweenawan sediments in the Lake Superior syncline. The orientation of this valley diverted the ice to the west into Minnesota. The highland in northern Wisconsin–Michigan inhibited southward movement of the ice, although ice eventually covered the highland and spread southward into central Wisconsin.

Successive advances of the ice deepened the basin to over 1,300 feet, some 700 feet below sea level. As in the Lake Michigan basin, it was necessary for the ice to carry the eroded material uphill nearly 2,000 feet onto the surrounding land surfaces. The ability to carry large amounts of material uphill is one of the ways in which glacial erosion differs from stream erosion. Erosion by the last advance of the ice has completely obscured the earlier history of Lake Superior.

During the Wisconsinan glaciation, Lake Superior apparently remained ice-filled during much of the earlier advances and retreats of the Lake Michigan glacier. Thus, Glacial Lake Chicago had been in existence for thousands of years before the Lake Superior Lobe melted back sufficiently for ancestral Lake Superior to form in front of the ice.

Glacial Lake Keweenaw is the name given to the ancestral Lake Superior. The lake had an elevation of 780 feet (nearly 180 feet above the present level of Lake Superior). The high lake level resulted in flooding of considerable areas in northern Wisconsin and Minnesota. The Brule and St. Croix Rivers served as the outlet for Lake Keweenaw into the Mississippi River (Figure 6–44). This level persisted until a lower outlet, the Whitefish River, opened across northern Michigan into the Lake Michigan basin (Figure 6–45). Thick deposits of red clay that accumulated on the bottom of Lake Keweenaw are present in the northern tier of counties in Wisconsin.

A readvance of the ice again completely filled the Lake Superior basin with ice. A rapid retreat of this ice formed Glacial Lake Duluth in the Lake Superior basin, with its outlet again through the Brule–St. Croix valley. The thick deposits of red clay on the lake bottom form the flat plain along the south shore of Lake Superior from Superior eastward nearly to Marquette, Michigan. Reopening of the Whitefish River outlet

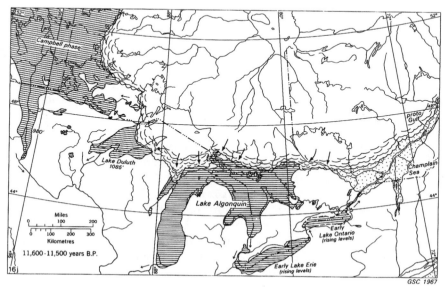

Figure 6-44: Map showing a higher level of Lake Superior when it's outlet was through the St. Croix River into the Mississippi. (From Prest, 1970)

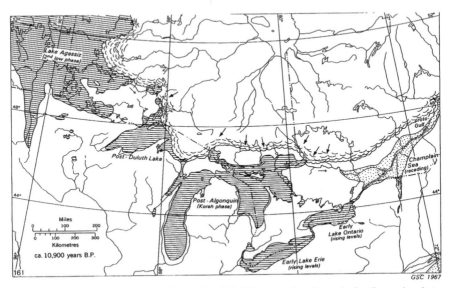

Figure 6-45: Map showing the Whitefish River outlet from Lake Superior into the Lake Michigan Basin. (From Prest, 1970)

again drained the lake into the Lake Michigan basin (Figure 6–45). The Whitefish River outlet was abandoned when the St. Mary's River at Sault Ste. Marie was freed of ice. At this time Lakes Superior, Huron, and Michigan were connected and drained through the Des Plaines River into the Mississippi. This large lake was called Lake Nipissing. Approximately 10,000 years ago the St. Lawrence River valley was freed of ice. Because of crustal subsidence, the valley was much lower than it is now. This resulted in a dramatic lowering of Lake Superior (and Lake Michigan) to several hundred feet below the present lake level. This low stage of Lake Superior is called Glacial Lake Houghton, which corresponds to the Lake Chippewa stage of Lake Michigan (Figure 6–42). Crustal rebound associated with continued melting of the continental ice sheet gradually raised the St. Lawrence outlet of the Great Lakes. Somewhere about 7,500 years ago the surface had rebounded sufficiently to give the Great Lakes essentially their present outline.

▲ PLEISTOCENE LIFE ▲

Pleistocene mammal fauna of North America were linked with South America by the Isthmus of Panama and with Eurasia by the land bridge at the Bering Strait. The land bridge was a result of the lowering of sea level due to glaciers tying up water on the land surface. Zebrine horses, modern camelids, hyena-type dogs, and beaver from Asia appeared during the lower Quaternary. Ground sloths and porcupines from South America appeared about the same time. By Kansan time, mammoths, horses, brown bear, saber-toothed cats, musk oxen, antelope, rodents, and bison had arrived from Asia along with giant armadillo and mammoths from South America.

Mastodon, moose, stag moose, giant beaver, deer, and bear lived in the subarctic forest near the ice front; elephants of the mammoth line, tapirs, deer, and carnivores lived farther from the ice sheet; while elephant, horses, bison, elk, antelope, ground sloths, and various small mammals lived in the more temperate steppe still farther removed from the ice. As the ice front (and climate zones) shifted south, these animal communities did likewise. When the glaciers melted back, the animals migrated northward again.

At least 200 genera of animals became extinct during late Pleistocene time. The extinctions were mainly among the large herbivores, which then caused some carnivores to become extinct. There was no corresponding loss of small vertebrates or of the plants. These Pleistocene extinctions were different from practically all previous extinctions in the geologic record in that no new groups of animals appeared to replace those that perished. This suggests that the extinctions were not the result of "natural" processes. Many extinctions occurred during the waning stages of the "ice age," which implies that they were not simply due to the more severe climate.

By the end of the Aftonian interglacial period, saber-tooth cats, mastodons, camels, dogs, pronghorn, and hyena became extinct. By the end of Kansan time the three-toed horse, zebrine horses, mastodon, and giant camel became extinct. By the end of Wisconsinan time, mastodons, camels, horses, giant beavers, giant short-faced bears, small ground sloths, giant armadillos, saber-tooth cats, mammoths, shrub oxen, pronghorns, tapirs, spectacled bears, moose, antelope, yak, caribou, and musk ox had all become extinct. Most of these extinctions took place before 11,000 years ago. Fluted-point hunters lived in the Lake Superior area by that time. Throughout the world there is a pattern that the mass extinctions occurred shortly after the arrival of primitive hunters.

Man's arrival in North America was probably from Asia by way of the land bridge across the Bering Straits. The time of his arrival is speculative, but probably between 12,000 to 100,000 years ago. Early man traveled southward from Alaska through the Yukon via an inland route between major ice sheets. These early men lived largely by hunting. It seems incredible, however, that these primitive hunters 10,000 to 15,000 years ago could exterminate more animals than modern man with his sophisticated weapons. Some archaeologists believe that individual kills were small before 7,000 B.C.. The native animals may have had no fear of early man. Until they developed an instinctive fear of this new predator, hunting may have been relatively easy. Later hunters evidently used the stampede as a hunting technique. Herds were driven over cliffs or across unfavorable terrane. Hundreds of animals were trampled to death, but the hunters may have used meat from only a few of the victims. This wasteful method may have hastened the extinctions. While it is possible that natural causes (disease or climatic change) might have contributed to the extinctions, the evidence points more strongly to man. An archeological site in France contains remains of 100,000 horses, which were used for food by early man. As civilization advanced and man began raising some of his food and domesticating animals, the slaughter of wildlife gradually diminished.

It is generally agreed that Paleo-Indians lived in the Great Lakes area by 7,000 to 8,000 B.C. Therefore, these early inhabitants must have witnessed the final retreat of the ice from this part of North America.

▲ ECONOMIC ASPECTS OF GLACIATION ▲

Glaciation has had a profound influence on the Great Lakes region and most of the remainder of central North America. Virtually all of the lakes for which the area is famous were formed as a result of glaciation. The abundance of lakes has been a major factor in the tourist industry in the region. Many thousands of people have summer homes on lakes throughout the area, and millions more spend their vacations in the "lake country."

The glaciated parts of North America, including the Great Lakes region, are perhaps the greatest food-producing area in the world. With few exceptions, the soils on which the crops are grown were formed on materials transported by glaciers. Large areas of rolling farmland in Minnesota, Iowa, Wisconsin, Illinois, Indiana, Michigan, and elsewhere have been developed on glacial till produced by direct deposition of materials carried by the ice. Other large flat areas, such as the famed Red River valley in western Minnesota and North Dakota, and extensive areas in central and northeastern Wisconsin, in Indiana, and in Michigan are former lake beds formed by deposition of sediment from meltwater from the ice sheets. Other areas are former outwash areas formed by streams flowing off the melting ice. Vast areas along and downwind from the Missouri, Mississippi, and other major river courses contain a thick blanket of loess (or windblown silt) that blew out of the major meltwater channels during low water periods. These loessial soils are probably the most fertile soils in the world, and along with an optimum climate, form the basis for the Corn Belt in North America.

The various sand and gravel deposits formed by meltwater streams from glaciers constitute a tremendous resource in the region. We tend to take for granted the seemingly inexhaustible supply of cheap "aggregate" with which we are blessed. One need only travel south or west of the glaciated area, however, to notice that in vast areas it is necessary to blast, crush, and screen hard rock to obtain the aggregate that the glaciers have provided for us in this part of North America. Many of the prime sources of sand and gravel have been worked out, have been covered by housing developments, or underlie prime farmland. Therefore, our once-abundant supply of sand and gravel is rapidly diminishing.

Finally, the underground water that we get from the innumerable wells in the Great Lakes region come, in many areas, from glacial deposits. The groundwater also contributes water to lakes, swamps, springs, and rivers throughout the region. In older times we could rely on good-quality water simply by digging, or drilling a well. The increase in industrialization, septic tanks, and more intensive farming has resulted, however, in pollution of the nearsurface groundwater in glacial drift in many areas. Lakes and streams have also become contaminated in much of the region. While natural systems have an amazing ability to purify themselves, it has become increasingly necessary to regulate the amount of contaminants added to these systems.

Few people in the upper Midwest think of this area as a potential source of diamonds, yet diamonds have been known to occur in the Lake Superior region for well over a century. Although the diamonds are not Pleistocene in age, the discussion of these intriguing minerals is included here. Most of the diamond discoveries have been in glacial deposits in southeastern Wisconsin, mainly in the late 1800s when water wells were dug in the glacial drift. Perhaps the well-digger took a break from his digging and looked at the interesting stones on the walls of his well. Some of the diamond discoveries provide very interesting stories. The following is excerpted from an unpublished report by M. G. Mudrey, Jr., of the Wisconsin Geological and Natural History Survey.

"The first documented diamond discovery in Wisconsin was made during the digging of a well in 1876 by Charles Wood, who was a tenant on the farm of Tom Devereaux, near Eagle, in southwestern Waukesha County. This first important Wisconsin diamond discovery is recorded in the files of the Milwaukee County Circuit Court, and the Wisconsin Supreme Court. The digging had passed through 10 to 15 meters of clay, and then through loose gravel of approximately 5 meters, when a 2-meter layer of hard yellow material was struck. While penetrating this stratum, a hard stone of unknown identity was struck. Clarissa Wood took this peculiar pebble to Col. Samuel B. Boynton, a jeweler in Milwaukee. Boynton identified the stone as "topaz," and purchased it for $1.00. Once the true identity of the diamond was disclosed, Clarissa offered to buy the diamond back, first for $1.00 and later for $1.50. Boynton refused, and Mrs. Wood sued. The Supreme Court ruled that the stone was Boynton's because he believed it was topaz when he bought it. He later sold the stone to Tiffany and Company of New York for $850. He had offered the stone to the State of Wisconsin for $1,000, but his offer was declined. The crystal, originally known as the Waukesha Diamond and later, the Eagle Diamond, is a warm yellow color and weights 16.25 carats."

"J. P. Morgan, the late 19th century financier, purchased the Eagle diamond from Tiffany's and ultimately donated the gem to the American Museum of Natural History in New York City. The stone was on public display at the museum until the evening of October 29, 1964, when "Murph the Surf" broke in, and departed with the Eagle Diamond and other gems. The stone has not been recovered."

"The stone which created the greatest interest in the possibility of diamonds in Wisconsin was discovered in 1888 by Louis Endlick of Kohlsville on or near the Green Lake Moraine and is known as the Theresa Diamond. The stone weighed 21.5 carats and is the largest diamond on record ever recovered in the State, and the fifth largest in the United States."

"This diamond was of further interest because of its unusual color. One side of the crystal was colorless, while the other portion was almost cream yellow. These differing color portions were separated by a flaw or distinct cleavage plane. The crystal was almost spherical in shape."

"Shortly after the Theresa Diamond was discovered, the Endlick family moved away from Kohlsville, taking the diamond with them. Later inquiries regarding the whereabouts of the diamond were fruitless until an article on the subject was published in a newspaper and was read by a son of Mr. Endlick (Olson, 1953). He explained that the family had moved to Kewaskum. In 1918 the Theresa Diamond had been cut into ten stones at a cost of $400. Total weight of the ten stones was 9.27 carats, divided as follows: 1.48 carats, 1.09 carats, 0.97 carats, 0.96 carats, 0.95 carats, 0.85 carats, 0.83 carats, and 2 stones weighing 0.65 carats each."

Because these, and the several other diamonds discovered in the Lake Superior region have come from glacial deposits, there has been much speculation on the source of the diamonds. Diamonds are very rare, and originate in distinctive rocks known as *kimberlites*. Kimberlites originate deep within the earth's mantle and are brought to the surface in violent, gas-charged eruptions. Most kimberlites emerge at the surface as roughly circular, pipelike bodies generally only 100 feet or less across. As the gas-charged magma approaches the surface the rock is typically broken into innumerable angular fragments. In effect, the pipe is composed of a breccia of various rock fragments. The diamonds, which also originate in the mantle, are carried up to the surface in these small pipelike bodies.

Considering the combination of the small size of the kimberlite pipes, and the fact that nearly all of the Lake Superior region is covered with glacial deposits, it is not surprising that the potential source of the diamonds remained unknown for many years. In 1970, two geologists, Klaus Schulz and William Spense, engaged in mineral exploration in northern Michigan, discovered a peculiar rock exposed by a bulldozer on a logging road near Lake Ellen, east of Crystal Falls, Michigan. The rock was badly weathered, but was extensively brecciated, and had a composition suggesting that it might be a kimberlite. Subsequent tests verified that the rock was indeed a kimberlite. Thus, nearly 100 years after the first diamonds were found in the Lake Superior region, a potential source of the diamonds was discovered.

Despite extensive testing on the Lake Ellen, Kimberlite, however, no meaningful diamonds were discovered. Extensive geological studies in northern Michigan and Wisconsin have resulted in the discovery of more than a dozen kimberlite bodies, mainly in the area from Crystal Falls to Escanaba, Michigan. Although some of the kimberlites contain small quantities of microdiamonds, none of them appear to have commercial quantities of diamonds. Therefore, the source of the large diamonds found in the glacial deposits of southeastern Wisconsin remains unknown.

The kimberlites make an interesting sidelight to the geology of the Lake Superior region. Age determinations conducted as part of the comprehensive study of the kimberlites indicate that they were emplaced during Cretaceous time, about 100 to 150 million years ago. Therefore, there appears to have been periodic violent eruptions of kimberlite volcanoes at a time when dinosaurs may have been roaming the landscape in the Lake Superior region.

In conclusion, we can say that geological events that have occurred throughout an incredibly long span of time have all had an influence on the lives of people who live in, and visit, the Great Lakes region. I have attempted to describe and explain some of the major events as I see them. Our geological heritage in the Lake Superior region is perhaps the longest and most colorful of any region in North America, and people living in the area should be aware of it.

SUGGESTED ADDITIONAL READINGS

Alden, W. C., 1918, Quaternary geology of southeastern Wisconsin, U. S. Geological Survey Professional Paper 106.

Attig, J. W., Mickelson, D. M., and Clayton, Lee, 1989, Late Wisconsin landform distribution and glacier-bed conditions in Wisconsin, Sedimentary Geology, vol. 62, pp. 399—405.

Attig, J. W., Clayton, Lee, and Mickelson, D. M., 1985, Correlation of late Wisconsin glacial phases in the western Great lakes area, Geological Society of America Bulletin, vol. 96, pp. 1585–1593.

Clayton, Lee, Attig, J. W., Mickelson, D. M., and Johnson, M. D., 1992, Glaciation of Wisconsin, Wisconsin Geological and Natural History Survey Educational Series 36, 4 p.

Clayton, Lee, and Attig, J. W., 1989, Glacial Lake Wisconsin, Geological Society of America Memoir 173, 80 p.

Clayton, Lee, 1984, Pleistocene geology of the Superior region, Wisconsin, Wisconsin Geological and Natural History Survey Information Circular 46, 40 p.

Dorr, J. A., Jr., and Eschman, D. F., 1970, Geology of Michigan, University of Michigan Press, Ann Arbor, MI.

Karrow, P. F., and Calkin, P. E., 1985, Quaternary Evolution of the Great Lakes, Geological Association of Canada Special Paper 30, 258 p.

Ojakangas, R. W., and Matsch, C. L., 1982, Minnesota's Geology, University of Minnesota Press, Minneapolis, MN, 255 p.

Wright, H. E., 1972, Quaternary history of Minnesota, in Sims, P. K., and Morey, G. B., Editors, Geology of Minnesota: A Centennial Volume, Minnesota Geological Survey.

REFERENCES CITED

Bickford, M. E., Van Schmus, W. R., and Zietz, I., 1986, Proterozoic history of the midcontinent region of North America, Geology, vol. 14, p. 492–496.

Bornhorst, T. J., Paces, J. B., Grant, N. K., Obradovich, J. D., and Huber, N. K., 1988, Age of native copper mineralization, Keweenaw Peninsula, Michigan, Economic Geology, vol. 83, p. 619–625.

Buckley, E. R., 1898, Building and Ornamental Stones of Wisconsin, Wisconsin Geological and Natural History Survey Bulletin No. 4.

Card, K. D., 1990, A review of the Superior Province of the Canadian Shield, a product of Archean accretion, Precambrian Research, vol. 48, p. 99–156.

Craddock, C., 1972, The Late Precambrian regional geologic setting, in Geology of Minnesota: A Centennial Volume, P. K. Sims and G. B. Morey, eds., Minnesota Geological Survey.

Dott, R. H., Jr., 1983, The Proterozoic red quartzite enigma in the north-central United States - Resolved by plate collision? in Early Proterozoic Geology of the Great Lakes Region, Geological Society of America Memoir 160, L. G. Medaris, Jr., ed., p. 129–141.

Flint, R. F., 1943, Growth of the North American ice sheet during the Wisconsin age, Geological Society of America Bulletin, vol. 54, p. 325–362.

Goldich, S. S., 1972, Geochronology in Minnesota, in Geology of Minnesota: A Centennial Volume, P. K. Sims and G. B. Morey, eds., Minnesota Geological Survey.

Green, J. C., 1982, Geology of Keweenawan extrusive rocks, in Geology and Tectonics of the Lake Superior Basin, Geological Society of America Memoir 156, R. J. Wold and W. J. Hinze, eds.

Han, T-M., and Runnegar, B., 1992, Megascopic Eukaryotic Algae from the 2.1-billion-year-old Negaunee Iron-Formation, Michigan, Science, vol. 257, p. 232–235.

Hanson, G. N., 1972, Saganaga batholith, in <u>Geology of Minnesota: A Centennial Volume</u>, P. K. Sims and G. B. Morey, eds., Minnesota Geological Survey.

Heyl, A. V., Jr., 1959, The geology of the Upper Mississippi Valley zinc-lead district (Illinois-Iowa-Wisconsin), <u>U.S. Geol. Surv. Professional Paper 309</u>.

Hutchinson, R. W., 1970, Mineral potential in greenstone belts of northwestern Ontario, 16th Annual Institute on Lake Superior Geology, Thunder Bay, Ontario.

Klasner, J. S., Ojakangas, R. W., Schulz, K. J., and LaBerge, G. L., 1991, Nature and Style of Deformation in the Foreland of the Early Proterozoic Penokean Orogen, Northern Michigan, <u>U.S. Geol. Surv. Bulletin 1904-K</u>.

LaBerge, G. L., Klasner, J. S., and Myers, P. E., 1990, New observations of the age and structure of Proterozoic Quartzites in Wisconsin, <u>U.S. Geol. Surv. Bulletin 1904-B</u>.

LaBerge, G. L., and Myers, P. E., 1983, Precambrian Geology of Marathon County, Wisconsin, <u>Wisconsin Geol. and Natural History Surv. Info. Circular 45</u>.

LaBerge, G. L., and Myers, P. E., 1984, Two early Proterozoic successions in central Wisconsin and their tectonic significance, <u>Geological Society of America Bulletin</u>, vol. 95, p. 246–253.

LaBerge, G. L., Robbins, E. I., and Han, T-M., 1987, A model for the biological precipitation of Precambrian iron-formations: Geological evidence, in <u>Precambrian Iron-formations</u>, P. W. Appel and G. L. LaBerge, eds., Theophrastus Publications, Athens, Greece.

Larue, D. K., 1981, The Chocolay Group Lake Superior region, U.S.A.: sedimentological evidence for deposition in basinal and platform settings on an early Proterozoic craton, <u>Geol. Soc. of Amer. Bulletin</u>, vol. 92, p. 417–435.

Larue, D. K., and Sloss, L. L., 1980, Early Proterozoic Sedimentary basins of the Lake Superior region, <u>Geol. Soc. America Bulletin</u>, vol. 91, p. 1836–1879.

Morey, G. B., and Ojakangas, R. W., 1982, Keweenawan sedimentary rocks of eastern Minnesota and northern Wisconsin, in <u>Geology and Tectonics of the Lake Superior Basin</u>, Geological Society of America Memoir 156, R. J. Wold and W. J. Hinze, eds.

Oftedahl, C., 1958, A theory of exhalative-sedimentary ores, Geologiska F_renin-gens I Stockholm F_rhaudlingar, Band 80, Hoftel.

Ojakangas, R. W., 1972, Graywackes and related rocks of the Knife Lake Group and Lake Vermilion Formation, Vermilion District, in Geology of Minnesota: A Centennial Volume, P. K. Sims and G. B. Morey, eds., Minnesota Geological Survey, p. 82–91.

Percival, J. A., and Williams, H. R., 1989, Late Archean Quetico accretionary complex, Superior province, Canada, Geology, vol. 17, p. 23–25.

Prest, V. K., 1968, Quaternary Geology, in Geology and Economic Minerals of Canada: Economic Geology Report No. 1, R. J. W. Douglas, ed., Geol. Surv. of Canada, Ottawa.

Sims, P. K., 1976, Early Precambrian tectonic-igneous evolution in Vermilion district, northeastern Minnesota, Geological Society of America Bulletin, vol. 87, p. 379–389.

Sims, P. K., Van Schmus, W. R., Schulz, K. J., and Peterman, Z. E., 1989, Tectono-stratigraphic evolution of the Early Proterozoic Wisconsin magmatic terranes of the Penokean Orogen, Canadian Journal of Earth Science, vol. 26, p. 2145-2158.

Sims, P. K., and Viswanathan, S., 1972, Giants Range batholith, in Geology of Minnesota: A Centennial Volume, P. K. Sims and G. B. Morey, eds., Minnesota Geological Survey.

Smith, E. I., 1978, Introduction to Precambrian Rocks of South-Central Wisconsin, Geoscience Wisconsin, vol. 2, p. 1–17.

Suszek, T. J., 1991, Petrography and Sedimentation of the Middle Proterozoic (Keweenawan) Nonesuch Formation, western Lake Superior region, Midcontinent Rift System, M.S. Thesis, Univ. of Minnesota, Duluth, 198 p.

Thwaites, F. T., 1943, Pleistocene of part of northeastern Wisconsin: Geological Society of America Bulletin, vol. 54, p. 87–144.

Weege, R. J., and Pollack, J. P., 1971, Recent developments in the native-copper district of Michigan, in Guidebook for Field Conference, Michigan Copper District, Sept. 30-Oct. 2, 1971, W. S. White, ed., Society of Economic Geologists, p. 19–43.

Wright, H. E., and Frye, J. C., 1965, The Quaternary of the United States, Princeton Univ. Press, Princeton.

Young, G. A., 1981, Sedimentary environments and regional tectonic setting of the Huronian Supergroup, North Shore of Lake Huron, Ontario, Canada: <u>Eleventh Annual Field Conference, Great Lakes Section, Society of Economic Paleontologists and Mineralogists</u>.

Young, G. A., 1983, Tectono-sedimentary history of early Proterozoic rocks of the northern Great Lakes region, in <u>Early Proterozoic geology of the Great Lakes Region</u>, Geological Society of America Memoir 160, L. G. Medaris, Jr., ed., p. 15–32.

GLOSSARY

accretion - the gradual addition of new land to old. In geology it refers to the gradual increase in the size of continental masses with time.

accretionary wedge - In plate tectonics: a complex group of sedimentary rocks formed in a subduction zone by materials being "scraped-off" the down-going plate.

aeromagnetic - Magnetometer observations made from a moving airplane.

anaerobic - living or active in the absence of free oxygen.

andesite - a volcanic rock composed of andesine and one or more mafic minerals. Commonly associated with subduction zones.

anorthosite - a plutonic rock composed almost wholly of plagioclase.

asthenosphere - a layer within the Earth's mantle about 100-200 Km (50-100 miles) below the surface that is partially molten. It is the plastic layer on which the lithospheric plates move, and is the source of basaltic lava produced at spreading plate margins.

basalt - an extrusive rock composed primarily of calcic plagioclase and pyroxene, with or without olivine.

batholith - a body of intrusive rock, typically granite, that is more than 40 square miles in area.

bedding - any form of layering resulting from deposition. Characteristic of sedimentary rocks.

caldera - a circular depression 10-30 miles in diameter, formed by collapse after extrusion of magma from underlying area. Common in rhyolite volcanoes.

chemical weathering - chemical disintegration of rocks as a result of interaction between rocks and oxygen, carbonic acid, and water at or near the Earth's surface.

chert - as a mineral: cryptocrystalline variety of quartz; as a rock: compact siliceous rock of varying color composed of microorganisms or precipitated silica grains.

conglomerate - A sedimentary rock composed of rounded, water-worn pebbles cemented together by another mineral.

continental glaciation - ice-sheet that covered a large part of a continent.

convergence - in plate tectonics: when lithospheric plates move toward each other.

craton - A large area of continental crust, composed mainly of granitic material, in contrast to basaltic oceanic crust.

cross-bedding - inclined bedding or laminae in sedimentary rocks. It is produced by currents.

dike - a tabular body of igneous rock that cuts across adjacent rocks or cuts massive rocks.

dip - the angle at which a bed or any planar feature is inclined down into the earth.

dolomite - a rock which is composed of the mineral dolomite (calcium magnesian carbonate).

drumlin - a streamlined hill or ridge of glacial drift with long axis paralleling direction of flow of former glacier.

epigenetic - a feature in a rock that was produced by conditions or processes different from those that produced the enclosing rock.

esker - winding ridges of gravel or sand marking former stream channels at the bottom of melting ice sheet.

facies - different types of rocks formed at the same time but under different conditions.

fault - a fracture or fracture zone along which there has been movement of one side relative to the other.

fault zone - an area of numerous small interlacing faults creating an area hundreds or thousands of feet wide.

firn - compacted, granular snow which has survived more than one season but has not become glacial ice.

fluvial - deposits or processes that result from the action of rivers.

foliation - laminated structure resulting from segregation or alignment of minerals.

fracture - manner in which a mineral breaks or a break in a rock due to folding or faulting.

gabbro - a plutonic rock consisting of calcic plagioclase (usually labradorite) and pyroxene.

glacial drift - a general term for all of the materials deposited as a result of glacial action. It included deposition directly by ice, meltwater streams, lakes, and wind.

gneiss - coarse-grained metamorphic rock with bands of minerals.

graben - a down-dropped block of rocks bounded by faults. Generally form in tensional environments.

granite - plutonic rock consisting of alkali feldspar and quartz.

graywacke - a dark sandstone that has grains of quartz and feldspars set in a clay matrix.

greenstone - typically metamorphosed basaltic rocks colored by chlorite, actinolite, and epidote.

horst - an uplifted block of crust bounded by faults on either side.

hydrothermal - heated or hot aqueous-rich solutions; typically contain dissolved metals.

interlobate - an area situated between two glacial lobes.

intrusion - a body of igneous rock that invades older rock and crystallizes below the Earth's surface.

island arc - curved chain of volcanic islands with a deep trench on the convex side. Usually associated with a subduction zone.

jasper - red, brown cryptocrystalline chemically precipitated quartz.

joints - fractures in rock along which no movement has occurred.

kame - a conical hill of gravel or sand deposited in contact with glacier ice.

kaolinite - a common clay mineral composed of hydrous aluminum silicate.

kettle - a steep-sided depression in sand or gravel formed by melting of a buried block of glacial ice.

limestone - a bedded sedimentary rock consisting mainly of calcium carbonate.

lithosphere - The lithosphere forms the plates at the Earth's surface. It is about 100 Km thick and contains the crust and part of the upper mantle.

loess - Wind deposited silt originating in glacial outwash plains or in desert regions.

magma - molten rocks that cool to form igneous rocks.

mantle - layer of earth between the crust and the core, composed of peridotite.

mantle plumes (hot spots) - in plate tectonics: stationary sites within the mantle where abnormal heat produces more or less continuous volcanic activity on the surface. Plates may move over a mantle plume and form a chain of volcanic islands, such as the present-day Hawaiian Islands.

metamorphism - process by which rocks are altered from heat, pressure, and chemical activity of fluids, usually at depth.

migmatite - A mixture of igneous (generally granite) and metamorphic rock (gneiss or schist) formed by intense metamorphism.

Moho discontinuity - a seismic velocity boundary between the crust and the mantle.

moonstone - varieties of feldspar that exhibit opalescent play of colors; used as a gem.

moraine - drift deposited by direct glacial action, usually exhibits linear topography.

obsidian - volcanic glass of rhyolitic composition formed by rapid cooling.

organic matter - carbonaceous remains of living tissue. May contain carbohydrates and other chemical ingredients.

orogeny - process of forming mountains by deformation, metamorphism, and igneous activity.

outwash - sediments deposited by meltwater streams beyond active glacier ice.

paleomagnetism - the study of fossil magnetism in rocks.

passive margin - in plate tectonics: the margin of a continent that is moving away from a spreading margin. Typically it is the site of deposition of sedimentary rocks on a continental shelf and rise.

pegmatite - coarse-grained, igneous rock, usually of granitic composition.

peridotite - a coarse-grained ultramafic rock consisting primarily of olivine and pyroxene.

pillow basalt - basalt that exhibits pillow structure (rounded or sack-like structures).

plate - one of the large segments of the Earth's crust.

plate margins - in plate tectonics: the edges of the lithospheric plates.

pluton - a body of igneous rock that has crystallized beneath the Earth's surface from magma.

porphyry - an igneous rock exhibiting two grain sizes: relatively large crystals (phenocrysts) and a finer-grained crystalline ground mass.

quartz monzonite - a coarse-grained igneous rock similar to granite containing major plagioclase, orthoclase, and quartz.

quartzite - metamorphosed sandstone consisting of quartz grains.

radiometric - age of material as determined by measuring the radioactive decay of certain elements in the rock.

recrystallization - the formation of new mineral grains in a rock while in a solid state.

regression - gradual retreat of a shallow sea resulting in emergence of the land as the sea level falls.

rhyolite - a fine-grained to glassy volcanic rock similar to granite in composition.

rift - generally an elongate valley produced by subsidence of a series of blocks in areas where the Earth's crust is being (or has been) pulled apart.

rock-forming minerals - Minerals that form the major rock groups: feldspars, quartz, ferromagnesian minerals, micas, and carbonates.

roof pendant - older rocks projecting down from the "roof" into a batholith.

sabkha - an Arabic term for a very flat, arid coastline characterized by deposition of gypsum, halite, and other evaporite minerals, and associated formation of dolomite.

saprolite - soft, clay-rich chemically weathered rock usually red or brown in color.

schist - metamorphic rock with foliation due to alignment of platy minerals like micas or amphiboles.

seafloor spreading - hypothesis that spreading at oceanic ridges and rises produces "new" oceanic crust and results in movement of plates.

sediment - solid material, both mineral and organic, that is transported and deposited.

shale - laminated sedimentary rock that is predominantly clay.

shards - curved, fragments of volcanic glass formed by expansion and fragmentation of gas bubbles during violent eruptions.

shield - a large area of exposed metamorphic and igneous rocks, surrounded by sedimentary platforms.

sill - a tabular igneous intrusion that is parallel to the layers it intrudes.

slate - a fine-grained metamorphic rock showing well-developed alignment of the clay minerals.

subduction - descent of one lithospheric plate beneath another.

sulfide - a compound of sulfur with a metal element such as iron, lead, zinc, or copper.

syenite - a plutonic igneous rock similar to granite consisting of alkalic feldspar with hornblende or biotite, but lacking in quartz.

syncline - a "down-fold" in which the limbs dip toward the axis, youngest beds are found in the axis of the fold.

syngenetic - mineral or ore deposits formed at the same time, and by the same processes, as the enclosing rock.

tectonic - pertaining to rock structure resulting from the deformation of the Earth's crust.

terrane - area or surface within which a particular rock or group of rocks is prevalent.

thrust - a type of deformation in areas of intense compression where slabs of rock are transported horizontally over underlying rocks.

till - non-sorted, non-stratified, sediment deposited directly by glacier ice.

transgression - gradual advance of a shallow sea resulting in a progressive submergence of land, as when sea level rises, or land subsides.

tuff - a rock formed of compacted volcanic fragments; may contain crystals, fragments of older rocks, and glassy fragments.

turbidity current - density current of sediment-laden water.

ultramafic - magmas and igneous rocks that have a high content of magnesium and iron and a low silica content.

vein - a long, narrow feature, usually quartz- or carbonate-rich, of secondary origin, cutting older rocks.

vesicular - containing small round cavities formed by gases escaping from lava flows.

volcanic - pertaining to a volcano.

xenolith - fragments of older rocks incorporated in intrusive rocks, resulting from magmatic stoping.

INDEX

Granites
  Amberg, 104
  Athelstane, 104
  Mellen, 160
  Red Granite, 125
  "red rock," 160
  "rotten," 138, 139
  St. Cloud, 104
  Wausau, 104
  Wolf River, 131
Graphite, 36, 87
Graywackes, 4, 32
Great Lakes — Glacial History, 286
  Lake Michigan, 287
  Lake Superior, 290
Greenstone belts, 22
  origin of, 44
  with granite batholiths, 37, 41
Greenstones, 25, 116
  Ely, 37
Grenville orogeny, 180

Hamilton Mounds, 117, 118
Hemlock Volcanics, 83, 90
Huronian Supergroup, 55

Igneous rocks, 8
Iron-formation, 35, 67
  banded, 67
  Biwabik, 69
  granular, 67
  Gunflint, 68
  Ironwood, 67
  Negaunee, 71
  Soudan, 35
Iron Mines
  Champion, 82
  Hull-Rust-Mahoning, 51, 79
  Quinnesec, 82
  Sunday Lake, 81
Iron ores, 78
  Clinton, 216
  formation, 78
  minerals, 78, 81, 83
  Neda, 216, 234
  Paleozoic, 234
  taconite, 84
Iron-mining districts
  Cuyuna, 66
  Gogebic, 66
  Gunflint, 66
  Iron River-Crystal Falls, 66
  Marquette, 66
  Menominee, 66
  Mesabi, 66
  Vermilion, 66
Island arcs, 93, 95, 97

Keweenawan, 145
Kimberlite, 297
Komatiite, 29
Kyanite, 112

Lava flows
  Keweenawan, 148
  Portage Lake, 168
Lead-zinc, 228
Life
  Cambrian, 196
  Devonian, 204
  Ordovician, 198
  Pleistocene, 293
  Precambrian, 60, 68, 71, 72, 73
  Silurian, 201, 220

Mahnomen Formation, 63
Mantle "Plumes," 17
Marquette Range Supergroup, 86
Massive sulfides, 39, 107, 108
Michigamme Formation, 86
Microbial mats, 69
Microfossils, 71
  Animikea, 72
  Eoastrion, 73
  Eosphaera, 73
  Gunflint, 68
  Gunflintia, 72
  Huronispora, 72
  Kakabekia, 73
  Nonesuch shale, 164
Migmatites, 47
Mineral wealth, 38
  Lead and zinc, 38, 228
Mississippi River, 267
Mylonites, 14, 109

Niagara Fault Zone, 110, 111

Oil, 164
  Nonesuch shale, 163
Oronto Group, 162

Paleomagnetism, 155
Paleozoic, 8, 183
  Cambrian, 8, 183, 195
  Devonian, 204, 225
  Economic Importance, 226
  History, 207
  Ordovician, 187, 198
  Silurian, 201, 219
Palms Formation, 63
Passive margin, 55, 93
Penokean Mountains, 110, 111
Penokean Orogeny, 110
Phosphate, 89